CARL HIAASEN

Dance of the Reptiles

Carl Hiaasen was born and raised in Florida. He is the author
of thirteen novels, including the bestsellers *Bad Monkey*, *Star
Island*, *Nature Girl*, *Skinny Dip*, *Sick Puppy*, and *Lucky You*,
and four bestselling children's books, *Chomp*, *Hoot*, *Flush*,
and *Scat*. He joined *The Miami Herald* in 1976 and worked
on the newspaper's magazine and investigations team before
starting his column in 1985. In 2010, he received a Lifetime
Achievement Award from the National Society of Newspaper
Columnists.

www.carlhiaasen.com

BOOKS BY CARL HIAASEN

FICTION

Bad Monkey

Star Island

Nature Girl

Skinny Dip

Basket Case

Sick Puppy

Lucky You

Stormy Weather

Strip Tease

Native Tongue

Skin Tight

Double Whammy

Tourist Season

FOR YOUNG READERS

Chomp

Scat

Flush

Hoot

NONFICTION

Dance of the Reptiles: Selected Columns (edited by Diane Stevenson)

The Downhill Lie: A Hacker's Return to a Ruinous Sport

Paradise Screwed: Selected Columns (edited by Diane Stevenson)

Kick Ass: Selected Columns (edited by Diane Stevenson)

Team Rodent: How Disney Devours the World

DANCE

OF THE

REPTILES

DANCE
OF THE
REPTILES

Selected Columns

CARL HIAASEN

Edited by Diane Stevenson

Vintage Books
A Division of Random House LLC | New York

A VINTAGE ORIGINAL, JANUARY 2014

All the selections in this work were previously published by the
Miami Herald Publishing Company, a division of Knight Ridder,
One Herald Plaza, Miami, Florida.

Library of Congress Cataloging-in-Publication Data
Hiaasen, Carl.
Dance of the reptiles : selected columns / by Carl Hiaasen ; edited by
Diane Stevenson.
pages cm
ISBN 978-0-345-80702-1 (pbk.)—ISBN 978-0-345-80703-8 (ebook)
1. Florida—Social life and customs—21st century—Anecdotes.
2. Florida—Social conditions—21st century—Anecdotes.
3. Florida—Politics and government—21st century—Anecdotes.
4. Florida—Humor. I. Stevenson, Diane, 1947–, editor of compilation. II. Title.
F316.2.H48 2013   975.9'064—dc23   2013024990

Book design by Joy O'Meara

www.vintagebooks.com

Printed in the United States of America
10 9 8 7 6 5 4 3 2 1

CONTENTS

INTRODUCTION

It's been almost twelve years since *Paradise Screwed* was published as the second collection of Carl Hiaasen's newspaper columns written for *The Miami Herald*, and almost fifteen years since the first, *Kick Ass*, appeared. Since then, Hiaasen has written some six hundred weekly op-ed columns for the *Herald*, in addition to five novels for adults, a nonfiction book about golf, and four novels for young adults. The first of those, *Hoot*, which launched Hiaasen's career in that genre, told the story of Mullet Fingers, a boy who relocates surveyors' stakes to stop an illegally cited development that would destroy the habitat of burrowing owls. *Hoot* won a prestigious Newbery Honor Book award, its plotline mirroring Hiaasen's own life: He did pull up surveyors' stakes with his friends in youthful opposition to the paving of Florida.

Over time, much of Hiaasen's attention has, in fact, been aimed at young people who always inherit a future and who invigorate him with the writing energy he needs to continue railing against the destruction of his beloved state. As Hiaasen says, "I want there to be something wonderful left of Florida for them to see and experience," perhaps as he himself did when he was just six and his father took him fishing in the Keys for the first time, an adventure recounted in his well-known essay "The Florida Keys: Something Precious Is Falling Apart." As he observes, "You stay and fight, because otherwise you're surrendering." Such continuity and consistency, essential to Hiaasen as a person and a writer, are clear in this latest collection of columns.

In *Dance of the Reptiles*, Hiaasen resumes his verbal war against greed, corruption, ignorance, and hypocrisy, addressing such issues as hurricanes, offshore drilling, and water, all of which occupy center stage nationally. Devastating storms like Hurricane Sandy, for example, roared across the northern states of New York and New Jersey, capturing national attention; for years, however, Hiaasen has written about massive storms in Florida not only flattening entire communities but also driving up insurance premiums by splintering flimsily constructed homes and flooding coastal properties overbuilt to begin with.

Offshore drilling is another topic Hiaasen tackled almost 30 years ago, his urgent warnings poignant now that British Petroleum's Deepwater Horizon inevitably blew, spewing some 206 million gallons of oil into the Gulf of Mexico. In a 1987 column entitled "U.S. Points Out the Bright Side of Oil Spills," Hiaasen lampooned a government report asserting there was only a 48 percent chance that a major spill would "smear the beaches within 35 years." The study also claimed that "offshore oil exploration is abundantly safe" and that advanced equipment "should minimize damage to reefs, tidal banks, water quality and marine life." A fifty-fifty chance for an ecological disaster isn't so bad, Hiaasen wryly stated, concluding with an invitation to the interior secretary to hurry on down before he had to "tiptoe through the tar balls."

And, of course, there's the issue of water. Surrounded on three sides, Florida remains vulnerable to all storms: Hurricanes can rip across oil derricks yet to be built or gas lines yet to be dug, with the potential for future catastrophe very real—to the coastline, the wildlife, the economy. Any construction in those sensitive waters makes Hiaasen cringe, especially since the state has problems with drinkable water; its supply is drying up. The sustained pollution of wetlands and rivers, which have been drained, paved, or contaminated by runoff and pulp residue—all permitted by questionable legislation—has reduced and diminished Florida. Nature is interconnected, Hiaasen would say, and fragile.

That most of Florida's concerns have gone national is nowhere more evident than in voting. As Hiaasen says, "The 2000 election . . . put this country in the hands of the people who invaded Iraq. Those non-existent weapons of mass destruction were this generation's Gulf of Tonkin's ruse." By only 537 certified votes, Bush and Cheney won the election, or so ruled the Supreme Court a month after actual balloting, in "one of the most contorted decisions ever written," Hiaasen says, with Florida and Secretary of State Katherine Harris, not to mention Palm Beach and its butterfly ballots, leading the way. "Anytime people say their vote won't matter, I tell them to go to Arlington and look at the thousands of graves of American soldiers who died in Iraq," Hiaasen says. "That war happened strictly because some impulsive, arrogant and not-very-smart people got into power."

An entire chapter in *Dance of the Reptiles*, entitled "Shock, Awe, and Swagger," chronicles the arguments for, as well as the consequences of, so many years invested in the Iraq war, and demonstrates what some consider Hiaasen's greatest strength as a journalist: He digests facts, presents them accurately and articulately, and draws clear conclusions. You know where Hiaasen stands. Perhaps this advocacy role is what earned him the Damon Runyon Award from the Denver Press Club, the Ernie Pyle Lifetime Achievement

Award from the National Society of Newspaper Columnists, and a place in the anthology *Deadline Artists: America's Greatest Newspaper Columns*.

At 60, Carl Hiaasen shows no signs of slowing down. As he says, "I haven't mellowed one little bit. Mellowing would be the worst thing that could happen to a writer like me." His novels allow him to create an ending that is morally satisfying for a change, though often wickedly funny and delivered with a punch by nature. His weekly newspaper columns allow him the immediacy of addressing issues as they arise, with humor and outrage. In both books and columns, Hiaasen acts as an agent of change; he is a person of integrity, dark irreverent humor, and passionate conviction based on the simple principles of loyalty, decency, and honesty. Always the first principle—and Hiaasen would agree—is one of continuity: As the columns in *Dance of the Reptiles* show, the world must be preserved for our children and theirs—environmentally, politically, geographically, and morally.

Diane Stevenson
Columbia, SC
July 2013

DANCE

OF THE

REPTILES

GO AWAY

Haul the Rampaging Nitwits Off to Tourist Court

Florida needs a special prison for tourists.

Not all tourists—just the ones who trash the place, rob, shoplift, vandalize, drive drunk, assault the cops, puke in the alleys, pee in the medians, and so on.

For some reason, Memorial Day brings out these troglodytes in droves.

This year it was South Beach that got the full treatment, but outbreaks of mayhem occur all over the state.

Maybe it's time to stop worrying about crimes committed against tourists and do something about the crimes committed by tourists.

As it stands, rampaging visitors are tossed in jail with local criminals. This plainly is cruel and unusual punishment, and it's only a matter of time before the criminals file a class-action suit.

Nobody deserves to be locked in a cell with obnoxious, whiny, ill-clad tourists. Such sociopaths belong in an institution of their own, a mini-Raiford specializing in hard-nosed discipline and social graces.

In fact, the entire justice system should recognize and deal with the uniquely repulsive nature of tourist misbehavior.

Say you're driving through the Keys and some dork in a neon-blue rental yells, "Yee-haw!" and hurls an empty Southern Comfort bottle off the Bahia Honda Bridge. Under current statutes, that's good for a wimpy charge of littering. It doesn't even rate any jail time, only a piddling $50 fine.

You want deterrence? Put fangs in the law. Let the police snatch the boor off the highway and drag his sorry butt straight to Tourist Court. Same goes for the drunks, stoners, and public urinators.

Tourist Court should be set up sort of like Drug Court, only not as lenient. The judges would come from smaller venues, such as Kissimmee, Key West, Naples; places that get a rush of visitors yet still have a vestige of hometown pride.

First-time offenders in Tourist Court would be permitted to plead guilty in exchange for a one-week hitch at Sandal Camp. This would be set up like Boot Camp, only much tougher.

Here, inmates would spend seven days and six nights being drilled on vacation etiquette. For example, they'd be taught how to read speed-limit signs; how to park within the parallel lines of a parking space; how to drink and dispose of alcohol; how to vomit inconspicuously; how to steer a Jet Ski and chew gum at the same time. . . .

The drill instructors would be selected from an elite pool of former Highway Patrol troopers, ex–Navy SEALs, and retired tour guides from Epcot.

Defendants who don't want to tackle Sandal Camp could instead risk a trial. However, all jurors in Tourist Court should be chosen from the hospitality industry—waiters, waitresses, bartenders, chefs, motel desk clerks, cabbies. Not easily fooled, those folks—and no tipping allowed in the courtroom!

Once convicted, it's off to Tourist Prison. Admittedly, finding a location for such a high-risk facility won't be easy.

In the event of an escape, you'd have renegade tourists scurrying all over the place with no cash or credit cards—a nightmare scenario for resort communities, especially during the season.

Consequently, the prison is more likely to end up someplace like Mims or Plant City than, say, Turnberry Isle.

Inevitably, the age-old debate will come to a boil: Is the

goal of incarcerating lawbreaking tourists merely to punish them, or should we make a good-faith effort at rehabilitation?

Many Floridians would argue, persuasively, that the conduct of some visitors is so abominable that they are beyond redemption. Yet a humane approach compels us to consider the possibility that a few of these nitwits might actually get the message if the screws are firmly applied.

It's even conceivable they might someday become lawful and productive vacationers who treat their holiday destinations with care and respect—no more stealing baby lobsters and flushing the heads down motel-room toilets!

Yet for the incorrigible ones, the hard-core slobs, a stretch in Tourist Prison will serve mainly to keep them off the streets, beaches, and waterways—temporarily.

Unfortunately, vigilante justice might be the only kind these outlaws understand: an angry mob in minivans and Winnebagos to chase them up the Turnpike, all the way home, and do to their backyards what they did so heedlessly to ours.

August 12, 2001
Stop Shark-Feeding Dive Expeditions

No summer would be complete without delirious shark hype, even though bumblebees and lightning bolts kill more people.

Still, in the wake of two harrowing attacks, it's significant to note that the Florida Fish and Wildlife Conservation Commission recently decided that there's no reason to ban shark-feeding dive excursions.

While of dubious scientific footing, the ruling was consistent with the state's anything-for-a-buck approach to marine management. At least four outfits in South Florida advertise shark-feeding scuba trips. These are promoted as "interactive experiences," meaning dive operators get to interact with your money.

Giddy explorers descend to a place where sharks are chummed in and hand-fed pieces of smelly dead fish. The sharks themselves have no interest in communing—they come strictly to eat, which is what nature so exquisitely engineered them to do. They are also engineered for hunting, not begging, like stray cats. That's why many dive captains and marine biologists oppose the chumming expeditions.

Supporters say the practice is educational, helping to raise appreciation for a creature that's being ignorantly slaughtered worldwide, but whose presence is vital to sustaining the bounty of our oceans.

No one can dispute that sharks are maligned and misunderstood. However, teaching them to seek snacks from humans doesn't seem like the smartest way to save them from extinction or to prevent future maulings.

Not that most suckers care, but a commercial shark dive is hardly a natural encounter. Sharks don't naturally behave like Central Park pigeons.

And pigeons, of course, can't sever a human limb.

In the Bahamas, where these dives have become popular, nine injuries were documented through 1996. Usually, the bitten party was the shark handler, not a paying customer.

The Florida expeditions concentrate on nurse sharks, a relatively slow and mopey species. Granted, it's not easy to get nailed by a nurse shark, but it does happen. Three years ago, an Illinois teenager snorkeling in the Keys decided to tug the tail of a baby nurse shark, which promptly whipped around and chomped him. It did not let go. With the fish firmly attached to his chest, the boy was rushed to a Marathon hospital. There the shark was surgically dispatched, and its jaws were pried off.

The lesson of the story is twofold: Never underestimate any shark, and never overestimate any human. These are two life-forms that were never meant to fraternize. It's telling that the supposedly advanced species is the one initiating eye-to-eye contact.

A shark easily can be conditioned to slurp mullet from a diver's hand. If one day that shark meets up with a diver who has no mullet, it might impulsively settle for the hand instead. They are primordially swift and opportunistic. The ones that mangled little Jessie Arbogast in Pensacola and Krishna Thompson in Freeport weren't rogues. They were doing precisely what sharks have been doing for 420 million years—chasing what they thought was supper.

With its crowded beaches, Florida leads the nation in unplanned shark encounters. The vast majority are nonfatal nips of surfers and swimmers in murky water.

Humans are not a shark's normal prey, and typically, it flees after the first taste—but not always. Last summer, a tenacious bull shark killed a man swimming in a canal near St. Petersburg.

Three Broward cities—Hillsboro Beach, Lighthouse Point, and Deerfield Beach—have outlawed the offshore feeding of sharks and other marine animals. State officials contemplated a similar ban, then backed off. Instead, the FWC asked the dive industry for guidelines ensuring that the excursions will be safe for both the divers and the sharks. The proposals didn't satisfy some commissioners, so the FWC is supposed to tackle the controversy again next month. Among the options are prohibiting feedings by hand and requiring chum zones to be located far from recreational beaches.

A smarter idea is stopping the dives, which are about as

educational as a rerun of *Jaws III*. Chumming sharks is nothing but a thrill gimmick designed to hook tourists.

Visitors to Florida needn't feel deprived of a swim with the ocean's most magnificent predator. They're out there every time you go in the water, all over the place.

If you're lucky enough to see one, be bright enough not to try making friends.

April 21, 2002
Even Death Doesn't Free Us from Crookery

Before you die, make sure your relatives install a LoJack transmitter in your casket. That way they can find your body if it gets swiped, dumped, or stripped for parts.

Even the dead are up for grabs in the Sunshine State.

Last week, agents from the Florida Department of Law Enforcement officially set up a crime scene at a cemetery in Palm Beach County. They found evidence of victims who are in no shape to testify.

The attorney general says that Menorah Gardens & Funeral Chapels has been burying people in the wrong plots, stacking coffins like Tupperware, reselling occupied grave sites, and cracking open private mortuary vaults to make room for more corpses.

It's hard enough to find a decent parking space when you're alive. Evidently, things only get worse after you pass away.

According to state investigators, Menorah Gardens failed to inform family members that 44 of 136 burials in one section of the cemetery had been staged in the wrong location. Other residents were roused from eternal slumber by backhoes. Former gravediggers have told authorities that they were ordered to use heavy machinery to break into vaults and then scatter the contents, including human remains, in nearby woods.

Not even the young and innocent are safe. At a Broward cemetery also operated by Menorah Gardens, two babies were allegedly buried in the same grave on two occasions. Soon we might have to redefine the term "sleazeball," or at least create a special odious category for those who treat the deceased like Dumpster fodder.

Menorah Gardens is owned by a huge Houston-based company called Service Corporation International. SCI disputes the sordid Florida allegations and says that it's cooperating with the state to correct any problems. Initially, the company suggested that the discarded bones and skull fragments videotaped by cemetery workers were actually those of dead animals. On Thursday, FDLE agents confirmed unearthing bones that were definitely human.

The sight of yellow crime tape strung around a graveyard is enough to make a person consider cremation as a less risky alternative to burial. In Florida, though, you might well be kissing your ashes goodbye—assuming you even get to the crematorium.

Professional corpse hauler Joseph Damiano is being investigated for allegedly taking bodies marked for cremation and selling them to an embalming class for $110 each. Damiano, who has previously been sued for misplacing human ashes, denies the new accusations and says he is the target of a vendetta by jealous competitors.

Family members and caretakers of 23 persons who recently died told the *Herald* that their loved ones were sent without consent to the mortuary school at Lynn University in Boca Raton. There the bodies were embalmed.

School officials say they thought that the families had given permission for the bodies to be used in the classes and have promised a full investigation. Damiano insists that he sold no corpses to Lynn without first consulting with relatives.

A North Lauderdale man has sued, claiming his wife was embalmed against her religious beliefs. Other problems face Damiano, who was recently arrested for illegally operating an incinerator, and had his state licenses revoked.

These latest scandals might not have happened if the death industry were policed even halfheartedly, but it's not. Funeral operators contribute heavily to politicians and finance lobby groups that help snuff most attempts at serious reform.

Service Corporation International, for instance, has its own political action committee. It donated more than $518,000 to chosen candidates around the country between 1996 and 2001.

Here in Florida, where the Legislature often appears embalmed, the funeral lobby continues to keep a death grip on top lawmakers. Again this year, all efforts to strengthen regulations and expand consumer rights died a swift death.

One bill was single-handedly snuffed by Rep. Mark Flanagan, R-Bradenton, who took $1,000 in campaign donations from funeral associations last year. Flanagan says the money didn't influence him one bit. Neither, apparently, did the heartrending stories of those who had learned that Menorah Gardens was allegedly playing musical tombstones with the remains of their relatives.

Approximately 163,000 persons will die in Florida this year, and most will end up in the urn or grave where they had planned to be. Sadly, some won't.

Because the state isn't protecting the public from unscrupulous human buzzards, we are left to worry about our loved ones long after they're dearly departed.

These days, there's no peace for the dead.

December 8, 2002
Perfect Film Locale: Florida's Roadways?

If you're a visitor to South Florida, you've undoubtedly noticed that some very busy roads are being closed to the public during peak driving hours.

That's because a Hollywood movie crew is here, and it needs highways for chase scenes. We apologize for the hassle, but you'll just have to stew in traffic with the rest of us.

Sitting there, you might be wondering what kind of nincompoops would casually turn over six miles of interstate to a motion-picture company between the hours of 9 A.M. and 3 P.M. for 10 days. Likewise the Florida Turnpike or even A1A.

On the surface, it might seem unfathomably stupid, but try to appreciate our situation. South Florida is rather desperately trying to make itself attractive to the motion-picture industry. To that end, we'll do just about anything that movie producers want, including blockading motorists from roadways paid for with their own tax dollars.

We're keenly aware that no other major urban center in the United States would inflict such unnecessary inconvenience upon its working people, not to mention tourists. If movie producers asked to barricade the Santa Monica Freeway for six hours on a weekday, they'd be laughed out of Los Angeles. And New York wouldn't shut down the FDR at rush hour if Woody Allen himself fell to his knees and begged.

But here in South Florida, we're blessed with numerous municipal officials who are basically rubes. Easily dazzled and starstruck, they're amenable to just about any goofball idea that showbiz tosses their way. Which is why we're now in position to become the No. 1 car-chase-and-crash location in cinema. It's a niche that is wide open, for obvious reasons.

It all started with a project called *Holy Man*, starring

Eddie Murphy. For that one, they actually shut down the MacArthur Causeway, the primary link between Miami and South Beach. Unfortunately, the movie tanked, and almost nobody got to see how lovely our roads are.

Then, a few months ago, we got another chance. The producers of *Bad Boys 2* asked to use the MacArthur for a wild chase sequence, and local big shots promptly agreed to seal off the busy causeway for several days. The resulting traffic snarl was chaotic, and motorists were pretty ticked off. But all that aggravation and wasted gas surely will be worth it once the movie comes out and there's Will Smith firing his gun out the car window, the S.S. *Norwalk* resplendent (though somewhat fuzzy) in the background.

Currently, South Florida is hosting a film called *2 Fast 2 Furious*. Unless you're an adolescent male with an IQ hovering in the mid-80s, you might have missed the original.

Although the reviews weren't especially kind, the movie made tons of money. The plot revolved around a group of daring young men who illegally raced their souped-up cars through crowded downtown streets in order to find their true inner selves.

Prominent in the cast was an actor named Vin Diesel, who has since ascended to big-time action stardom. Diesel opted out of the sequel, which instead will feature the major-screen debut of Ludacris, the hip-hop performer.

Okay, so we're probably not talking Oscar bait.

Yet "FF2," as it's fondly known around town, offers a grand opportunity to show the screen industry how far we'll go to get their stunt-driving business. Who needs Merchant and Ivory when you've got fast cars, hot babes, and miles of sunny expressways? And what better way to showcase South Florida's natural vistas than through the windshield of a nitro-powered Civic barreling a hundred miles an hour down the Turnpike extension?

Those who gripe about the roadblocks should be reminded that the movie production is pumping good money into our economy—hopefully enough to offset the thousands of work hours lost by commuters stuck in the gridlock.

And for those who say local film promoters ought to aim for something loftier than brainless action flicks, remember that the highest-grossing movie ever made down here was a 62-minute epic called *Deep Throat*, which earned more than $400 million.

In other words, things really could be worse.

This week, drivers in West Broward will be detoured from certain sections of I-75 and I-595, where the cast of FF2 is shooting yet another thrilling race scene. If we're nice to them, they might even come back next year for FF3.

In which case we'll loan them the entire Dolphin Expressway, if they want, because no sacrifice is too large in the name of art.

October 23, 2005
Will Pythons Deter Visitors? Let's Hope So

Lock up the kids, put a GPS on your Jack Russell, and make way at the top of the food chain.

The killer pythons are here.

Visitors to South Florida recently clicked on the television to see an X-ray of a 12-footer that had eaten a rotund Siamese cat named Frances.

It was the lead story on the local news, hot on the heels of an incident in which another large python exploded after devouring a six-foot alligator in Everglades National Park.

The grisly photos of that gastronomical Vesuvius received front-page play all over the world.

Finally, the word is getting out that pythons are amok in the Sunshine State. Will this scare anyone away? We can only hope. Shark attacks, gator maulings, West Nile—oozing mosquitoes, flesh-eating bacteria, killer hurricanes every three or four weeks—none of these threats has significantly dented Florida's insane growth rate.

An infestation of ravenous pythons, however, might deter potential newcomers to our state. Large mammal-eating snakes trigger a special primal fear in our otherwise cocky species. Sharks cruise and gators lurk, but at least we know where they hang out. Snakes, on the other hand, go wherever they please. They swim, they slither, they dig, and they climb.

Humans are as stunningly ignorant about reptiles as they are intrigued by them. About 144,000 Burmese pythons were imported by the pet trade into the United States last year, and many of those will either escape or eventually be freed by their owners.

That's why Florida is crawling with the beasts today. Most people who buy them as babies are clueless about how fast they grow and how much space they require.

As one who owned snakes for years, I steered clear of exotic constrictors. Sharing a house with a 90-pound carnivorous predator required a deeper personal commitment than I was willing to make, not to mention a steady supply of full-grown rabbits.

Friends up north who've been reading about our python plague have asked if they eat humans. The same question, I suspect, is being worriedly pondered at the breakfast table in many South Florida households.

The answer is yes, though rarely. In one documented case, a teenager was devoured by a 31-foot reticulated python in Indonesia. Ten years ago, a 23-footer killed and tried to swallow a worker at a rubber plantation in Kuala Lumpur.

More recently, Internet snake freaks eagerly disseminated a graphic photograph purporting to show a man's corpse being removed from a dead anaconda in South America. Some experts believe the photo was faked.

In any case, it's important to remember that snakes are primitive and undiscerning. They tend to eat whatever is available, sometimes without regard for proportions or digestibility. Witness the inflated ambitions of the now-famous Everglades python that expired after gobbling the alligator.

Tragically, there have been many cases of hungry pet snakes behaving like hungry wild ones. In 1984, an 11-month-old baby was strangled in bed by the family's 10-foot pet reticulated python. This happened in Iowa, not the ideal climate for an active tropical reptile.

A New York man was killed in 1996 while trying to feed a live chicken to his 13-foot python, which mistook him for supper. A Colorado python owner suffered the same fate, his pet wrapping around him so tightly that it took a team of firefighters to pry the coils from his body.

In 1999, a 3-year-old Illinois boy was choked to death by his parents' pet African rock python. Two years later, an 8-year-old Pennsylvania girl was critically injured by a 10-foot Burmese—one of five big snakes kept at her home—that wound around her neck and wouldn't let go.

Obviously, a multitude of good reasons exist for parting company with an unmanageable python. The best way is to take it to a veterinarian or give it to an experienced reptile keeper.

Simply opening the car door and letting the snake go might be convenient, but it's also profoundly stupid. Pythons have few natural enemies, Miami being short on wild jaguars and tigers. The small python you set free today could be inhaling your neighbor's prize parrot next year.

While eradication efforts are under way in the Everglades, some herpetologists believe it's too late. They say the pythons, which breed prolifically, are here to stay.

As a public service, dire warnings should be issued to tourists and all those considering a permanent family move to Florida. Perhaps it will do some good, but who knows.

It was 16 years ago that I first wrote about the python invasion, after a 20-footer and a 17-footer were captured in local suburbs where they'd been feasting on raccoons and domestic pets.

The news didn't seem to frighten a soul. People kept arriving, and so did the snakes.

Now we're overrun with both, setting the stage for a classic Darwinian duel. Having seen big pythons in action, I definitely wouldn't bet against them.

May 21, 2006
Folks Freak Out as Gator Panic Sweeps Florida

Full-bore alligator panic is sweeping Florida in the aftermath of three fatal attacks on humans.

Last weekend, a woman near Bradenton fired a handgun four times at a three-foot gator that she said was chasing her golden retriever. (If you see a gator that small eat a full-grown dog, call Ripley's immediately.) The reptile survived the gunfire, and the woman was cited for hunting without a license.

The next day, a Pasco County sheriff's deputy shot a nine-foot alligator in the head. The animal had entered the yard of a 75-year-old woman, supposedly "trapping" her in the home. (We must assume that the house had only one door.) In any event, the cop's bullet failed to dispatch the gator, which was later captured by a professional trapper.

On Wednesday, a Miramar police officer actually managed to kill one of the critters, plugging it in a residential neighborhood where it was allegedly menacing a Labrador retriever. The owner of the dog said his wife is so upset that she wants to sell the house and move away. To find a place that's gator-free, they'll have to leave the state.

Fear is a predictable public reaction to the recent spate of attacks, but you're more likely to be hurt by someone shooting at a gator than you are by the gator itself.

They are not easy to kill. Their hide is thick and their brains are small, and if you miss the target, you'll have succeeded in ticking off one of the earth's most efficient predators.

That won't stop a few people from trying. It will be a miracle if we get through the next few weeks without some half-wit shooting himself, his truck, or his drinking buddy instead of the alligator at which he's aiming.

Considering how much of their native habitat has been drained and bulldozed, the hefty saurians have behaved themselves fairly well for a long time in Florida. Since 1948, 17 persons had been killed by gators—a remarkably low figure, given the constant interaction between the species. Then, this month, three women died in gruesome attacks. It's not surprising that people are freaking out. The same thing happens after a wave of shark incidents. The difference is that sharks don't crawl out of the water to sun themselves in your backyard.

The sight of even a puny alligator is now cause for delirium. The state's Nuisance Alligator hotline is being flooded with calls—225 in one day last week.

Wildlife experts interviewed by the media are asked again and again: What's going on out there? The dark implication is that gators have suddenly turned on humans, in revenge for us turning so many of them into handbags, shoes, and belts.

In reality, the answer is much less sinister. Florida has been experiencing uncommonly dry weather, and alligators are moving around in search of water and food. It's also mating season, when they become more aggressive.

Still, the biggest factor in the attacks is the continuing encroachment of humanity. For eons the critters had the wetlands to themselves, and now the wetlands are subdivisions, and the subdivisions are full of people.

As primitive as they are, gators have adjusted to our presence far better than we've adjusted to theirs. That's the problem with suburban specimens such as the one that tragically killed a jogger in Sunrise—they see so many people that they're not particularly afraid of them anymore.

As reckless kids, my friends and I used to go bass fishing from inner tubes in the canals along Alligator Alley. We spotted plenty of gators, large and small, but they stayed away. Today they'll follow you around like hungry mutts. It is definitely inadvisable to float among the lily pads, dangling one's legs while dragging a stringer of fish.

One reason that alligators don't mind people so much these days is that people feed them. This is an act of profound stupidity, and it's also against the law. Hand-fed gators lose all fear and will, in the absence of table scraps, eagerly go after a pet poodle or even a child. Anybody caught feeding an alligator should be bound with duct tape and hauled off in the back of a pickup truck.

The smartest way to deal with gators is to avoid them,

which isn't always easy in Florida. They were here first, and obviously, they're not going anywhere.

Humans have always had a primal curiosity about the beasts that we dread, whether it's a great white or a grizzly bear or a king cobra. This isn't necessarily an unhealthy curiosity, unless it manifests itself in perilous behavior.

Alligators are fascinating animals to see up close, one of the last living dinosaurs on the planet. And they are the pre-eminent icon of Florida's wilderness.

But they're also killing machines. In millions of years, they haven't changed their agenda, and they're not going to change for us.

January 13, 2008
Good News: Fewer People Moving to Florida

The mad stampede of new residents into Florida is finally slowing down, the inevitable result of high taxes, miserable traffic, overcrowded classrooms, and other unappealing urban problems.

According to the Census Bureau, the state's population grew by only 1.1 percent during the 12-month span ending last July 1. That's a significant dip from the 1.8 percent increase recorded the previous year, and it drops Florida's growth rate to 19th in the nation.

This is a cause for relief, not panic. Any lull in the avalanche of incoming humanity should be eagerly welcomed by the 18.3 million souls already living here. The last thing we need is more warm bodies clogging the roads, schools, courts, jails, and hospitals.

A break is long overdue. It's not a crisis but rather an opportunity. At long last, state and community leaders might be forced to intelligently confront the economic blowback from decades of inept planning and greed-fueled runaway growth.

With each passing day, Florida is becoming a less desirable place to live. For the first time in modern memory, moving companies report that they're transporting more families out of the Sunshine State than into it.

The disenchantment is widespread and deep-seated, judging by a new Mason-Dixon survey that was released by Leadership Florida, a group founded by the state Chamber of Commerce.

Of more than 1,100 residents interviewed by telephone in November, 43 percent said their quality of life has declined over the last five years. That's an eye-popping number, up 7 percent from 2006.

More evidence that lots of people see their Florida dream dissolving: Of those surveyed, only 24 percent said they think things will get better during the next five years. Thirty-seven percent believe the state will become a worse place to live during that time.

The increasingly glum outlook of many Floridians isn't just a reaction to off-the-chart property taxes and insurance rates, as politicians want us to believe.

More and more folks are figuring out what serious urban planners have known for a long time: Run-amok growth doesn't pay for itself. Taxpayers always get stuck with the bill for sprawl and also with the hometown ills it brings. By an overwhelming margin of nearly three to one, Floridians polled in the Leadership Florida survey oppose higher population densities in their neighborhoods—a view that resonates fairly evenly among registered Democrats, Republicans, and independents.

A majority of residents—52 percent—believe local governments are "not effectively managing growth" in their communities. The figure is unchanged from 2006, and the Mason-Dixon pollsters describe the sentiment as "strong and and consistent among all groups and across the state."

Respondents were divided evenly when asked whether new people moving into Florida was good or bad. The question is rarely even whispered among politicians, many of whom live in fear of antagonizing the developers, bankers, and road builders who bankroll election campaigns.

The beleaguered sense among many Floridians—that they're not only being overtaxed but overrun—will not soon go away. Politicians who resist calls for strict land-use reforms and continue to shill for special interests risk being dumped from office by those whom they've ignored. It's happened already in scores of municipalities where voters got fed up watching their green spaces malled and paved while the waterfronts went condo.

The social equation isn't complicated. The more people you cram into a place, even a place as vast and geographically diverse as Florida, the more stressful life becomes for everybody. It also becomes more expensive. Ask anyone in New York or California what happened to their taxes as the populations of those states swelled.

A bipartisan group that advocates semi-sane growth policies, 1000 Friends of Florida, last year predicted that the state's population would double to 36 million by 2060, and that 7 million acres of agricultural land and wilderness would be converted to concrete and asphalt.

That was before the real-estate market tanked and the sub-prime mortgage racket imploded, but there's no denying that even an overcrowded Florida continues to hold some mythical allure, whether you live in Dubuque or Port-au-Prince.

Despite their rising disillusionment, about 62 percent of

those interviewed for the Leadership Florida poll said they'd still recommend the state as a place for friends or relatives to live.

For strangers? Maybe not. Because growth is an exalted industry unto itself, rather than the natural result of a broadening economic base, lawmakers have always focused on attracting hordes of new residents at all costs. The first casualty of such a fast-buck mentality is the quality of life.

One out of five Floridians surveyed in November say they are "seriously considering" moving elsewhere.

This is what's known as a message. And for those who've sold out Florida's future to enrich their campaign coffers, it breaks down like this:

Enough.

March 15, 2009
Strange Doings Down on the Farm

Sometimes it's not easy to admit that you live in Florida.

Last week, our state Senate boldly took the first step toward making it illegal for a person to have intimate relations with an animal.

Although such a law might thin the dating pool in certain counties, it should ultimately serve to protect household pets and domestic livestock, which evidently are at far greater risk than most of us had imagined.

The cry for justice first arose from the small Panhandle community of Mossy Head, where in 2006 a 48-year-old man was suspected of abducting a neighbor family's pet goat and accidentally strangling it with its collar during a sex act.

I wish I were making this up, but the story is true. The poor goat's name was Meg.

After outraged citizens demanded that the suspect be arrested and locked up, local authorities were alarmed to discover that Florida was one of only 16 states that had no laws against bestiality. While our moldy statute books still prohibit "unnatural and lascivious acts" between consenting adults, there's apparently nothing you cannot do with a four-legged partner.

More unwanted publicity came to Mossy Head when a local entrepreneur began selling T-shirts that said BAAAA MEANS NO! Residents demanded that the suspected goat rapist be charged at least with animal cruelty, but DNA samples collected from the crime scene proved inconclusive.

Shortly after the fatal encounter with Meg, the same man was arrested while trying to sneak off with another goat. This time he was sentenced to 364 days for theft.

Enter Sen. Nan Rich, a Sunrise Democrat and longtime advocate for animal rights. Soon after the bizarre abductions in Mossy Head, she set out to write a law imposing tough criminal penalties on those who seek out animal companionship with carnal intent.

Although the bill died in the 2008 legislative session, this year it has a better chance of passing. A Senate agricultural committee has approved a version that would make bestiality a third-degree felony, punishable by up to five years in prison and a $5,000 fine.

However, the discussion among lawmakers of this rather delicate topic already has provided a few uncomfortable moments. As Rich's bill was being amended to make sure that some common animal-husbandry practices were exempt, Sen. Larcenia Bullard of Miami spoke up in puzzlement. "People are taking these animals as their husbands? What's husbandry?" she inquired.

The committee chairman, Sen. Charlie Dean of Citrus County, patiently explained that animal husbandry was a term used for the rearing and care of domestic animals.

Still, Bullard appeared confused. "So that maybe was the reason the lady was so upset about that monkey?" she asked, an apparent reference to the recent incident in which a pet chimpanzee was shot by Connecticut police after it went berserk and mauled a visitor.

Bullard has taken some ribbing about her loopy comments, but in fairness, she represents a big-city district in which neither goats nor chimps often make an appearance. (Miami does have a scattered population of chickens, which the proposed law would presumably protect from human sexual advances.)

Given the many urgent matters confronting the Legislature, it's easy to make light of the bestiality deliberations; lots of Internet correspondents have been chiding lawmakers for wasting time on such a silly subject. Yet Rich asserts it's anything but silly, citing "a tremendous correlation between sexually deviant behavior and crimes against children and crimes against animals."

I'm not familiar with those statistics, but it's safe to assume that anyone with a burning sexual passion for farm critters has insurmountable psychological problems and would not be a welcome presence in most neighborhoods.

As fervently as we might hope otherwise, the goat-sex attack in Mossy Head wasn't an isolated incident. Rich says other disturbing acts against animals have been reported throughout the state, including the molestation of a horse in the Keys and of a Seeing Eye dog in Tallahassee.

The latter case involved a 29-year-old blind man who four years ago was charged with "breach of the peace" after admitting to police that he had sex on numerous occasions with a yellow Labrador named Lucky, his guide dog.

You needn't be an animal lover to be left aghast by such accounts. Sure, we all knew Florida was crawling with sickos—but boinking a Seeing Eye dog?

Okay, Sen. Rich, you win. We definitely need a law.

And a drink.

October 22, 2011
A "Lead Cocktail" or Old Sparky Not a Laughing Matter

Every time Florida starts to fade from the national spotlight, somebody like Brad Drake comes along and gets everybody laughing at us again.

Drake is the state representative who is sponsoring a bill to give Death Row inmates the choice between the electric chair or a firing squad—"a lead cocktail," in Drake's words.

Not even Clint Eastwood could say the phrase "lead cocktail" with a straight face, but Drake claims to be serious. He says he's frustrated by the questions about whether lethal injection, Florida's current method of execution, is actually painless.

"I say let's end the debate," Drake said in a prepared statement. "We still have Old Sparky. And if that doesn't suit the criminal, then we will provide them a .45-caliber lead cocktail instead."

Drake is a Republican and a proud Baptist from the Panhandle community of Eucheeanna. At the tender age of 36, he has already been named one of the World's Worst Humans by TV commentator Keith Olbermann.

For supporters of the death penalty, the first problem with Drake's proposed legislation is that it will generate so many court challenges as to effectively halt all executions in Florida. The second problem with the idea is his lack of originality.

If you want grisly executions, come up with something fresh. Drake's Web page says he's a NASCAR fan, so why not make use of the speedway at Daytona? Strap the doomed inmate to the track and let Jeff Gordon run him over for a hundred laps.

Florida's electric chair was retired because the chair malfunctioned, causing some ghastly moments in the death chamber. Firing squads lost favor in this country for the same reason—they were messy and not always instantaneous. Inefficiency of an execution method has been viewed by some courts as "cruel and unusual punishment," which is barred by the U.S. Constitution.

Says Drake: "Don't tell me I have to be sympathetic and humane to people who do something so heinous that a judge orders them to be executed."

You can see why death-penalty opponents are secretly elated to have this guy spouting off. All that's missing is flecks of spittle on his lips.

Back in 1983, when Drake was in elementary school, I watched a man named Robert Austin Sullivan put to death in Florida's electric chair. Old Sparky worked fine that day, but it was a Gothic ceremony that unsettled witnesses and journalists. Some saw smoke rise from one of Sullivan's legs. I didn't, probably because I was watching his hooded face.

Sullivan had been convicted in the brutal robbery-murder of a Howard Johnson's manager in Miami. If the victim had been a member of my family, I would have been in the front row of the death chamber to watch Sullivan die.

Capital punishment doesn't deter anybody else from committing murder, but that was never the point. I would have no problem with the death penalty if it were administered consistently, regardless of race, and if the guilt of the condemned were a certainty.

Unfortunately, that isn't how it works. According to the Death Penalty Information Center, 115 condemned inmates have been exonerated in this country since 1973. Seventeen were freed when DNA evidence proved their innocence (after they'd served a combined 209 years in prison). One man, Frank Lee Smith, died on Florida's Death Row after serving 14 years for a rape and murder he didn't commit. DNA testing cleared his name too late.

Numerous studies show that blacks are more likely than whites to receive a death sentence for similar crimes. Two of the most famously wronged Death Row inmates were Freddie Pitts and Wilbert Lee, who were ultimately pardoned after the late *Herald* reporter Gene Miller punched holes in the double-murder case against them in the Panhandle.

A commonly heard complaint is that it takes too long to have somebody executed, often more than a decade. The appeals process is slow and grueling for victims' families, but it has saved persons who are indisputably innocent from the death chamber. A good Christian like Drake ought to be grateful for that.

Taxpayers already spend a fortune on legal battles before an inmate is actually executed. Getting the hated serial killer Ted Bundy from his cell to Old Sparky cost the state an estimated $5 million. It would have been much cheaper to lock him up and throw away the key.

Given past miscues, the odds of conducting a flawless firing squad in Florida would appear to be shaky, unless the shooters were allowed to stand five feet from their target. There surely would be no shortage of volunteers and no shortage of lawsuits.

Drake says he got his idea for the "lead cocktail" from lunchtime chatter at a neighborhood Waffle House. Perhaps he should have gone to the IHOP.

June 2, 2012
Nude Face-Eating Cannibal? Must Be Miami

All of us who live in Florida struggle to explain this bizarre place to distant friends and family.

The task got somewhat easier after the 2000 presidential election, which showcased the state's unique style of dysfunction to a vast international audience. Since then, people who live elsewhere seem not so easily mortified by anything that happens here.

Take the dreadful case of the naked cannibal.

I'd be willing to bet that in no other city but Miami would the following quote appear matter-of-factly in a crime story: "Rudy was not a face-eating zombie monster."

Those words come from a high school friend of Rudy Eugene, who chewed the flesh off a homeless man's face on Memorial Day weekend. Eugene first removed his own clothes and then tore off the trousers of his victim, 65-year-old Ronald Poppo.

The gruesome biting attack, reported by passersby, took about 18 minutes. It didn't end until Eugene was shot dead by a policeman and physically separated from the gravely injured Poppo.

All this occurred on a Saturday morning on a ramp of the MacArthur Causeway, practically within fast-break distance of the American Airlines Arena, where the Miami Heat plays.

Naturally, the gory assault was captured on video by security cameras mounted on buildings. And naturally, it's all over the Internet.

For a nontabloid headline writer, the perverse facts of the crime make it almost impossible not to sensationalize. The case is grotesque even by the extreme standards of South Florida.

In my many years of working for the *Herald*, I can't honestly recall anything quite so demented occurring in broad daylight at such a public location.

Numerous heinous crimes have a nude perpetrator or a nude victim and occasionally both. At least one murder case I remember involved a grim bit of cannibalism. But the combination of nudity and cannibalism along a busy highway should be, well, shocking.

Which isn't a word often heard when journalists who cover Miami get together and tell stories. People down here do things that are sick, warped, disgusting, twisted—but rarely shocking. Not anymore.

However, a zombie-like face-eating attack would be major news in any city. And had it happened in Des Moines or Spokane, the worldwide reaction would have been one of plain revulsion.

The initial response to the MacArthur Causeway bloodbath was the same kind of horror, but then—after the dateline was noted—almost a sigh of relief: Oh, this was in Miami? Well, that explains it.

Even some New Yorkers I know, who read daily about strange and violent events in their own zip code, expressed the view that South Florida would have been their first guess as the location for a nude face-eating incident. Is it the vibe of this place that promotes such a bounty of derangement, or do the deranged simply move here for the vibe?

The subject frequently comes up in interviews. It's a legitimate question—how to account for the unrelenting weirdness?

Reporters looking at the life of Rudy Eugene have found

a pot-smoking, Bible-reading guy with money problems and a relatively minor rap sheet. So far there is no indication that the 31-year-old man was fixated on zombie lore, werewolves, vampires, or Hannibal Lecter.

The most likely explanation for Eugene's vicious behavior was a dose of bad drugs. A police officer speculated it was LSD, which in the old days wasn't famous for causing spontaneous cannibalism. Maybe there's a new version on the streets. Another widely suggested culprit is "bath salts," synthetic crystals sold in some convenience stores that can cause hallucinations and violent outbursts.

Still another possibility is that Eugene wasn't high on anything. Perhaps he suffered a severe mental breakdown before confronting Poppo, who'd lived on the streets for four decades and had his own problems with the law.

The autopsy's toxicology report will provide some answers, but it won't get South Florida off the hook.

Whatever factors compelled Eugene to strip naked and gnaw on another man's face, the hideous crime truly could have occurred anyplace where there's bad dope and mental illness—which is to say, anyplace.

It didn't, though.

And as the story (complete with video) continues to rocket through the blogs, posts, and tweets, the lack of disbelief resonates.

Of course it's Miami. Where else?

SURROUNDED ON
THREE SIDES

Bush: Big Business's Top Shill

Seldom does a president turn out to be just as bad as predicted, but George W. Bush is rapidly making prophets of his shrillest enemies.

During the election campaign, Democrats warned that a new Bush administration would be friendly toward polluters and hostile toward the environment.

That's what Democrats always say about Republicans, so many voters didn't take it seriously. Who would have imagined that, in only three months, Bush would start to make Ronnie Reagan sound like Marjory Stoneman Douglas?

In his budget package unveiled last week, George II asked Congress to cripple the Endangered Species Act by suspending the deadlines when government must respond to petitions for protecting imperiled wildlife. Echoing a complaint of the Clinton administration, the Bush White House says the Interior Department is swamped by lawsuits seeking "endangered" status for rare species of fish, plants, birds, reptiles, and mammals.

Bush officials want a one-year moratorium that would effectively forestall any new court order protecting specific animals and their habitats. They say such decisions should come from within the agency, not from outside litigation.

Unfortunately, litigation is the only thing that seems to work. The Endangered Species Act is despised by powerful segments of the business community, and the Interior Department never has been independently aggressive about enforcing it.

If it weren't for legal action by citizen groups and environmental organizations, no federal protection would exist for the Atlantic salmon, the northern spotted owl, and most of the 1,200 species that the U.S. Fish and Wildlife Service now lists as threatened.

That's not to say the law isn't abused or that the listing process doesn't need reform. But the notion of entrusting the fate of the nation's dwindling wildlife to a political appointee—especially Interior Secretary Gale Norton—is laughably brazen.

Critters sometimes get in the way of bulldozers, and that's unacceptable to those who bankrolled Bush's presidential campaign—developers, energy companies, the timber and mining industries. They'd love to see the Endangered Species Act trashed completely, and there's no reason to expect Bush won't try to oblige. Judging by his brief track record, he'll do absolutely anything that industry wants.

One of the president's first executive actions was to throw out the federal rules on how much arsenic can be dumped in drinking water by hard-rock mines. Bush decided it won't hurt people in Utah and Nevada to swallow 80 percent more of the soluble poison.

Next, he casually reneged on a campaign promise to reduce carbon-dioxide emissions from power plants. Overruling his new chief of the Environmental Protection Agency, Christie Todd Whitman, Bush said that adding smog controls would be a financial hardship for utilities.

He made the same argument for weaseling out of the Kyoto Protocol, an international agreement to limit the volume of greenhouse gases released into the global atmosphere.

Predictably, the two industries that will gain the most from Bush's backpedaling—mining and electric power—were responsible for two-thirds of the 7.7 billion pounds of toxic chemicals spewed into the environment in 1999, the last year for which statistics are available. That report was issued Wednesday by the EPA itself. Naturally, President Asterisk wants to cut the agency's budget by 6 percent, a big chunk coming from enforcement.

As dangerous to the public health as his actions appear, Bush is refreshing in a peculiar sort of way. He wasted no time showing his true colors, which was considerate of him. We've had plenty of presidents who didn't give a damn about the environment but pretended otherwise.

Not Bush. He's proving to be a rare species himself—a politician who is exactly what his critics said he was: in this case, a stalwart and unapologetic shill for big business.

His priority is simple and unambiguous: to fatten corporate profits at all costs.

Nobody can say he isn't decisive. Nobody can say he doesn't have a well-defined policy.

Look at the bold moves he has made in only three months:

More toxins in the water we drink, more crud in the air we breathe, less wilderness for refuge—and fewer birds and animals to share it with.

And to think this is only the beginning.

June 3, 2001
George W. Does the 'Glades Thing

President Bush travels to Florida tomorrow on a new campaign to prove he really doesn't hate nature.

Buoyed by his triumphant communing with a giant sequoia tree in California, the president plans to celebrate federal efforts to restore and preserve the Everglades.

Concerned that Bush is perceived as indifferent to environmental concerns, the White House carefully has crafted a Florida itinerary that will show the president as a caring, sensitive friend of the earth:

8 A.M. *Air Force One* arrives at Miami International Airport.

Photo opportunity: President cradles a small burrowing owl that has been digging a nest near runway Nine-Right.

Prepared comment: "Imagine such a tiny thing living among these huge noisy jumbo jets—what better example of nature and mankind coexisting in harmony!"

9:05. Motorcade enters Everglades National Park.

Photo op: President pauses to admire a mangrove.

Prepared comment: "While perhaps not as imposing as the great sequoias, this humble tree plays a unique role in nurturing marine life.

"That's why it is vital to continue clear-cutting our vast federal forests in Montana and Idaho, so that these precious mangroves will never be needed to meet our nation's burgeoning timber needs."

10:15. Motorcade stops at a wetland.

Photo op: President poses with the wetland.

Prepared comment: "My administration is firmly committed to restoring the river of grass to its previous lush glory, so that it may be cherished by future generations.

"That's why it is imperative to move ahead with drilling in the Gulf of Mexico and the Arctic Preserve, thus ensuring there will always be plenty of gasoline for Americans who wish to drive to Florida and see the Everglades."

10:30. Motorcade stops at a slough.

Photo op: President poses with a garfish.

10:45. Motorcade stops by a canal.

Photo op: President poses with a turtle.

10:55. Motorcade stops at a cypress hammock.

Photo op: President poses with a palmetto bug.

Noon: Box lunch, followed by airboat ride.

Photo op: President pauses to admire sawgrass.

Prepared comment: "Wouldn't it be a tragedy if Americans could no longer tour this national treasure because there wasn't enough aluminum for making airboat hulls, or copper for wiring the engine coils?

"That's why our mining companies must not be crippled by unnecessary regulations and pollution controls. A little extra arsenic in the water is a small price to pay for the pleasure of airboating among garfish and turtles on a spring day."

1:15. Motorcade stops at gator pond.

Photo op: President points out several alligators swimming nearby.

Prepared comment: "It wasn't so many years ago that these magnificent animals were almost extinct. Today they're so plentiful, we're making shoes and purses out of 'em again!

"Now, that's how the Endangered Species Act is supposed to work."

2:30. Kayaking excursion on Whitewater Bay.

Photo op: President swims with a manatee.

Prepared comment: "We must do everything in our power to help this gentle giant endure.

"That's one reason why I'm committed to leasing millions of public acres dirt-cheap to America's cattle ranchers, so that these precious manatees will never be needed to meet our nation's burgeoning demand for protein."

4:05. Motorcade arrives at a Seminole Indian village.

Photo op: More endangered species.

Being allergic to cats, the president will be unable to commune with a captive Florida panther. Alternatives include a gopher tortoise, a baby indigo snake, and some sort of large moth.

In the event that no endangered animals are available, the president has consented to be photographed with a raccoon.

4:30. Tribute to Marjory Stoneman Douglas.

Photo op: The president and Interior Secretary Gale Norton will perform a dramatic reading from Douglas's classic Everglades essays.

This will be followed by a small riot.

5:15. Presidential tour ends at park headquarters.

Photo op: President is greeted by his brother, Florida Gov. Jeb Bush, who will be wearing a grocery bag over his head.

November 28, 2001
War Has Been Declared on the Humble Sea Cow

"We need to define just how many manatees you need."

That revelatory remark was made two years ago by a fellow named Wade Hopping. He's a big-time Tallahassee lobbyist who was speaking on behalf of the National Marine Manufacturers Association, which represents makers of boats and outboard engines. Asserting that Florida's manatee population was "stable and growing," Hopping suggested that the mammal be removed from the endangered-species list.

Incredibly, both the U.S. Fish and Wildlife Service and the Florida Fish and Wildlife Conservation Commission now seem to be sliding in that direction.

War quietly has been declared on the humble sea cow.

Influential special interests fear that their profits will be threatened by regulations designed to protect the hulking, easygoing animal.

Last month, the Coastal Conservation Association disgraced its own name by petitioning the state to demote the manatee from "endangered" to "threatened." The CCA claims to stand for the views of thousands of recreational anglers, but on this issue, the group is hauling water for boating and sportfishing suppliers.

It's part of an anti-manatee backlash that began after authorities decided to beef up efforts to protect the species. Hammered by lawsuits from environmental groups, state and federal agencies agreed to devise broader regulations. Among them: more low-speed boating zones in areas of heavy manatee activity and the creation of several manatee sanctuaries where human activity would be banned or limited.

Another controversial provision would have imposed special fees for new docks, the revenues to be used for enforcing manatee laws. That plan was scrapped after an outcry from developers of marinas.

The new proposals have earned the manatees some prickly enemies:

* Boaters who don't like to be told to slow down.
* Fishermen who don't like to be told where to fish.
* Trade groups whose members sell fast boats and fishing tackle.

While the efficacy of some manatee protection measures can and should be debated, it's ridiculous to argue that the critter is no longer endangered.

Florida has more than 800,000 registered boats and only about 3,200 sea cows. Even when you're lucky enough to see one in the wild, it's usually striped with prop scars.

Advocates of "delisting" cite an increase in the manatees counted during aerial surveys. They say that the population has reached a level at which strict regulations are no longer necessary. In other words, there are enough manatees swimming around that we can start killing them off again with impunity.

The Fish and Wildlife Service recently bucked its own scientists by approving a plan that would allow the delisting of manatees even if their population wasn't growing.

The FWS said that an annual mortality of 200 to 300 adult males is acceptable (to all, presumably, except the doomed manatees). Meanwhile, state wildlife officials also have agreed to reassess the species' designation as endangered.

The irony is, there wouldn't be any sea cows left to argue about if they hadn't been protected for the last three decades.

No less important than the laws and the speed zones is the heightened public awareness that resulted.

Today the manatee is a beloved Florida icon, celebrated with license plates, Jimmy Buffett tunes, and cuddly stuffed toys. Homely as they are, sea cows are adored by tourists and natives alike.

Idling my boat through a channel instead of racing full throttle is a small sacrifice for the thrill of sharing the water with these ancient and fascinating behemoths.

In 1999, the year that glib Mr. Hopping and the marine manufacturers declared war, 82 manatees were killed by boaters—the most ever. During the last 23 months, 150 more have perished by propeller.

Such sad accidents are inevitable. Sea cows go wherever they please, and it's impossible to protect them all the time. That doesn't mean that we should stop trying.

Despite what lobbyists say, saving a few more manatees won't endanger Florida's huge marine industry. With input from anglers and boaters, as well as biologists, it shouldn't be hard to come up with a sensible long-term plan.

How many manatees is enough? What an insipid question.

It's more appropriate to ask just how many Wade Hoppings we need.

May 16, 2004
Fishy Tale About Timber Lobbyist, Wild Salmon

President Bush has found an intriguing way to skate around the Endangered Species Act, the wildlife-protection law that has caused so many headaches for his pals in timber, oil, and real-estate development.

In a move that surprised residents of the Pacific Northwest, the administration has decided to start counting hatchery fish when determining whether certain types of wild salmon should remain on the federal endangered list.

This proposal didn't come from biologists, many of whom consider hatchery fry to be genetically inferior to wild salmon. Nor did the plan come from the administration's own appointed panel of experts, whose findings were dismissed by the president's men.

Actually, it was a lawyer named Mark C. Rutzick who first dreamed up the idea of including hatchery-bred salmon when counting the species. The intent was to boost the reported fish population to such levels that the species might be removed from the endangered list and no longer be protected.

At the time, Rutzick's prize clients were timber companies, often under fire for trashing streams and rivers. He led the fight against conservation rules intended to protect fish and animal habitats from the effects of forestry operations.

Presented with such credentials, it's no wonder that President Bush appointed Rutzick as a legal adviser to the National Marine Fisheries Service. Who better than an agent of the logging industry to oversee the future of America's 26 imperiled species of salmon?

Here in Florida, we have no salmon, but we do have a variety of wildlife at risk of being wiped off the planet, including the panther, the Key deer, the Miami blue butterfly, and the homely short-nosed sturgeon.

In all, federal and state officials have classified at least 57 Florida species as either endangered or threatened. None stirs more emotion than the ponderous manatee, which is at the center of a battle pitting environmentalists against the recreational marine industry and waterfront developers.

The Legislature's sympathies were never in doubt. Last

month it passed a bill that would severely limit the ability of state wildlife authorities to set boating speed zones or restrict dock building in areas where manatees congregate.

The measure, now on Gov. Jeb Bush's desk, is endorsed by some of the same interest groups that have been lobbying to get manatees scratched off the endangered list altogether. Could their campaign be given new life by the administration's novel hatchery concept?

Obviously, farming manatees would pose some unique challenges. For starters, sea cows are considerably larger than salmon—an adult specimen weighs anywhere from 800 to 1,200 pounds. Even newborn manatees are chubby, averaging more than 60 pounds. Consequently, the holding tanks will have to be very spacious.

Then there's the fertility issue. A female salmon lays 2,000 to 10,000 eggs every spawning season, but the average female manatee gives birth to only a single calf every two to five years. So the process of accumulating baby manatees will take a very long time.

And while mother salmon typically lay their eggs and take off, mother manatees insist on sticking around for a couple of years to nurse and raise the calves. This could get expensive, because manatees eat the equivalent of 10 to 15 percent of their own body weight every day.

So the grocery bill for fresh greens will be very high.

Finally, there's the problem of adaptability. When you put baby salmon into a river, they almost always swim away— even the dumbest, most inbred hatchery fish. Manatees are more likely to be confused by their sudden freedom, especially after being fed and pampered for so long. The spectacle of hundreds of young sea cows moping around a river, waiting for handouts, could be a definite problem, PR-wise.

None of these hurdles is insurmountable, though. Just as

the White House relied on a timber advocate for advice on salmon, perhaps it could turn to the makers of Jet Skis for guidance on manatee management.

If such a bold approach were successful, we might see a day when a hatchery-style census is applied to Florida's remaining panthers and Key deer, perhaps counting zoo specimens as part of the natural population.

Anything is possible when we've got a president so clearly committed to pruning the nation's roster of endangered species down to a manageable two or three critters.

May 29, 2005
Vigilance Falls Woefully Short

If Miami-Dade commissioners sell out to developers and vote to move westward the county's Urban Development Boundary, thousands of acres of wetlands will be open to destruction.

The decision would effectively sabotage the $8 billion Everglades restoration plan and would further imperil South Florida's future water supply.

In theory, wetlands are supposed to be protected under the Clean Water Act by the U.S. Army Corps of Engineers. Since the federal government is an equal partner with Florida in the much-hyped Everglades project, you might reasonably assume that the Corps would make at least a token effort at vigilance.

But you'd be wrong.

If the UDB gets moved, all remaining wetlands along the rim of the Everglades are in danger. Judging by its past actions, the Corps will bow to the developers as meekly as the politicians do.

A series of superb articles in *The St. Petersburg Times* has documented that at least 84,000 acres of wetlands in Florida have been obliterated since 1990. That was the year that the first President Bush unveiled a federal initiative called "no net loss." The idea was that developers would be required to replace the pristine marshes and swamps that they destroyed.

"It's a huge scam," Steve Brooker told the *Times*. For 15 years he reviewed wetlands permits for the Army Corps in Florida. "A make-believe program," agreed Vic Anderson, who spent 30 years with the Corps.

Basically, here's how it is meant to work. Through a process known as mitigation, developers are allowed to drain and pave a wetland if they agree to re-create another one somewhere else.

Unfortunately, constructing a shopping mall is much easier (and much more lucrative) than constructing an ecologically healthy swamp. Many of the artificially devised wetlands are nothing but glorified rain puddles.

Not that the Army Corps would ever notice. To this day, the agency has no system for tracking the success or failure of mitigation projects. Usually, it's content to take the developer's word.

According to the *Times*'s investigation, the feds approve more wetland destruction in Florida than in any other state.

How easy is it to turn a marsh into asphalt and concrete? Between 1999 and 2003, the Corps approved more than 12,000 wetland destruction permits here.

Number rejected: One.

Agency officials say their job is not to "impede" development but, rather, to work with developers during the permitting process to minimize the project's impact.

Look around Florida and see what a swell job they've done.

In Pensacola, a top Democratic fund-raiser named Fred

Levin and his brother were allowed to erect five 21-story condos on prime beach marshlands, despite the objections of the Environmental Protection Agency, the Fish and Wildlife Service, and the National Marine Fisheries Service.

The mitigation was a flop. The man-made wetland was so feeble that it was destroyed by the first hurricane to blow through.

Here's how the "no net loss" policy really works: Developers call up their congressman or senator, to whose campaigns they've generously donated, and whine that the Army Corps is dragging its feet on a wetland permit. The congressman or senator promptly picks up the phone or fires off a letter, and magically, the developer's permit is expedited.

This scenario was documented in shameful detail by the *Times*. Both Republicans and Democrats (Sen. Bill Nelson, Rep. Alcee Hastings, even Everglades champion Bob Graham) have intervened to hasten the demise of a wetland.

A classic example was the time in 1995 when then–U.S. Sen. Connie Mack chewed out Col. Terry Rice, then head of the Army Corps in Florida, for taking too long on a permit application from Florida Gulf Coast University.

Plans for the new university called for removing 75 acres of wetlands near Fort Myers owned by Ben Hill Griffin III, the citrus heir and a heavyweight political donor. Griffin had offered the tract to the university and wanted to build a huge development around it. Not long after Mack's angry phone call, Rice approved the wetlands destruction.

Construction commenced, and soon three feet of water covered the site. The problem hasn't gone away. Since FGCU opened, it's been cited three times for illegally pumping water from its campus into nearby marshes.

That's what you get for building on a swamp, a long and greedy tradition here. Most of western Broward, including the whole community of Weston, was once wetlands that nurtured the Everglades.

Which is why those seeking to dissolve the UDB in Miami-Dade aren't terribly worried about the feds interfering with their plans later on. Shoma Homes, Lowe's Home Improvement Centers, D. R. Horton—all have lobbyists who know exactly whom to call in Washington, D.C.

No developer has more clout than Lennar Corp, which is itching to cram thousands of homes on 981 acres outside Florida City, along the edge of Everglades National Park.

That single project could be fatal to Everglades restoration, but don't expect the Army Corps to ride to the rescue. The agency is merely a minor nuisance for big developers with friends in high places.

The record speaks for itself: In only 14 years, 84,000 acres of wetlands wiped out.

No net loss? Only for those pocketing the profits.

September 25, 2005
In a Storm, We're All Sitting Ducks

The only predictable thing about this hellish hurricane season is how soon its lessons will be forgotten.

Communities flattened by Katrina and Rita will be rebuilt gallantly but with little thought given to the next storm. You and I will pay for this with our federal taxes and usurious insurance premiums.

And when the next hurricane hits, we'll suck it up and do it all over again. That's how it goes.

Once upon a time, the vulnerable temperate shores of North America were protected by dunes, barrier islands, and vast wetlands that absorbed tidal surges and also served as windbreaks. Today much of the natural buffer against hurricanes is gone, wiped out in the name of progress. Millions of acres of wetlands have been drained and paved. Many barrier islands are now resort developments, and the beachfront dunes have been replaced by high-rise condos and hotels.

Densely populated urban centers have arisen in locations that are best not inhabited year-round. It's hard to imagine the ancient Romans constructing a city nine or 10 feet below sea level without planning for floods, but that's what happened in modern New Orleans.

For sheer arrogance toward the weather, no place beats Florida. Every millimeter of our 1,300-mile coastline is at risk of getting slammed by a killer storm, but that hasn't discouraged us from building to the water's edge.

And then rebuilding in the same dumb place if a hurricane knocks down what was there.

You'd think we would have learned more from Andrew, which pulverized South Miami-Dade in 1992. The storm exposed shocking incompetence and negligence by some home builders, and also those who were supposed to regulate them. Stronger building codes were finally passed, but no effort was made to reduce density along the coastline or prevent future overdevelopment. Just the opposite has been happening.

Today wetlands in Florida are being bulldozed at a record pace. Since Andrew, thousands upon thousands of new residents have been packed into burgeoning coastal communities, many of which were raked by last year's quartet of storms. Even the sturdiest structure isn't safe from the Biblical-scale storm surge delivered by Katrina or Rita. If you're on the coast, you're toast.

Gov. Jeb Bush wants a special panel to examine the way in which Florida's shorelines are being developed, with an aim of better hurricane protection. It would be a fine idea if it weren't 50 years too late. We're sitting ducks, all of us.

Much of the lower eastern seaboard and Gulf Coast are in the same predicament, as evidenced by the astounding scenes of mass flight first in Louisiana, then in Texas—millions of people jamming the highways, trying to get away. What else is there to do when a hurricane comes? With no remaining natural barriers to shield us, the only intelligent option is to run like hell.

No matter how much death, destruction, and dislocation occur, nothing changes to make things safer. We can't undo what's already been done to the coastlines, but why keep repeating the same dangerous mistakes?

The cost of hurricane relief to taxpayers this year alone will exceed $100 billion, but there is no talk of wetlands policy reform among the so-called conservatives in Washington. Greed always trumps common sense and science. Waterfront property is the Holy Grail of the real-estate trade, and few politicians are courageous enough to argue for sane growth regulations.

In 1989, Hurricane Hugo destroyed scores of luxury homes on the barrier islands of South Carolina. Most were grandly rebuilt, an act of impudence subsidized by you and me. Eventually, those houses will be wrecked by another storm, and we'll again pay for new ones. It's quite a system.

Trent Lott, the Republican senator from Mississippi, lost a stilt cottage on the Gulf to Katrina. In one of his now-weekly visits to the region, President Bush predicted that Lott will have a "fantastic" new home on the same site. I'm sure that's a big relief to the senator's constituents, many of whom are sleeping in shelters these days.

Whenever a disaster strikes, there are two kinds of victims:

those who had the opportunity to be somewhere else and those who didn't.

Years ago, I moved to the Keys in full command of my faculties, knowing that my house would get thumped every now and then by a hurricane, which it has. I've got no excuses and deserve no sympathy.

Save it for those who have no choice. Often they're held in place by poverty or a hard-won job. You saw them by the thousands in the gut-wrenching footage from the Superdome and Gulfport and Biloxi.

Many who evacuated will never go back to where they lived before. Those who do might find themselves fleeing again someday, in advance of another terrible storm.

Unwilling to control the foolish way we exploit our coastlines, the government can't do anything about hurricanes except tell us when to run.

October 9, 2005
How to Kill a Perfectly Good Florida River

The killing of the St. Lucie River is deplorable but hardly unique. Other Florida rivers are being destroyed, although the symptoms aren't so arresting.

The St. Lucie is dying as a man-made slime trail, a huge vein of effluent streamed with blue-green algae. The remaining fish are increasingly sick and ulcerated, the birds have flown, and residents of neighboring counties are being warned to keep their children away from the water.

Unlike some of Florida's rivers—poisoned slowly by mines and paper mills—the St. Lucie is dying very publicly and in a heavily populated region. Many thousands of people live on or near the waterway, and some are protesting loudly.

It's uncomfortable for state authorities. Often a river can

be killed off without much fuss; only a few stout souls in mill towns dare to protest, and the enviros downstream don't get much play in the local media.

But the St. Lucie is different. Palm Beach County TV stations have been avidly covering the story, sending up helicopters—helicopters!—to take video of the churning crud.

This is bad. This is ugly stuff.

The source is Lake Okeechobee, a humongous latrine for ranches, farms, groves, and, more recently, massive residential developments in central Florida. For decades the state has tolerated the dumping of cattle manure, pesticides, and fertilizers into the big lake. Tons of foul sediment were stirred up by last year's hurricanes, and water is now being pumped at up to 26,000 gallons per second into the St. Lucie River.

Water managers blame the weather. Months of heavy rain have forced them to keep flushing Lake Okeechobee so it won't overflow, they say. The runoff can't be sent elsewhere because the high phosphorus levels exceed the limits imposed for the Everglades restoration project.

So where does all that bad water go? Down the Caloosahatchee River to the Gulf of Mexico, and down the St. Lucie to the Atlantic.

What the good people of Martin and St. Lucie counties see and smell on their river is the disastrous culmination of generations of lousy planning, worse management, and slimy politics. Florida has a squalid record of letting special interests exploit and contaminate our public waterways, and the state remains an unfailingly enthusiastic partner in such pollution. Georgia-Pacific, which empties up to 36 million gallons of crap every day into a creek near Palatka, now has a permit to pipe its waste directly to the St. Johns River. Meanwhile, International Paper in Pensacola has a green light to build an outfall pipe to wetlands along Perdido Bay.

The most outrageous case is in Taylor County, up in Florida's Big Bend. There, the Buckeye paper mill, which manufactures fluff for disposable diapers, has annihilated virtually all life in the once teeming Fenholloway River. In a grievously belated attempt to restore the Fenholloway to a "fishable-swimmable" waterway, the state has brilliantly decided to let Buckeye pipe its toxins straight to the Gulf of Mexico, a swath of which has already been deadened by noxious dumping.

For these upcoming atrocities, you can thank pro-industry stooges at the federal Environmental Protection Agency and Florida's assiduously gutless Department of Environmental Protection (the former chief, David Struhs, left for a job at International Paper). The rivers will go black before any Bush brother notices.

Rather than requiring big companies and governments to clean their waste, it's much easier (and cheaper) to pipe it somewhere less noticeable. Somebody would have already suggested that remedy for the St. Lucie River were it feasible to build a sewer pipe from Lake Okeechobee to the sea. With property values along the St. Lucie in jeopardy and much of the river unsafe for human recreation, plenty of folks in Martin and St. Lucie counties are angry.

Officials of the South Florida Water Management District say that they're at the mercy of the rains and of the timetable for Everglades restoration. On the drawing board is the C-44 reservoir, which supposedly will cleanse about 13 billion gallons of Lake Okeechobee poo before it reaches the St. Lucie. Unfortunately, the project isn't due for completion until 2010, and many fear it will be too late. The Martin County commission has discussed suing the water district for wrecking the St. Lucie, and similar action is being considered by a group called the Rivers Coalition.

Meanwhile, the Stuart/Martin Chamber of Commerce has enlisted a big-time lawyer, Willie Gary, to join the river battle. Gary lives along the St. Lucie and has offered his counsel for free, which is not happy news for the state.

In what many residents perceive as a blunt threat, some water managers have suggested that litigation could result in the postponement of the C-44 reservoir construction. In other words: Shut up, be patient, and trust us.

It's not easy.

The history of Florida waters is one of greedy abuse and neglect. Surely there must be a way to save the Everglades without killing the rivers that border it.

The ruination of Lake Okeechobee took 70 years, but the St. Lucie is deteriorating much faster. Completion of the filtering reservoir is a minimum of five years away, which is an awfully long time to wait if you're a kid who wants to fish or go swimming.

An awfully long time to sit by and watch a river die.

June 11, 2006
No Reason to Rejoice over Manatee Ruling

Let the celebration begin.

Manatees, those lovable, bewhiskered icons of Florida waterways, are officially no longer endangered!

The news is all the more amazing because the state's own biologists fear "a significant decline" in the manatee population due to increased threats from boats, red tide, and habitat loss.

That doesn't sound like much of a reason to break out the champagne, but it's only because we don't understand the advanced scientific logic used by state regulators: Reducing the number of manatees in the wild simply means there will be fewer of them to die later.

That's obviously what members of the Florida Fish and Wildlife Conservation Commission had in mind last week when they voted unanimously to downgrade the pokey sea cow to the status of "threatened."

Cheering estimates that the burly aquatic mammals now number about 3,000, commission chairman Rodney Barreto said, "I believe the manatee has recovered. We should be rejoicing."

So far, the only ones rejoicing over the panel's decision are waterfront developers, marina builders, and representatives of the marine industry, who for five years have been waging an expensive political campaign to get the manatee "downlisted."

They were miffed by strict rules imposed in some places while manatees were on the state's endangered list. Speed zones were established that inconvenienced fishermen and weekend boaters, while restrictions were imposed on permits for new docks and marinas in certain areas.

As adorable as they might be, the sea cows had become a nuisance. They were getting in the way of big plans by people with big bucks. The more slips that you can cram into a marina, the fatter your profit margins. And the larger the marina is, the more boats will be sold to fill it.

Everybody makes out dandy except for the nearsighted manatees, which tend to gather and breed in the same quiet waters along which developers like to build their projects.

So, heavyweight lobbyists such as Wade Hopping were hired to promote the notion that manatees are doing just great. Last week the seven FWCC commissioners, all appointed by Gov. Jeb Bush, agreed.

A nonscientist looking at the mortality data might wonder why they're so upbeat. Last year, 396 manatees—more than 10 percent of the estimated population—died. Of those, only

81 fatalities were classified as natural. This year, manatees are perishing at a record pace. As of May 31, there were 195 known deaths in Florida.

Those sorts of statistics don't exactly make you want to dance a jig with Rodney Barreto. Nor does the final report of the state Biological Review Panel, which says there's a better than even chance that the manatee population will shrink by 20 percent over the next 30 years. But sunny optimism rules at the wildlife commission, which prefers to trumpet a 100 percent increase in the annual aerial manatee census over the last 20 years.

Yet if the protection program is working so well, why scrap it? Isn't it insane to eliminate the very rules that resulted in such impressive results?

It is if you want the manatee population to continue growing—but that's plainly not the goal of coastal developers, the recreational marine industry, or state wildlife managers.

By their count, we've got enough sea cows. What we need more of is boats, docks, ramps, marinas, and condos. To the softhearted, the lobbyists might say: What better way to reduce the number of manatee deaths than to start reducing the number of manatees? Scratching the species off the endangered list was the first step, but no restrictions on building or boating can be lifted until the state comes up with a management plan.

Meanwhile, the manatee remains on the federal endangered species list, although the U.S. Fish and Wildlife Service is under pressure from members of Congress who are shilling for the same special interests that prevailed in Florida.

At last week's meeting in which the manatee's rebound was heralded, state wildlife officials elevated the gopher tortoise to the list of threatened species. They did not, however, suspend the policy of permitting developers to bury the animals alive in exchange for paying into a conservation fund.

More than 74,000 gopher tortoises have been "entombed" with state approval, which might explain why the species is in trouble. Commissioners promised to find a less cruel way to deal with the critters one of these days.

Presumably, we can look forward to another round of rejoicing.

April 1, 2007
If You Like Polluted Rivers, You'll Love This

Say goodbye to the days when you dipped a toe in a lake to see if it was warm enough for a swim. Soon that toe will be the only part of your anatomy that you'll dare immerse in certain waters, and only then if you're not especially worried about arsenic, cyanide, or fecal bacteria.

Florida's Department of Environmental Protection is steaming ahead with plans to reclassify state waterways for the benefit of corporate and agricultural polluters.

Rather than requiring paper mills, phosphate mines, and ranches to clean up their effluent, the DEP has devised a ranking system that could forever surrender some of the most damaged rivers, lakes, and canals to those who are using them as a sewer.

Florida waterways now fall into one of five classes, depending on cleanliness and safety. Class I is drinking water, followed by shellfish harvesting (Class II); recreational uses such as swimming, boating, and fishing (Class III); agricultural (Class IV); and industrial (Class V), which currently is not used.

It's noteworthy that the state has more rigorous aquatic

health standards for oysters than for humans, a policy that would be creatively expanded under the DEP's new proposal.

Under the plan, Class III recreational waters would be divided into three "Human Use" categories with escalating degrees of risk. Waterways classified as HU-3 theoretically would be safe for all fishing and swimming activities. Full-body contact with the water would not be considered danger-ous, so you could dunk all your extremities, not just a toe. However, an outing to a river rated HU-4 would be more adventurous. Fishing would be permitted, but the state would recommend only "limited human contact."

By way of elaboration, the DEP says an HU-4 waterway would be considered "splashable"—meaning a splash or two won't be toxic. You still shouldn't go in the water, but a few random drops won't necessarily blister your flesh.

Fun, huh? And I bet you can't wait to reel in one of those two-headed carp and fry it up for supper.

Things could get seriously interesting on waterways rated HU-5—"boatable," though unswimmable and unfishable. No human contact would be advised, so forget the shoreline picnic unless you've got hazmat suits for the whole family.

DEP insists that a new rating system is necessary because some Florida waterways are misclassified. The agency says it's unrealistic to expect water in an urban drainage canal, for example, to be as clean as that of an estuary or a natural spring.

But critics such as Linda Young of the Clean Water Net-work say the proposed Human Use categories could be a gift to polluters, allowing them to continue poisoning waterways at levels hazardous to fish, wildlife, and humans. Instead of cleaning a polluted river to make it safe for all swimming and fishing—as the rules now putatively require—heavy industry and agriculture will be able to lobby for the more lenient splashable or boatable rating.

Such an option would have been a godsend to the Buckeye pulp mill in Perry, on Florida's northwest coast. Built in 1952 by Procter & Gamble, the mill dumps 58 million gallons of dioxin-filled waste daily into the Fenholloway River, a foul, lifeless spume that threatens the Gulf of Mexico.

For years, state and federal regulators looked the other way while Young and fellow conservationists tried to make Buckeye stop killing the Fenholloway and restore it to the standards of a Class III waterway.

Buckeye wants to bypass the river and pipe its filth directly into the Gulf, a ludicrous idea approved by the boneheads at DEP. The case remains tangled in court, but Buckeye would have prevailed a long time ago if the Fenholloway were designated anything less than fishable-swimmable.

Under DEP's draft plan, companies will be able to flush substantially heavier loads of contaminants into HU-4 and HU-5 waterways. The limits haven't been set, but the long list of acceptable chemicals and compounds include benzene, arsenic, methylene chloride, chloroform, mercury, lead, copper, nickel, PCBs, pesticides, fertilizers, and that yummy old favorite, fecal coliform bacteria.

At a time when pollution threatens virtually every important body of water in Florida—from the St. Johns to Lake Okeechobee to Florida Bay—it's incredible that the state wants to make life easier for the polluters.

Well, not really so incredible.

Just gaggable.

May 13, 2007
Overcrowding? Nature Will Fix That

In the absence of a sane growth-management policy, nature is becoming the great equalizer in Florida.

A 17-month drought has made a puddle of Lake Okeechobee and has parched the Biscayne Aquifer. Parts of the Everglades are drying up, while advancing seawater endangers the well fields that serve hundreds of thousands of residents in Broward and Palm Beach counties.

Water managers warn that, unless consumption is drastically reduced, the taps could run dry—or, at the least, start spitting salt—in several coastal communities. Forget about watering your lawn; you won't be able to water your kids.

The emergency is so dire that even a busy hurricane season may not make it go away. Florida, one of the wettest states in the country, is running dry.

Drought cycles here are nothing new, but this is the first one to occur with 18 million people encamped on the peninsula. They might cut back on sprinkling their geraniums, but they won't stop taking showers or washing their laundry.

Not many politicians are brave enough to cite overpopulation as a cause of the current crisis, though it is. There are too many people using too much water, but it's easier to blame the weather.

The state's primitive, low-tech economy revolves around cramming as many humans as possible onto every available acre. Few in Tallahassee have the guts to admit that it's time to change course.

This is where nature steps in. Try selling a new home or a condo when briny crud is dripping from the spigots.

Since its infancy, Florida has had a contentious relationship with water. The Everglades were diked and dredged to sabotage the natural flow, first for the benefit of agriculture and later for the benefit of land developers. The Everglades promptly began to die, and only when the financial ramifications became manifest did those same special interests rally behind the current restoration program.

Unlike California and other fast-growing states, Florida can't hijack big rivers to supply its thirsty cities. Much of our water is pumped from porous rock underground, and without moderate rain, the levels keep dropping and salt intrusion progresses.

Once a contaminated well is shut down, it can take years to bring it safely back online. Said Jesus Rodriguez, spokesman for the South Florida Water Management District, "The scenario is a grim one. We could be talking about bottled water for the municipalities for a long time."

One way to gird for the future—and protect families who already live here—would be to impose building moratoriums in those counties where the water shortage is most acute.

This is way too simple and sensible. Moratoriums can't be enacted unless local leaders are willing to stand up to developers, a rare occurrence indeed. The state is requiring counties to recycle water for nonpotable uses, but that doesn't curb the liquid appetite of sprawl.

It's lunacy to continue carving out subdivisions and erecting high-rises when the wells are drying up, but that's the plan: Keep Florida growing, no matter what. Once the rainy season begins, everything's gonna be fine, right?

Wrong. The state was soaked by hurricanes and tropical waves during 2004 and 2005, yet where's all that water now?

As we all know, newcomers aren't easily spooked away from Florida. Despite predictions of another terrible storm season, the state's population soared last year by nearly

431,000. That's the same as adding two more cities, each the size of Orlando.

According to the University of Florida's Bureau of Economic and Business Research, the state will have 20 million residents within three years and almost 25 million by 2025.

Don't let anybody tell you this is good news, unless you yearn for more taxes, higher insurance rates, and water bills as hefty as your car payment. That's the future, and it's not so far off.

Rains will come this summer, as they always do, providing temporary cover for politicians who don't want to confront the water crisis. Experts say it could take years of heavier than normal precipitation to restore safe levels in Lake Okeechobee and saturate the aquifers sufficiently to stave off encroaching seawater.

Shortages will hit some communities sooner, and harder, than others. Eventually, state water managers will be forced to take action on a bolder scale than rationing sprinkler use.

Twice as many people are moving here as are moving out. The net population continues to expand at the dangerous rate of about 1,000 souls a day, and they'll keep coming until there's a full-blown water panic.

By then, we'll all be sucking air.

March 8, 2009
Public Spigot Stays Open for Water Bottlers

You probably thought there was a serious water shortage in Florida.

It's why we're spending billions to repair and repurify the Everglades, right? It's why we're not supposed to run our lawn sprinklers more than once or twice a week.

But hold on. It turns out there's a boundless, virtually free supply of Florida water—though not for residents. The public spigot remains open day and night for Nestlé, Coca-Cola, PepsiCo, and 19 other corporations that bottle our water and sell it for a huge per-unit profit.

The stuff is no safer or tastier than most municipal tap water, but lots of us buy it anyway. You know all the brands: Deer Park, Dasani, Zephyrhills, Aquafina, even Publix. Common sense would suggest that a company with a balance sheet like Coca-Cola's or Pepsi's ought to pay for the water they take, the same as homeowners and small businesses do.

Nope. Every year, state water managers allow large bottling firms to siphon nearly two *billion* gallons from fresh springs and aquifers. The fees are laughably puny.

For example, it cost Nestlé Waters of North America the grand sum of $150 for a permit to remove as much water as it pleases from the Blue Springs in Madison County. Every day, Nestlé pipes about 500,000 gallons, enough to fill 102,000 plastic bottles that are then shipped to stores and supermarkets throughout the Southeast. Even by Florida standards, the scale of this public rip-off is mind-bending.

Protected by lawmakers, the bottling companies get a free ride—more precisely, a free guzzle of about 5.4 million gallons a day. Up until December, the Department of Environmental Protection kept no data on water-bottling operations and, of course, imposed no regulation.

Three years ago, House Democrats sought a fee on bottled-water producers, but the bill was quietly drowned by Republicans in the Senate. Vermont and Michigan have already passed such a measure, and Maine is currently considering it.

Now the issue is floating up again in that dreary annual IQ test otherwise known as the meeting of the Florida Legislature. Gov. Charlie Crist is pushing for a modest 6-cents-per-gallon tax on water taken by commercial bottlers.

The governor's office calls it a "severance fee" that would treat water like phosphate, oil, and other natural resources extracted by private companies. Crist predicts the tax would raise $56 million the first year, much-needed funds that could be used for projects like desalinization plants.

Crist's fee would also apply to water purchased by bottling companies from municipal supplies—basically tap water. Though bottlers don't advertise it, some of the water they sell with fancy labels comes from the same treatment tanks as the stuff from your kitchen faucet, only it's outrageously more expensive.

Perceptively noting that the budget is in shambles and the state is desperate for revenue, even some Republicans have expressed support for cashing in on the bottled-water craze. In a charming understatement, Sen. Evelyn Lynn of Ormond Beach said "it's somewhat of a contradiction" for Florida to let bottling firms have all the water they want while curtailing use by homeowners.

However, Lynn wants to tax water bottles at the point of sale, meaning the money would come from the pockets of consumers. Crist's proposed fee is fairer, laying the burden where it belongs—on the companies that are getting rich from tapping Florida's underground aquifers.

Not surprisingly, the industry greatly prefers a sales tax over an extraction fee. Its lobbyists are fiercely working to kill the governor's plan. Bottlers say it's wrong to single out one group among the many private and public users of spring water. Although agriculture does draw billions of gallons from the same sources, few ranches or farms enjoy the spectacular profits that water bottlers do.

The times are jittery for corporations such as Nestlé and Coca-Cola, under fire for contributing a waste stream of plastic containers to the nation's landfills and dumps.

It also appears that consumers are starting to figure out what experts have long asserted—that bottled water is no bargain, and no better for your health than what comes from the tap. Nestlé's sales of its water brands dropped about 1.6 percent in 2008.

Don't worry, though. Those companies that use Florida springs are still mopping up. It's easy when you don't have to pay for your product.

Next time you open your family's water bill, think about that little bottle of Zephyrhills that you bought for $1.69. How does it taste now?

December 12, 2010
Florida Fights for Rights of Polluters

Farms, mills, and municipalities that use Florida waterways as a latrine got more good news last week from their stooges in Tallahassee. The latest battle to stop the enforcement of federal pollution laws will be funded by state taxpayers.

Outgoing Agriculture Commissioner Charles Bronson— backed by Attorney General Bill McCollum—has sued to prevent the Environmental Protection Agency from imposing revised clean-water standards for Florida's rivers, creeks, and lakes.

Standing stoically in support of the polluters, McCollum and Bronson say the new water rules are too costly and based on flawed science (interestingly, data provided by the state itself). Endorsing that lame position are their successors, Attorney General–elect Pam Bondi and Agriculture Commissioner–elect Adam Putnam.

To hear all this whining, you'd think the EPA had ambushed Florida businesses with the new water regulations. Not even close. Back in 1998, the EPA ordered all states to cut back pollution of so-called surface waters with damaging nutrients from farms, ranches, septic tanks, and sewage-treatment facilities. The agency set a deadline of 2004 and then—in the anti-regulatory spirit of the Bush era—basically did nothing to follow up. In 2008, environmental groups finally sued the EPA in order to compel enforcement of the federal Clean Water Act.

It's not some new piece of radical legislation. It was born in 1948 as the Federal Water Pollution Control Act, and expanded significantly under Richard Nixon in 1972, and again in 1977.

Floridians who aren't familiar with the Clean Water Act can be forgiven, because it has never been taken seriously here by companies that dump massive volumes of waste into public waters, or by the politicians who are supposed to care about such crimes.

The Everglades wouldn't be in its current dire condition if authorities at all levels hadn't skirted and even ignored the law, permitting ranchers, sugar farmers, and developing cities to flush billions of dirty gallons of runoff into the state's most important watershed.

With good reason, after decades of getting their way, polluters became cocky and complacent. But they're not stupid, and the writing has been on the wall for some time. The EPA has worked with the administrations of both Jeb Bush and Charlie Crist to come up with new water rules, often bowing to industry concerns.

Under fire in court, the EPA in 2009 finally agreed to set pollution standards for lakes and streams this year, with regulations for saltwater bays and estuaries to take effect in 2011. The agency estimates only about 10 percent of Florida's farms and fewer than half the waste-treatment plants would be affected.

Still, the outcry from heavy industry and agricultural interests was instant and predictable, as was the agency's response: another delay.

Both of Florida's U.S. senators, Democrat Bill Nelson and Republican George LeMieux, pushed for the EPA to back off, and polluters won a 15-month reprieve.

Heck, it's only water. Try not to think of the crud in it as fertilizers, pesticides, and human waste. Embrace more benign terms, like phosphorus and nitrogen. That's what the industry lobbyists prefer.

And while they haggle with scientists over how many numeric parts per billion is a tolerable stream of pollution, try not to worry about its impact on the public waters that your children and grandchildren will inherit and rely on.

It's not easy if you live along the St. Johns River, the St. Lucie waterway, the Caloosahatchee, or any number of Florida rivers and streams that for generations have been used to transport man-made waste. Nutrient pollutants spawn algae blooms, kill wildlife, choke out native vegetation, and cause nasty health problems for humans.

Because of toxic freshwater runoff, the state's southwest coast has experienced caustic red tides that littered the beaches with dead fish and sent coughing tourists scurrying back to their hotel rooms—and then to the airport.

Among the many harsh lessons of the BP oil spill was that pollution—not regulation—is a more devastating job-killer. Florida's upper Gulf Coast received a relatively small bombardment of tar balls, but it was enough to cripple tourism and the commercial fishing trade for months. It didn't help property values, either.

The argument that it's morally indefensible to foul natural waters is futile against the outsized political clout of the polluters. Whether it's a phosphate mine, pulp mill, or cane field, Florida's leaders—Democrats and Republicans—have traditionally been happy to offer our rivers and wetlands as free sewers.

However, the blowback—that dirty water is endangering the economy—is increasingly difficult to brush aside.

That didn't stop Bronson and McCollum from suing the EPA. They're not doing it for the citizens of Florida; they're doing it for the polluters.

And they're paying for it with your tax dollars, at a time when the state budget is strapped for revenue.

Try not to think of this as pure crud. Just try.

September 7, 2012
Dolphins at the Mercy of the Clueless and the Cruel

Earlier this summer, in the Gulf waters near the Florida-Alabama border, somebody stabbed a screwdriver into the head of a bottlenose dolphin.

Sightings of the injured mammal occurred for a couple of days until it turned up dead in Perdido Bay. The crime, which remains unsolved, is notable for more than its extreme cruelty. Years ago it would have been unusual for a human with a weapon in his hand to get near enough to wound a wild dolphin. That was before people began following and illegally feeding the animals, a practice recklessly adopted by a few tour-boat captains in the Panama City area.

The result was to train communities of dolphins to be not just lazy but dependent on handouts for survival. Instead of teaching their offspring how to hunt schools of baitfish, momma dolphins taught the little ones to wait for boatloads of tourists bearing buckets of chum.

Dolphins are smart and opportunistic. When the tour boats weren't around, they started bothering commercial fishermen, who, with their paychecks on the line, didn't regard the voracious acrobats as fondly as visitors did. According to the National Oceanic and Atmospheric Administration, the government in recent years has prosecuted three fishermen for attacking dolphins. Guns are the favored method, and in one case a pipe bomb was thrown.

The screwdriver killing is a first. Experts believe the mortally wounded dolphin came from a place near Orange Beach, Alabama, where feeding the protected marine mammals has become popular.

In most places you seldom hear of a dolphin being struck by a boat propeller. The adult specimens always teach the calves how to keep a safe distance from the engines—you can see these lessons in progress when a pod comes together in your wake. Likewise, it's uncommon in most waters for a dolphin to take a bait on a fishing line. They know better than to bite anything with a piece of barbed steel in it.

Except when they've lost their natural wariness of humans.

Increasingly, necropsies on dead dolphins reveal fishhooks in their stomachs or monofilament line tangled around their fins. Stephen Nohlgren of *The St. Petersburg Times* recently wrote of the troubles facing a resident group in Sarasota Bay. This summer, four dolphins were struck by boats. One was a calf that later disappeared from the pod and is presumed to have died.

Local marine scientists haven't seen such a spate of deaths in 42 years of research. The animals hit by vessels hadn't been known to follow humans for food. However, dolphin feeding did become more common in the region after a red tide in 2005 wiped out many small-prey fish. In hunger, some dolphins learned to mooch around piers and charter boats.

Nohlgren tells the story of an old-timer, the aptly named Beggar, who works a busy section of the Intracoastal Waterway in Nokomis, between Sarasota and Venice. Beggar accosts passing boaters who think he's adorable and obligingly toss goodies from the bait well. So far he's bitten 33 of his benefactors.

It's been illegal to feed wild dolphins since 1991, but despite the well-publicized penalties (jail time and fines up to $20,000), state and federal authorities have had trouble stopping it.

The Panama City area remains the epicenter. Stacey Horstman, bottlenose dolphin conservation coordinator for NOAA Fisheries, says sometimes a single dolphin will be surrounded by 30 to 50 humans in the water. "A pretty tough scene," she said.

The evidence is plentiful on YouTube, where partiers with submersible cameras like to share their cross-species encounters. The dolphins in these videos behave more like raccoons at a garbage dump.

A few months ago, a tour operator in Cape Coral and two more in the Panhandle got fined $5,000 for feeding dolphins. Vendors in Panama City continue to promote swim-with-the-dolphin tours while publicly saying that no feeding is allowed.

What they don't say is that the only reason any dolphin swims with a human is to sponge a handout. Contrary to myth, Flipper has no interest whatsoever in being your friend, unless the payoff is a juicy sardine.

Still the congenitally clueless—tourists and locals alike— continue to flop into the Gulf and mess with these phenomenal creatures, dooming them to a future of begging, sloth, and worse.

A dolphin that swims close enough to take a treat from your fingers is also close enough to be stabbed by a scumbag with a screwdriver.

DRILL, SPILL, AND KILL

May 2, 2004
Pipeline to the Bahamas Spells Disaster

Sometime in the near future, two companies will begin trenching heavy pipelines across the ocean bottom from the Bahamas to South Florida.

Not only will the construction scar the reefs and disperse marine life; the pipes will be used to carry millions of cubic feet of natural gas, which ignites rather spectacularly when exposed to oxygen and a spark.

Nonetheless, both projects have won hearty approval from the state Department of Environmental Protection, an agency that obviously needs to change its name.

In endorsing the Bahamas-to-Florida pipelines, the DEP conceded that the drilling might cause "potential damage to the coral reefs and other important marine resources." Yet those concerns were outweighed by the rosy conclusion that the pipelines "will help satisfy the growing demand for natural gas in Florida."

How these goofball schemes got the go-ahead so swiftly, and with minimal public input, would seem a mystery. But not really.

The idea was to transport the gas in liquid form from Africa and other places to the Bahamas. There it would be converted to vaporized fuel and piped to Florida, for distribution along the eastern seaboard.

One of the plans was first hatched by those fine corporate citizens at Enron and has since been taken over by an outfit called Tractebel. It calls for 90 miles of underwater pipe running from a gas plant on Grand Bahama all the way to Port Everglades.

The second pipeline would cross 54 miles from Ocean Cay, near Bimini, to Dania Beach. The company that's building it is a subsidiary of AES Corp, whose chairman is Richard Darman, a heavy Republican playmaker who was budget director when the first George Bush was president.

Given the current George Bush's chummy relationship with the gas and oil industry, it's no surprise that the Federal Energy Regulatory Commission breezily approved both Florida pipelines.

Yet for one fleeting moment it appeared that the president's own brother might throw a wrench in the works. In mid-March, Gov. Jeb Bush delayed a cabinet vote on the pipelines, saying he was concerned about the environmental impact as well as dangers to humans.

Bush heard a presentation by Raymond McAllister, professor emeritus of ocean engineering at Florida Atlantic University. McAllister had stated that the pipelines could not be built without permanently damaging the reefs, and that leaks could create a potentially lethal hazard for boaters and beachgoers.

Evidently, the governor's worries evaporated after what pipeline officials characterized as a period of "education." Whatever malarkey they told Bush in private, he apparently bought it. Two weeks ago, the cabinet approved both Bahamas pipelines with little debate. A third pipeline, to be operated by a unit of Florida Power & Light, will soon be up for a vote.

Each company insists that its project will be safe, secure, and kind to the deep blue sea. AES and Tractebel say they'll clear a path for the lines by drilling horizontally beneath the reefs, then fitting the pipes through the rock. To make things even more interesting, the segments must be laid through the Gulf Stream, against a current of three to four knots. No problem, the companies say. Don't you fret about a thing.

Right. They're going to chew through 90 miles of ocean

bottom and leave it just the way God made it. Who are they kidding?

Here's a well-known fact about coral reefs: Silt and sediment can kill them deader than a doornail. Nothing stirs up sediment like a humongous underwater drill, yet we're supposed to believe that all that suspended debris—millions of tons—will be transported harmlessly away from the reefs.

No way.

The last bureaucratic hurdle for the pipeline builders is the Army Corps of Engineers, an agency that probably knows which questions to ask. Whether it is immune from the clout of Darman and the others is doubtful, however.

Under their agreement with the state, the pipeline companies can't sell or transfer the easement rights if the projects go bust. They will also be liable for up to $1.5 million for any damage done to the marine habitat. Unfortunately, because of the extreme distances and depths of the pipe, the damage is likely to be irreparable at any price. Dead coral tends to stay dead, and the sea life that depends on it never returns.

Florida is home to the last of the continent's living reefs, a fact we boastfully trumpet to lure tourists. It's startling that Gov. Bush and the cabinet would so casually put this already imperiled treasure at risk for so little gain to the public.

It's even more disturbing that, with the future of our shores and ocean waters at stake, Bush would dismiss the concerns of scientists and trust the word of energy hustlers. They might call it an "education," but it smells like a sellout.

July 9, 2006
Energy Policy: Political Tide Favors Big Oil

On the same day that the U.S. House voted resoundingly to lift the 25-year ban on offshore oil and gas drilling, it also rejected a measure that would have boosted the minimum average gas mileage of American cars.

That's all you need to know about U.S. energy policy and who drives it. Consumption is king; conservation, an afterthought.

Fourteen representatives from Florida supported the pro-drilling bill, which would allow oil and natural gas rigs 50 miles from the Atlantic coast and Panhandle. Polls show that most Floridians strongly oppose offshore drilling, but lawmakers who voted for the legislation insist it's the best possible compromise. A battle looms in the Senate, where Florida's two senators—Democrat Bill Nelson and Republican Mel Martinez—have vowed to block the bill unless tougher restrictions are added.

There's no dispute that the political tide has turned in favor of Big Oil. High gasoline prices and the worsening bedlam in the Middle East have galvanized enemies of the moratorium that has kept derricks far away from Florida's ecologically fragile shores.

The pot was sweetened when House leaders agreed to share a fat chunk of future gas and oil lease royalties with states that open areas between three and 100 miles offshore to energy exploration.

According to the Congressional Budget Office, the royalty split could cost the federal government $102 billion during the next decade. Even the Bush White House, which is basically an arm of Big Oil, expressed dismay at the deal. Once that kind of heavy money starts flowing into the moist, eager paws of local legislators, be assured that energy lobbyists will get whatever they want, whenever they want it.

Floridians fear a nightmarish spill like that of the *Exxon Valdez*, the tanker that lost nearly 11 million gallons of oil and fouled 1,300 miles of Alaskan coastline back in 1989.

Such an accident would be devastating both to Florida's marine environment and to tourism. Vacationers tend to avoid smelly black beaches littered with dead, tar-covered seabirds.

The energy industry, and the politicians who pimp for it, say there's no reason to worry. The technology of extracting and shipping fuel has improved, they say, and so has the safety record.

Even if the platforms and tankers are better built, the infrastructure required to transport and store billions of gallons of oil is inherently vulnerable to acts of nature. After hurricanes Katrina and Rita hammered the Gulf Coast last summer, authorities responded to at least 595 oil, gas, and chemical spills in the region, according to a study by *The Houston Chronicle*.

The leaks came from offshore platforms, storage tanks along the coast, and even fuel trucks that overturned in the storm surge and high winds. In all, an estimated nine million gallons of oil was released, contaminating homes, farm soil, waterways, and wetlands.

An estimated one million gallons leaked from a Shell Oil facility in Pilottown, Louisiana.

Another 1.4 million gallons spilled from a Murphy Oil plant near Chalmette. Another 991,000 gallons poured from a Chevron terminal near Empire, on the Mississippi River.

The worst spill happened at Cox Bay in Plaquemines Parish, where 3.8 million gallons of sweet crude spewed from two storage tanks owned by Bass Enterprises Production Co. About 450,000 gallons slopped into nearby marshes.

Energy companies said they hadn't anticipated—or prepared for—the vast spillage caused by the hurricanes. It was not a confidence-inspiring response. Given Florida's lively history of hurricanes, residents here deserve to know where all that oil being raised offshore will be stored, and whether those facilities will be able to withstand a storm stronger than Katrina, a Category 3 when it made landfall. Even if oil taken from Florida waters is transported directly to Louisiana or Mississippi, the risk of a catastrophic spill at sea can never be eliminated.

Exploration for natural gas, which is odorless and colorless, poses a lesser threat to waters and beaches. Yet even the feds admit that the drilling operation raises tons of sludge containing potentially harmful heavy metals.

Thanks to a last-ditch push by Florida representatives, the House bill that passed June 29 prohibits drilling closer than 200 miles from the west coast. The 50-mile buffer along the east coast and the Panhandle may be expanded to 100 miles by the Legislature, but it must be renewed every five years.

Some of the GOP lawmakers howling for offshore drilling have scoffed at the resistance in Florida. They say the energy needs of America must come first and that exploiting the Outer Continental Shelf will help free us from dependency on foreign oil.

What a crock. Offshore drilling will provide short-term boosts in supply, but little relief from our perilous reliance on oil producers in the Mideast, South America, and the Eastern Bloc.

Inevitably, rigs will go up somewhere off Florida's coast, but only a dithering fool would believe that the price of gasoline will come down.

Those same folks who've been getting rich from Dick Cheney's energy policy will get richer, while Floridians are left to hope and pray that these geniuses do a better job of protecting our waters than they did in Louisiana and Mississippi. The odds stink.

July 20, 2008
Drilling Offshore Won't Help Us Much

Raise your hand if you actually believe that offshore oil drilling will bring down gasoline prices at the pump.

Raise your other hand if you believe in Peter Pan, unicorns, and variable-rate mortgages.

Last week, President Bush strode into the White House Rose Garden and announced that he was nullifying the moratorium on offshore oil drilling that his father initiated 18 years ago following the *Exxon Valdez* disaster in Alaska.

"The time for action is now," proclaimed the younger Bush, though of course the gesture was largely symbolic. The moratorium stays in place until Congress decides not to renew it. And Congress, declared our fearless leader, is "the only thing standing between the American people and these vast oil resources."

Wow. And we thought the gas crisis was more complicated. Apparently, it's the fault of those merciless fiends on Capitol Hill who continue to persecute the poor energy companies. Those companies, by the way, currently lease more than 90 million acres of public land for exploration. According to a House report, only about one-quarter of that leased acreage is being used.

Naturally, some "obstructionist" Democrats want the oil companies to explain why they aren't drilling in all these other places before they start drilling off the coasts of Florida, California, and along the eastern seaboard.

It seems like a good question, but the president had nothing to say on the subject.

Listening to Bush and now John McCain, you'd almost forget that the oil companies already do lots of offshore drilling. In fact, they currently have access to more than

71 billion untapped barrels of recoverable oil believed to lie beneath coastal waters. That means four-fifths of all known offshore deposits are available to industry exploration efforts, according to the federal Mineral Management Service.

So why aren't they concentrating on the oil leases that they already control? Another good question, and one for which the explanations are typically murky.

Politically, what's happening is simple. The energy companies want to score big before their two guardian angels, Bush and Dick Cheney, leave power. With the public pounded by gas prices surpassing $4 a gallon, industry lobbyists see a golden opportunity to dismantle the offshore moratorium.

Still, even if the restricted zones on both coasts were opened to drilling and the yield were good, it would be years—probably decades—before the pump price of gasoline might be affected.

For seaside communities, the prospect of drilling has always meant weighing the risks against the possible rewards. In both Florida and California, which suffered a horrendous spill at Santa Barbara in 1969, most residents have opposed near-shore oil exploration.

The current moratorium on drilling, which affects the lower 48 states, was imposed to protect not just coastal environments but tourist economies that depend on clean seas and clean beaches. Florida, with its dangerously narrow economic base, can't afford a major spill. One *Valdez*-type accident in the Gulf of Mexico could foul miles of beachfront with tarry gobs; the news video alone would cost the state millions in hotel bookings.

And then there's the incalculable long-term damage to the real-estate market and commercial fisheries.

Energy companies say the technology of extraction has improved substantially, making unlikely the chances of a serious mishap. Gov. Arnold Schwarzenegger of California is unpersuaded and remains outspokenly opposed to drilling there.

Yet in Florida, fellow green Republican Charlie Crist, a longtime foe of offshore drilling, recently announced that he—like McCain—has had a change of heart. "Floridians are suffering," Charlie said, as if oil companies will kindheart-edly deflate gas prices once their derricks rise off Destin and Tampa.

Ironically, both the industry and the government believe leases within 100 miles of Florida's coasts hold mostly natural gas, which will do nothing to help lower the cost of crude. Such details are seldom noted by politicians who disingenu-ously peddle offshore drilling as a cure for high gas prices. The only cure is to radically reduce demand and to develop alternative energy sources.

The United States owns only about 3 percent of the world's oil reserves, yet it guzzles 25 percent of global produc-tion. Every day Americans burn up 20 million barrels of oil, which is what keeps us slaves to OPEC.

Folks filling up their cars are understandably worried and alarmed. That's a bad combination in an election year because it encourages candidates to offer false hope and sham promises.

Undoubtedly it's possible to safely extract more oil from beneath our oceans, but there's not enough down there to free the United States from its crippling dependence on Mid-east reserves.

Drilling in the Alaskan wilderness won't save us; nor will drilling off the beaches of Florida and California. The main result would be a temporary boost in domestic product, which the oil companies will eagerly sell us at whatever price the market will bear.

Only a sucker would believe otherwise.

May 2, 2010
Gulf Spill Can Kill Our Tourist Season

Oops.

That's the official position of British Petroleum.

It turns out that oil is gushing from that blown-out rig off the Louisiana coast at a flow of at least 5,000 barrels a day, five times more than BP first estimated. Oh, and if you're keeping count, by Friday there were three leaks—not two—in the mile-long pipe that connected the platform to the wellhead.

The slick is larger than Rhode Island, and a shift of wind is pushing it into the wetlands of bayou country, imperiling birds, marine life, and commercial fishing. Tourist beaches in Alabama and northwest Florida are also at risk.

Barely a month ago, President Obama announced plans to expand offshore oil operations in the eastern Gulf of Mexico and along the Atlantic coast as far south as central Florida. Fabulous idea! It won't bring down the price of gasoline one penny at the pump, and it won't yield enough crude oil to light up America for even a year—but, hey, what harm could it do?

Oops.

The oil companies know how to find oil, and they sure know how to drill. The only part of the underwater operation that they haven't really nailed down is how to clean up their spills.

Soon after the Deepwater Horizon rig caught fire and

sank, killing 11 workers, BP sent remote-controlled subma-
rines to shut a master valve near the source of the outflow. It
didn't work.

Plan B is to dig a relief well in the hope of intercepting
the oil before it reaches the fractured pipe. Plan C is to plug
up the spewing hole with mud, concrete, or a heavy liquid.
At a depth of 5,000 feet, either project will take weeks or
months, during which time the oil would continue leaking.

Meanwhile, as this column is being written, BP is lighting
parts of the Gulf of Mexico on fire, to burn off some of the
slick. So much for high-tech. The company is also assem-
bling an extremely large dome—I swear—that engineers
could lower to the ocean floor and place over the leak in an
attempt to capture the oil. Maybe when they're done, they
can give it to Wile E. Coyote so he can use it to trap the Road
Runner.

BP says everything possible is being done to stop the leak
and contain the spill. That's probably true, which is sobering.
Despite all the assurances from Big Oil and the politicians
who are in its pocket, the technology of undersea drilling is
dangerously lagging when it comes to protecting the coastal
communities whose economies depend on clean water, clean
beaches, and healthy fisheries.

Last week, BP's chief executive, Tony Hayward, tried to
ease the fears of Gulf residents by saying that the approaching layer of oil was as light as "iced tea." Good luck trying to
sell that line: "Hey, folks, that brown stuff all over the beach?
Don't think of it as tar. Think of it as Snapple."

On Friday, with the spill blooming into a disaster, the
White House announced that no new offshore drilling will be
authorized until the Louisiana incident is fully investigated.
Under the plan announced in March by Obama, drilling in
Florida's eastern Gulf would expand but remain at least 125

miles offshore. On the Atlantic side, rigs could be erected within sight of the coast.

In Tallahassee, where Big Oil's lobbyists have been spreading gobs of money, several geniuses in the Legislature will next year continue their push to permit drilling within five miles of some prime Florida beaches. Perfectly safe, they say. Y'all just relax.

Two days after exploding, the Deepwater Horizon went down on April 22 about 50 miles from mainland Louisiana. It took only a week after that for the first streaks of oil to reach the shore.

Miles of protective booms have been laid along the marshes. Officials are considering cannon fire to scare away birds, so they don't land in the goo. Another idea is to recruit local shrimp boats as oil skimmers.

Because BP hasn't been able to cap the leak, the Obama administration is sending U.S. military assistance. In other words, the Louisiana spill is an official emergency. If it had happened near Jacksonville or Daytona Beach, Naples, Sarasota, Key West . . .

Oops.

By all means, let's surround Florida—a virtual hurricane magnet—with drill rigs. According to the U.S. Minerals Management Service, hurricanes Rita and Katrina destroyed 113 Gulf platforms, damaged 457 pipelines, and caused 146 spills that dumped 17,652 barrels of petroleum. One medium-sized blowout could trash miles of shoreline and kill a tourist season. Nothing sells seaside hotel rooms like YouTube videos of gunk-covered turtles and dead pelicans.

This is a no-brainer. Florida can't afford offshore drilling. The risk to the economy is ludicrous, compared to the relatively small amounts of oil to be found.

With the crud from the Louisiana accident slopping ashore, Obama should fly down to experience the scene firsthand. I'm sure someone will help scrape the "iced tea" off his flip-flops.

May 16, 2010
BP: And a Child Shall Lead Them

An absolutely true news item: British Petroleum says it is considering a plan to plug the main leak on the sunken Deepwater Horizon oil rig by shooting it full of shredded car tires, old golf balls, and knotted ropes.

British Petroleum announced today that it has fired its top engineer for safety design and replaced him with Jody McNamara, age 12, a sixth-grade honors student at the Dwight Eisenhower Middle School in Tulsa, Oklahoma.

McNamara, who will earn about $350,000 a year in salary and stock options, was offered the BP job after a panel of industry experts selected his 250-word essay, "How to Stop Undersea Oil Leaks Really Quick," over thousands of other entries.

"Jody is clearly on the cutting edge of deepwater energy technology," said BP chief executive Tony Hayward. "We couldn't be happier to have him join our team at such a critical time."

McNamara was introduced to reporters at a lunch-hour press conference in the school cafeteria. He said his first priority would be devising a new strategy for dealing with the oil spill in the Gulf of Mexico. "I don't want to talk trash about these other guys," he said, "but come on—golf balls and car tires? Seriously?"

It was not clear whether McNamara has any prior experience advising major petroleum companies. The school year-book lists him as a member of the Science Club, the Chess Club, and 4-H. His interests are said to include "soccer, skateboarding, and collecting really cool arrowheads."

The hiring of an outsider didn't surprise industry insiders, who say BP had run out of ideas in its increasingly desperate efforts to plug the mile-deep Deepwater Horizon. A four-story dome that was supposed to fit over the gushing wellhead became clogged with icy crystals and had to be towed away. Burning off the floating crude has had only limited success, as gobs of tar are threatening shorelines and marine life all along the Gulf Coast.

"What Jody brings to the table," said BP's Hayward, "is a completely fresh viewpoint on problem-solving. The principal showed us his class project from last semester—the hamster-powered lightbulb? I'm telling you, this kid is scary smart."

In his winning essay, McNamara proposed several possible options for sealing the ruptured oil pipeline. He said the most promising plan would require "a super-long straw" and approximately 3,700 metric tons of Quaker oatmeal. "You ever let that goop sit in a cereal bowl for an hour or two? It turns to rock," the sixth-grader explained at his press conference. "There's nothing that stuff won't clog up."

McNamara said he successfully tested the technique using a homemade LEGO model of the Deepwater Horizon, submerged in a 30-gallon aquarium in his brother's bedroom. "Don't worry, we took out all the fish first," he said.

Hayward later conceded that the aquarium experiment was more sophisticated than any that BP had undertaken. "It could have saved us the fortune that we blew on that stupid dome," he added ruefully.

Classmates describe McNamara as studious but not stuffy. One recounted a prank that occurred on a recent "Burger

Day" when McNamara loosened the cap on a bottle of mustard before handing it to an unsuspecting companion at the lunch table.

"We all fell on the floor laughing," the classmate said. "Jody's an awesome dude."

Said another: "So what if it's, like, his first really epic oil spill? He couldn't possibly do worse than those grown-up dorks did."

Critics of BP expressed guarded optimism about the company's decision to put a 12-year-old boy in charge of the Deepwater Horizon containment project.

A spokesman for the Department of Interior released a statement saying, "Jody McNamara seems like a bright young fellow, and we are encouraged by BP's willingness to give him a chance. God knows their own people don't have a clue what to do."

Before leaving for an orthodontist appointment, McNamara showed reporters his first memo to BP executives, written as an extra-credit assignment for his English class: "Please don't build any more offshore oil rigs until you figure out how to shut them off."

McNamara received an A on the paper.

He promised to get busy working on the oil-spill plan right away, as soon as he finishes his homework and cleans the hamster cage.

June 12, 2010
Now You Don't Trust BP, but It's Too Late

Every time a BP executive appears on television, I think of the garage scene from the movie *Animal House*.

An expensive car belonging to Flounder's brother has just been trashed on a drunken road trip, and the smooth-talking

Otter comforts the distraught Delta pledge with these cheery words: "You f—— up! You trusted us! Hey, make the best of it."

If only the BP guys were half as honest.

Incredibly, almost eight weeks after the Deepwater Horizon oil rig exploded in the Gulf of Mexico, the company that caused the disaster remains the primary source of information about it. Predictably, much of that information has been stupendously, tragically wrong, starting with the low-ball estimates of how much crude was leaking into the sea. BP didn't know the answer when the rig went down, and it doesn't know the answer now. Nobody does.

Every day we see streaming underwater video of that mile-deep gout of oil, billowing and unstaunched. The image is only slightly less sickening than the pictures of dead sea turtles and gagging pelicans. Some people I know can't bear to watch anymore, so painful are the feelings of helplessness and frustration. What's happening before our eyes is the slow murder of one of the world's most bountiful bodies of water, a crime precipitated by reckless corporate decisions and abetted by our own government.

Imagine a so-called regulatory process that allows oil companies to sink a drill 5,000 or even 10,000 feet through a living ocean without any reliable backup for when a blowout preventer fails to prevent a blowout.

Duh, let's build us a big ol' steel dome and drop it on the leak.

If that don't work, we'll blast us some golf balls and shredded tires into the hole.

Or maybe a giant sody straw might do the trick!

Obviously, these geniuses didn't have a workable Plan B. Worse, nobody in government figured that out until it was too late. This is what millions of dollars in campaign contributions buys—a free pass from Washington. The federal Minerals Management Service basically worked for Big Oil.

It was a relationship that flourished during the Bush-Cheney years, and not much changed when Barack Obama took office. Despite serious safety issues throughout BP's North American operations, the MMS blithely accepted the company's word that everything was peachy on Mississippi Canyon Block 252 in the Gulf of Mexico.

Even today, in the midst of the worst oil spill in history, the Obama administration is still relying largely on BP's word, although by necessity and not choice. CEO Tony Hayward continues to say things that would merely be silly if not for the dire context. Last week he declared that, despite the findings of several sets of researchers, no submerged plumes of petroleum are spreading through the Gulf. "The oil is on the surface," Hayward said. "There are no plumes."

He sounds just like the pet-shop owner in the famous Monty Python sketch who is trying to convince a disgruntled customer that his extremely dead parrot is only napping.

As of this writing, the latest news from BP concerns its new oil-collecting contraption, which is said to be siphoning 15,000 barrels daily from the fractured wellhead. The company has promised that, within days, it will be capturing "a vast majority" of the flow from the Deepwater Horizon.

Unfortunately, attaching the new device required recutting the riser in a way that actually increased the volume of the leak. Many experts believe that millions more gallons than before are now pouring into Gulf waters.

So, at the end of the day, all we really know for certain is this: The oil keeps gushing, and nobody's figured out how to stop it. That much we can see for ourselves on the dreary underwater video. Back on land, not a soul is able to state with certainty how much has been spilled, where it will end up, or what the ultimate damage will be to the Gulf and beyond.

Meanwhile, the coastal marshes of Louisiana are dying, and brown glop soils the beaches of Alabama and northwest Florida. The seafood industry is being crippled, and tourism is reeling.

And our government, which possesses neither the technology nor the expertise to plug the leak, is stuck in a grim alliance with the perpetrators.

Oil spills are like hurricanes: One is all it takes to change everything.

From the president to the industry's cheerleaders in Congress to all those state and federal regulators, too many people accepted the oil executives' sunny assurance that deepwater drilling posed no serious threat to this country.

In the immortal words of Otter, you f—— up.

You trusted them.

June 27, 2010
Oil Spill: The Nightmare Becomes Reality

A friend walked out on Pensacola Beach and took a photograph of the oil—miles of oil—on the morning that the gunk first washed ashore.

He e-mailed the picture to me with a note that said it all: "Sickening."

Pensacola is his home, and the unthinkable has happened. Louisiana's misery is now officially Florida's misery, too. For many residents of the Panhandle, the dreadful wait is over, and their worst fears have come to pass. In a calamity lasting so long and unfolding so inexorably, emotions swing from anger to sadness to grim acceptance. There's simply nothing to do except struggle to clean up the mess—as Pensacolans quickly did—and pray for the day when it's over.

The polls say most Americans (although not all) are outraged by the oil spill. Those untouched by the disaster may, if they choose, keep a distance. Along the Gulf shores, workers are scooping up dead dolphins and trucking them off for necropsies. The pictures aren't easy to stomach, and the impulse is to look away.

It might be difficult for someone who was born and raised far from a beach or a bayou to visualize a place they cherish being poisoned and defaced on such a massive scale. Or maybe not so difficult. Imagine if 120 million gallons of crude oil were flushed into the Minnesota headwaters of the Mississippi River, and for months the sludge was allowed to seep down through the veins of America's Midwest.

Now you begin to get the picture—the heartbreak, the helplessness.

Far from Pensacola Beach, where tears were shed last week, a certifiable idiot named Joe Barton was apologizing to BP because President Obama had pressured the company into creating a $20 billion compensation fund for victims of the Deepwater Horizon accident.

Barton is a Republican congressman whose district in Texas includes Arlington and parts of Fort Worth, a long way from the Gulf of Mexico. Although he later was forced to apologize for his apology to BP, Barton was cheered by some Tea Party bloggers and others who accuse Obama of shaking down the oil giant.

Talk about misplaced sympathy. Being clueless is one thing. To showcase such an obscene insensitivity to suffering is something else.

With the encroaching oil slick comes a mugging for all whose livelihood depends on the robust health of the Gulf. Hotels stand nearly empty, shop and restaurant workers are being laid off, and fishing boats sit idle at the docks. The folks staring out at a befouled horizon have mortgages, car payments, medical bills, and kids who need clothes for school. Their lives are upended and might never be the same.

Marine experts say it will take many years for the Gulf waters to heal, long after the tar balls and glop are cleaned off the beaches. A spill so deep and so torrential has no precedent, so no model exists to tell us what happens next.

For the millions of Americans who live on or near the ocean, from Kennebunkport to Seattle, the consequences of the accident don't need to be elucidated. The environment is the economy.

Interestingly, those who denounce Obama's "shakedown" of BP use no such criminal terms for what the oil company has done to the coastal communities of Louisiana, Alabama, and northwest Florida. Assault would be the word for it. Negligence would be the cause.

Once the oil arrives and the nightmare becomes reality, those who must deal with the stink and the slop are moving past the questions that preoccupy cable news and radio talk shows.

No deep, dark mystery remains.

The rig blew up because somebody made a terrible mistake, period. The well is still gushing and will keep gushing until August, at the earliest. Exactly how many barrels a day is now an academic debate; the volume remains so immense that it's virtually impossible to comprehend, a number that fluctuates from one press release to another.

Just get the damn leak plugged. That's what matters.

Meanwhile, the tropics are heating up. Who knows how

many storms will rip across the Gulf or how far they'll spread the oil.

Gov. Charlie Crist traveled to Pensacola Beach last week, not far from where my friend took the photograph. Standing among the tar puddles, the governor said, "It's pretty ugly."

Sickening is a better word.

You shouldn't have to be there to feel it.

April 23, 2011
A Year Later, Little in the Gulf Has Changed

One year and 206 million gallons of oil later, all that gushes from the wreck of the Deepwater Horizon is blame. Lawyers appear to outnumber the ocean microbes.

Everybody's suing BP, while BP sues the rig owner and the maker of the blowout preventer that failed to prevent the blowout. Some folks who barely got grazed by the disaster have received settlement checks from the oil giant, while others along the Gulf who got wiped out are still waiting for compensation.

The beaches have been cleaned, but miles of once fertile marshlands in Louisiana remain goopy and barren. Elsewhere, the shrimp and fish are rebounding, but samples show elevated levels of petroleum-based hydrocarbons. Nobody is sure how much of the BP oil remains suspended in the dark depths, or what the long-term effects will be on marine life.

In its own way, the aftermath of the Deepwater Horizon accident is as messy and maddening as the spill itself. Gulf Coast politicians who bashed the Obama administration for the way it handled the cleanup have also blasted federal efforts to prevent another devastating blowout.

The moratorium on deep-water drilling—which affected

only a fraction of the wells in the Gulf—was denounced as a dagger in the heart of the Louisiana oil industry. Yet dire predictions of massive job cuts proved to be wrong.

A stunted view, favored by those who rely on right-wing talk shows for political instruction, is that the government's role should have been to mop up the slop and then butt out. But for many who live near coastlines where oil companies drill (or want to), it would be reassuring to think that the feds are using at least some of our tax dollars to protect us from future calamities. That was, in fact, a widely held assumption before the Deepwater Horizon blew up.

The truth, as we now know, is that the agency that was supposed to be monitoring offshore oil exploration had been neutered into basically a jobs program for ex–industry employees. In the wake of the Gulf spill, Obama ordered a makeover of the lame Minerals Management Service and a more aggressive agenda.

Unfortunately—and this is the scariest part of the BP story—little has changed. Another major blowout could occur in the Gulf today, with the same harrowing results. On that point, the experts agree.

The Minerals Management Service is now called the Bureau of Ocean Energy Management, Regulation & Enforcement. It has a new director and a tougher slate of rules but remains disgracefully underfunded and critically short of staff members who are experienced in petroleum engineering.

"They changed the name, but all the people are the same. It's embarrassing," said William K. Reilly, a former chief of the Environmental Protection Agency and co-chair of the bipartisan presidential commission investigating the BP disaster.

During the 87 excruciating days it took to cap the

Macondo well, the administration was forced to rely too heavily on BP's version of events. That's because the government was woefully short of expertise and technology. It still is.

Far from the beaches and bays of the Gulf, members of the new Congress are working doggedly on behalf of oil lobbyists to minimize federal oversight of offshore operations. It's as if the Deepwater Horizon blowout never happened, as if those 11 men never died.

The House is considering legislation that would expedite the approval of drilling permits along both the Atlantic and Pacific coasts. Another measure would weaken environmental requirements for exploration in Alaskan waters.

Given the attitude in Washington, there's no mystery why the accident rates for offshore drilling projects in the United States are higher by several times than in Norway, Canada, the United Kingdom, and Australia, where strict safety rules are better enforced. Somehow the oil companies operating in those countries manage to cope with the regulations and still make mountainous profits. How amazing.

Here in the United States, politicians fronting for the industry are counting on $4-per-gallon gas prices and a short public memory. Their optimism is well founded, if recent polls are accurate. The images of dead sea turtles and starved pelicans are fading. Ironically, though, the BP spill cannot disappear entirely from the news as long as people are fighting over who gets the blame and who gets the money. It will take years to clean up that part of the mess.

In Mississippi, the city of Biloxi, which escaped the brunt of the spill, nonetheless used BP payouts to buy 14 trucks and SUVs, including a new Chevy Tahoe for the mayor. Rip-offs like this are inevitable when billions of dollars are up for grabs.

Of greater worry is a future in which coastal communities must depend on the Bureau of Ocean Energy Management—and the disinterested Congress that funds it—to prevent another nightmare like the Deepwater Horizon.

Only one year later, it's way too soon to start forgetting what happened and why.

Never is too soon.

FESTIVAL OF WHORES

Who Would Pay Top Dollar for a Swamp?

Miami-Dade school officials are being humiliated daily in Tallahassee, where lawmakers are examining the district's bizarre and suspicious land-buying practices.

Last week the Senate voted to ban the county from spending any state funds on school construction without prior approval of an oversight board. If the House concurs, the nation's fourth-largest school system will be forced to grovel for money to expand—this, while nearly a fifth of its 368,000 students are stuck in portable classrooms.

Blame falls largely on Miami-Dade's school superintendent, Roger "The Dodger" Cuevas, whose mealymouthed appearance last week failed to persuade a Senate panel that the county's schools were in competent hands.

The outrage is totally justified. A recent audit of 14 land deals revealed that the Miami-Dade school district overpaid in 11 instances by a total of $7 million, based on average property appraisals.

Staffers were said to make a "practice" of ignoring appraisals that were less than the amount sought by the sellers, and methodically shopping around for higher estimates. It's certainly an unusual negotiating technique—highballing the opposition—and one that would be challenging to explain to a grand jury. According to state auditors, the Miami-Dade school system's land-buying procedures are so wasteful of tax dollars that they ultimately impede efforts to open new schools and relieve overcrowding.

The most disgraceful example is the purchase of the West Miami-Dade site for the future John Ferguson High. In August 1999, the district bought the 60-acre tract for almost $7 million—about $2.35 million more than the sellers originally had paid. It was a nifty profit, considering that the sellers had acquired part of the land only days before it was resold to the School Board.

One appraiser said the site was overpriced by $2 million, but Tabitha Fazzino, then one of the district's land-acquisition directors, never shared that report with board members. Later she said she must have forgotten about it because she was preoccupied with wedding plans. Two other low appraisals were submitted to the board, which nonetheless approved the sale at a higher price.

The landowners were represented by an influential lobbyist, Dusty Melton, who was kind enough to take Fazzino to lunch. She later said that no lobbying for the Ferguson site took place.

The deal turned out even worse than initially feared. Not only did the School Board get reamed on the price of the land; it overlooked a crucial detail regarding the location, at Southwest 56th Street and 162 Avenue.

Turns out that the property has a serious problem with flooding. The new school cannot be built until the district spends another $5.6 million raising the elevation with dirt fill. In other words, these idiots paid top dollar for a swamp.

This seems incomprehensible unless you realize that, until recently, Miami-Dade school officials routinely purchased property without physically inspecting it.

Astounding but true.

The county is fond of blaming classroom overcrowding on the Legislature's stinginess. But judging by their extravagant conduct in dubious land deals, local school officials can't be trusted with unsupervised access to tax dollars. As the audit noted, more than $97 million that could have been used for new classrooms instead has been funneled to pet projects of School Board members, including two gymnasiums.

Cuevas claims he has made changes to tighten the process by which the district selects and purchases property. He says he has hired new staff to handle land acquisitions and reactivated a citizens' site-selection committee.

These moves are long overdue. Only after two years of embarrassing headlines has it dawned on the superintendent that he's in trouble. He should have been canned long ago, but he has been kept afloat by protective School Board members with as much to fear from scrutiny as Cuevas himself.

A few of the district's land purchases are so illogical that they can be explained only as political favors, acts of boggling stupidity, or acts of corruption.

The Legislature would be irresponsible not to step in with a noose. Every dollar squandered by school administrators is a dollar stolen from the kids crammed into those classrooms and portables.

April 22, 2001
Get Ready for Marlins Rebate II

The Florida House of Representatives has a committee known as the Council for Smarter Government.

I'm not kidding. That's what these people call themselves— the Council for Smarter Government. Want to know how smart they are? Last week they voted 7-5 in favor of a humongous tax rebate to help the Florida Marlins build a new stadium. Thanks to a previous cave-in by the Legislature, the state already shells out $2 million a year in tax rebates for baseball renovations to Pro Player Stadium, where the Marlins now play. Here's the punch line: The way the law was written, subsidies to Pro Player will continue for another 22 years even if the Marlins abandon the ballpark for a new site, as anticipated. That means taxpayers will be forfeiting

$44 million to improve a Major League Baseball facility where baseball is no longer played. As a bonus, they'll be bankrolling a new stadium to the tune of at least $122 million and probably much more.

Does that sound like smart government or dumb government?

It sounds like lovable, gullible government if you're John Henry, the owner of the Marlins, or Wayne Huizenga, the owner of Pro Player Stadium. These two fairly wealthy fellows will be the prime beneficiaries of the rebate double play pushed by lobbyists and now on its way to the floor of the House.

The original legislation, passed in 1988, was designed to entice big-league sports franchises to relocate to Florida. It has evolved into a welfare slush fund for rich team owners threatening to pack up and move someplace else. So far, nearly $90 million in sales taxes that could have been used for worthy public programs has been kicked back to private sports operations and entrepreneurs. Many millions more are committed for decades to come.

In addition to his baseball boondoggle, Huizenga scored a long-term $60 million break for the Panthers hockey arena in west Broward. To show they don't play favorites, lawmakers awarded a like sum to billionaire Micky Arison to help him pay for the Heat's latest basketball arena.

When deciding which sports to underwrite, the Legislature is anything but snobby. In 1996 it presented a $15 million tax break to something called the World Fishing Center in Dania, where stuffed replicas of lunker game fish are on display for public enrichment.

Last year, Gov. Jeb Bush joined lawmakers in magnanimously making room at the trough for spring-training camps in Dunedin, Clearwater, and Lakeland. The same old pitch worked like a dream. Those towns said they feared losing their seasonal major-league visitors to competing markets, and beseeched the state for money to help spruce up the ballparks.

Now John Henry wants a minimum of $122 million over the next 20 years. Given the Legislature's past unquestioning generosity, one can hardly blame him for asking—and expecting to get it. True, he once said he'd build the Marlins a new stadium with private financing. That was probably before he realized he was dealing with politicians who are pushovers, at least in the House.

The road doesn't look quite so smooth in the Senate. President John McKay and Majority Leader Jim King both have expressed misgivings about funding major-league baseball at a time when social and health programs are being hacked because of revenue shortages. An added embarrassment is that outrageous arrangement with Pro Player Stadium—guaranteed $2 million a year for baseball improvements, even if the team has moved elsewhere.

Marlins Rebate II would derive from sales taxes on merchandise sold at the ball games, roughly estimated at $6 million annually. That's a total of $8 million a year that any other business would be required to send to the state treasury, which needs every nickel.

Proposed Republican budget cuts threaten benefits and services for poor pregnant women, autistic kids, epilepsy patients, minority college applicants, and public school teachers, among others. In such lean times, subsidizing a new baseball stadium seems impossible to justify. Subsidizing two of them would be obscene.

Yet that's the majority recommendation of the House Council for Smarter Government. If only we had a House Council for Smarter House Councils.

June 22, 2003
How Many Legislators Could Pass the FCAT?

Nothing is more frustrating to Florida parents than the idea that politicians are the ones deciding what it takes for a student to be properly educated.

The absurdity was underscored last week as state lawmakers once again "debated" the merits of the Florida Comprehensive Assessment Test, otherwise known as FCAT.

No deliberative body is manifestly less qualified to make decisions about public education than our state Legislature. With a few shining exceptions, most of these clowns don't read, can't write, and clearly can't add. That's why lobbyists for special interests author so much of the legislation. Half the politicians in Tallahassee are too illiterate to type their own fund-raising letters.

Here's a fun idea for some mischievous state senator or representative: Propose a law requiring every elected official in Florida to pass the FCAT exam. It makes sense. Those who spend our taxes and write our laws ought to be at least as academically fit as the average high school senior.

Dreading the embarrassment, many politicians wouldn't sit still for any sort of standardized test. Yet they've got no problem dictating to our kids how knowledge should be measured, and the price of failure.

The main cheerleader for the FCAT movement has been Gov. Jeb Bush, one politician who could actually pass the test. Just a few days ago, Bush was praising statewide improvements in FCAT scores, especially among children in school districts plagued by poverty and unemployment. No mother or father who saw those results wasn't cheered by the news and thrilled for her or his children. But it's only part of the story.

Another side is the roughly 12,000 high school seniors in Florida who failed the FCATs and, by law, weren't allowed to collect their diplomas. Some people said tough luck—a test is a test. You either pass or flunk.

And certainly it was unsettling to see students and parents taking to the streets to protest the results. Attacking the test isn't attacking the problem, which is much larger and more systemic. Only a handful of states spend less money per pupil than Florida, an abominable statistic. While Bush has consistently pushed to increase education funding, the money hasn't kept pace with the state's rampaging population growth.

Students are packed like sardines into classrooms, teachers remain overworked and underpaid, and parents are perpetually ticked off—even parents whose children sailed through the FCATs. The schools are in crisis, and everybody knows it. That's why the amendment to cap class sizes passed so thunderously last fall.

Bush and Republican legislative leaders assert that the state can't afford to build all the new schools needed to meet the prescribed caps on class size. Yet they're the ones who have been cutting taxes for businesses and stock investors, reducing state revenues at a time of dire budget shortfalls.

Lawmakers dealt with the FCAT uproar in a predictable, slapdash way. Facing the wrath of disappointed parents and a threatened economic boycott by blacks, the Legislature last week tossed a life preserver to high school seniors who failed the test.

About 400 who met all scholastic requirements and attained a marginal score on a college entrance exam will be cleared for graduation. The remaining 11,000–plus students must complete all coursework and eventually pass the FCAT, or score high enough on SAT or ACT college tests. Some seniors who didn't pass the FCATs and are recent immigrants to the United States will get a rush course in English this summer before they retake the test. Good luck.

The bill affects only this year's seniors, but it's still a political retreat for the governor. Obviously, he didn't foresee the emotional and very public reaction of those whose kids came up short on the FCATs.

I've got no doubt that Bush is both serious and sincere in his quest to improve education, but far too much weight has been put on this single test. Because the FCAT is also used to rate and reward individual schools, teachers and administrators are also under pressure to produce high scores. It doesn't automatically mean they're producing the smartest, most well-rounded graduates.

In any case, the protests of this spring promise to become an annual event. Students will keep flunking the FCAT by the thousands as long as the Legislature continues to shortchange our schools in the budget.

All those lawmakers who tout the FCAT as the best academic yardstick should demonstrate their faith in the test by taking it themselves. Their scores would be most instructive to the rest of us when we grade them at election time.

May 1, 2005
DCF Policy: Forcing Babies to Have Babies

Forcing babies to have babies is now the official policy of Florida's child-welfare agency.

The sadists running the Department of Children and Families are trying to stop a 13-year-old girl under foster care from getting an abortion. They say that she's too immature to decide whether or not she should have the baby.

The logic is diabolically cockeyed. If the girl isn't mature enough to make a sensible choice about her pregnancy, how can she possibly be mature enough to care for a newborn infant? An even better question for the extremists at DCF is this: How can any 13-year-old child, from any background, be ready for motherhood?

The girl is publicly known only as L.G., and her life so far hasn't been a picnic. According to records, her parents lost custody of her years ago, and she has been raised under state care.

The girl was residing in a group home in St. Petersburg when she became pregnant 14 weeks ago. She got the news during a medical examination.

Her attorneys say L.G. immediately told her DCF case-worker "that she wished to terminate the pregnancy." The procedure had been scheduled for last Tuesday, but then the morality police from Tallahassee arrived. That very morning, DCF lawyers filed an emergency motion with Palm Beach Circuit Judge Ronald Alvarez. He signed a temporary order blocking the abortion and ordered a competency examination for L.G.

She is represented by lawyers from Palm Beach Legal Aid and the American Civil Liberties Union. They say that L.G. has never been found to be incompetent or institutionalized for mental problems. They say she should be allowed to make up her own mind about the pregnancy. The Florida Supreme Court has ruled that the state constitution offers a shield of privacy in such cases.

DCF insists that it's forbidden by law to let any person under its supervision undergo an abortion or sterilization procedure. Apparently, this is to ensure that the agency will never run out of clients. Forcing children in state custody to have babies against their will guarantees that there will be a whole new generation of abused, abandoned, and neglected kids for taxpayers to support. It's quite a clever plan.

Unfortunately, DCF can't keep up with the thousands of cases that it's already got—cases such as L.G.'s. In a way, she's one of the lucky ones; she only got pregnant. Others in state care have been tortured, raped, killed, or, in the case of Rilya Wilson, vaporized into thin air.

With nightmare stories leaking out every few weeks, one would think that DCF had its hands full. Wrong.

The zealots picked by Gov. Jeb Bush to run the agency are never too busy to play politics with somebody's private agony. The Terri Schiavo case was the most recent debacle, but there have been others. Two years ago, DCF fought to block a severely retarded Orlando woman from having an abortion. In that case, the agency litigated for so many months that the operation could not be safely performed. The woman gave birth, and the infant was put up for adoption.

Such ruthless intrusion into the most private matters is a trademark of the new Republican right, which seldom wastes an opportunity to whip the pro-life crowd into a tizzy. It will likely happen again with L.G.'s case.

With the governor's political image in mind, DCF carefully tries to mask its meddling as the act of a caring and concerned overseer. In fact, the driving but unspoken philosophy behind most of the new abortion restrictions is punitive: You got knocked up, kid. That's what you get for fooling around. Now everybody but you gets to decide your future.

That's basically what the state of Florida is telling L.G.

We know what's best for you, kid. You're going to carry this baby for the next six months, and we don't care whether you want it or not. We don't care whether you're old enough, responsible enough, sober enough, stable enough, or financially secure enough. You can give it up for adoption, or you can keep it. If you turn out to be a lousy mom, we'll simply take it away and stick it in a foster home, just like we did to you.

A spokeswoman for DCF Secretary Luci Hadi said the agency is doing "what we believe is in the best interest of the child." Sure. If you happen to believe that unplanned pregnancy is a real character-builder for teenage girls.

Don't be surprised if DCF uses the same cold-blooded tactics against L.G. as it did against the retarded woman in Orlando—dragging the case out in court until it's too late for a safe abortion.

If someone put your 13-year-old daughter through that kind of cruelty, you'd know exactly what to call it: Child abuse.

November 13, 2005
When Will We Be Ready for the Next One? Never

With its usual foresight and timeliness, the Florida Legislature is now grappling with the issue of hurricane preparedness.

We all know what that means: absolutely nothing.

The Democrats are blaming the Republicans for the halting response to Hurricane Wilma, and the Republicans are blaming the citizens for not heeding calls to be ready.

There's a breath of truth in both arguments—and plenty of hot air.

The fact is, urban South Florida will never be prepared for a major hurricane. The idea of evacuating six million people is ludicrous, and the vast majority will be either stuck on the highways or stuck in their homes.

If a slow-moving Category 4 or 5 storm strikes head-on any

place from West Palm Beach to South Miami, plan on mass destruction, long-term shortages of fuel and food, disorder in the streets, and, of course, darkness.

There's no other possible scenario, unless they bulldoze the whole peninsula, boot everybody out and start over. Catastrophic mistakes have literally been set in concrete, as has our fate.

How many cities and counties in South Florida govern development with future hurricanes in mind? The road systems are designed purely to feed growth. High-rises and subdivisions are mapped to maximize density. The result is sprawl, suffocating congestion, and—when the storm hits—the collapse of an overburdened infrastructure. Big surprise.

For decades, the state's governors and legislative leaders have avidly encouraged reckless coastal growth, beholden as they've been to mega-developers, road builders, banks, and others getting rich from cramming more people into Florida. Now our lawmakers sit around, scrounging for somebody to blame for the havoc caused by Hurricane Wilma. What boneheads.

I love the comments from Sen. Alex Diaz de la Portilla of Miami and Sen. Paula Dockery of Lakeland. They say Floridians need to take more personal responsibility for hurricane preparation. Are you slackers listening? Next time a tropical storm is brewing, rush out and buy your three days' worth of food, ice, and D batteries. You'll be just fine after the storm hits.

For 72 measly hours, at least. After that, good luck.

And here come the Democrats, carping about the Federal Emergency Management Agency and demanding to know why some supply trucks didn't get where they were supposed to go. Sure, there was some bungling and confusion, but it's hard to envision a smooth operation in the absence of traffic signals and fuel for the relief vehicles.

Meanwhile, Florida Power & Light has been asked to explain how so many of its substations got knocked out and why so many of its power poles snapped like matchsticks, leaving more than 3.2 million people in the dark. The utility probably isn't taking the inquiry too seriously, having been awarded last week a whopping rate increase of 20.6 percent for the average residential customers. Interestingly, the company had asked for less.

It was with the same unbridled generosity that the so-called Public Service Commission earlier decided that FPL should be handsomely compensated for revenues lost from the massive outages caused by the 2004 hurricanes. So, even though your electricity was off, the meter was still running.

Many thousands of private businesses took huge hits from Wilma, yet only a select few are being rescued by our concerned leaders in Tallahassee.

Take Citizens Property Insurance, the shambling, state-run outfit that will likely receive a humongous rate hike, including increased assessments on innocent policyholders using other coverage. Citizens was set up because real insurance companies were bailing out of Florida, which wasn't unexpected. Only gamblers or fools would write windstorm policies in Hurricane Central, so it's fitting that the state leaped into the void.

You won't be shocked to learn that Citizens is teetering toward insolvency, with losses projected to exceed $1 billion. To bail out South Florida's largest home insurer, we'll all be opening our wallets.

See, it's not just the next hurricane we should prepare for. It's the inevitable reaming that follows.

Wilma wasn't a cataclysmic event on the scale of Katrina smashing the Gulf Coast. It was a Category 1 storm swiftly raking across an insanely overpopulated swampland. Imagine a hurricane exponentially stronger and slower. Imagine sustained winds of 120 mph instead of 85 mph. Imagine four feet of rainfall and streets flooded for weeks.

When the big one arrives—the *really* big one—plan on the pits. Plan on devastation. Plan on mayhem. Plan on bungling by those who've been telling you how to plan. And plan on way more than 72 hours of grief and gouging.

Be prepared, they're warning us. Next time, you'd better be prepared. Know how to prepare? Stock up on Prozac, that's how.

Because it's going to be real bad, both miserable and tragic, and there's nothing to be done except wait.

February 25, 2007
Stadium Giveaway Idea Won't Go Away

Yikes. It's baaaaack. Like movie ghoul Freddy Krueger, the Florida Marlins Stadium scam refuses to die.

Republican leaders in the new Legislature have enthusiastically exhumed the oft-snuffed plan to throw away $60 million of public funds on a Major League Baseball park in South Florida.

Forget that the state is already shelling out $60 million in sales tax "rebates" to Dolphins owner Wayne Huizenga, ostensibly for having renovated his football stadium to accommodate the Marlins. Huizenga wants the Marlins out (though he'll keep the money, thank you very much), and the Marlins want a new stadium. Every year they come to Tallahassee begging for tax dollars, and up till now they've been shut out.

The big obstacle was Jeb Bush, who peevishly opposed

spending public funds on professional sports palaces. In 2005, Senate President Tom Lee actually uttered the term "corporate welfare" when discussing the money grab, and he helped send it to its deserved doom.

But Bush and Lee are gone, and a new breed of free-spending, jock-waving Republicans are poised to resubsidize not only the Marlins but every other pro-sports franchise in the state. Apparently, it's a good time to be a team owner in Florida, sniffing for a handout. Despite forecasts for a tight budget and possible cuts in social services, the needy billionaires of baseball, football, hockey, and basketball are finding friends in Tallahassee.

In contrast to his predecessor, Gov. Charlie Crist says he's got no problem with the concept of public payouts to help the Marlins build a new, publicly owned stadium. House Speaker Marco Rubio of Miami is gung ho for the idea, too.

In the Senate, Alex Diaz de la Portilla of Miami introduced the latest incarnation of the frequently spurned package that would award the Marlins $2 million annually over the next 30 years.

"It's a question of pride for our whole community," said Diaz de la Portilla, who has either conveniently forgotten or never bothered to read the Senate's own 2005 analysis of publicly financed arenas and stadiums. "These kind of activities do not yield a net economic benefit," concluded economist Ross Fabricant, who reviewed 40 national studies for his report.

Team owners, not their communities, reap bankable rewards from stadium subsidies. Taxpayers are already on the hook for not one but two Miami basketball arenas, neither of which sparked the promised revitalization of the downtown area.

A $60 million handout would supposedly help seal the

deal for a new Marlins ballpark, the total cost of which will easily surpass $500 million. The remainder of the financing would come from Miami-Dade taxpayers and team owner Jeffrey Loria, though in what proportion is uncertain.

We're constantly warned that the Marlins can't survive financially without a new stadium—but what they can't survive without are ticket buyers. Whether the seats are old or new doesn't matter if they're empty, which is the prevailing situation at home games.

Except for a small devoted core, South Florida baseball fans are easily distracted and even more easily discouraged. Three summers from now, if the club's in fourth place and fighting to reach .500, the new stadium will be as quiet as the county morgue and possibly less crowded.

But a lavish morgue it will be, complete with retractable dome.

One GOP legislator who opposed the Marlins legislation last year now says that such double dipping would help all nine major-league franchises in the state. Sen. Mike Fasano of New Port Richey has filed a bill that would give every team, including his local Tampa Bay Lightning, a second $60 million sales-tax subsidy.

Either Fasano is auditioning to be a comedian, or he's in dire need of a math tutor. At a time when legislators are discussing drastically cutting or even abolishing homeowner property taxes, this guy stands ready to kiss off $540 million in future state revenues.

If Fasano's bill passes, Floridians will involuntarily increase to more than $1 billion their total gift to rich sports owners such as Huizenga and Loria. When you think of how many schoolteachers could be hired with that money over the next 30 years, it's enough to make you hurl your ballpark hot dog.

While past polls have shown strong public opposition to sports subsidies, the Marlins and other teams are counting on Gov. Crist's support to turn the tide.

In an early display of optimism, the Senate Commerce Committee last week unanimously approved Diaz de la Portilla's bill, and also one filed by Sen. Rudy Garcia of Hialeah.

Hurdles to full passage lie ahead, but without Jeb around to drive another stake through its greedy heart, the monstrous stadium giveaway might finally claw its way into law.

Note: The stadium got built, at an ultimate cost in public funding of more than $2 billion.

February 17, 2008
Our Reputation for Flakiness Is at Stake

In a move that could endanger Florida's flaky backwater reputation, the state Board of Education is poised to endorse the teaching of evolution as a science.

This is a dangerous idea—not the presentation of Darwinism in schools but the presentation of Florida as a place of progressive scientific thought.

Over the years the Legislature has worked tirelessly to keep our kids academically stuck in the mid-1950s. This has been achieved by overcrowding their classrooms, underpaying their teachers, and letting their school buildings fall apart.

Florida's plucky refusal to embrace 21st-century education is one reason that prestigious tech industries have avoided the state, allowing so many of our high school graduates (and those who come close) to launch prosperous careers in the fast-food, bartending, and service sectors of the economy.

By accepting evolution as a proven science, our top educators would be sending a loud message to the rest of the nation: Stop making fun of us. Is that what we really want?

On Tuesday, the Board of Education is scheduled to vote on a proposed set of new standards that describe evolution as the "fundamental concept underlying all of biology" and "supported by multiple forms of scientific evidence."

Certainly that's the position of every reputable academic group on the planet, including the National Academy of Sciences, the American Association for the Advancement of Science, and the National Science Teachers Association.

But forget the fossil record, okay? Forget DNA tracing. Forget the exhaustively documented diversification of species. This battle is about pride and independence; about boldly going against the flow, in defiance of reason and all known facts.

In recent weeks, the Board of Education has been swamped by e-mails and letters from religious conservatives who advocate teaching creationism or intelligent design, and who believe evolution should be discussed strictly as a "theory." For those who wish to see Florida standing still, if not sinking, this is a fantastic strategy. In fact, it could be expanded to revise other educational doctrines.

Let's start teaching gravity as a "theory," too. And don't forget the solar system—what proof do we really have, besides a bunch of fuzzy, fake-looking photos, that Mars really exists?

At a recent public hearing in Orlando, opponents of evolutionary teaching rose one by one to assail the proposed curriculum standards. Some had traveled all the way from the Panhandle, and were, like presidential candidate Mike Huckabee, exclusive believers in the Bible's version of creation.

According to *The St. Petersburg Times*, one speaker compared Charles Darwin, the father of evolutionary science, to Adolf Hitler and Joseph Stalin, well-known tyrants and mass murderers. Such loony gibberish is actually good for the anti-evolution crusade, providing the best evidence that the human species has not advanced one iota in the last 100,000 years.

With this in mind, several school boards in North Florida have passed resolutions opposing the teaching of evolution as fact. True, students in those same districts have produced some of the worst science scores on the Florida Comprehensive Assessment Test, but who needs Newton or Copernicus when you've got the Corinthians?

The notion that humans descended from apes has never been popular among fundamentalists, but what of the apes themselves? Given the gory history of Homo sapiens on earth, no self-respecting chimp or gorilla would claim a genetic connection to us.

The outcry against evolutionary instruction has been so heated that 40 members of the committee responsible for the new science standards felt compelled to sign a letter stating, "There is no longer any valid scientific criticism of the theory of evolution." Caving in to groups that question the soundness of science, the letter warned, "would not only seriously impede the education of our children but also create the image of a backward state, raising the risk of Florida's being snubbed by biotechnology companies and other science-based businesses."

Nice try, pinheads, but there's no sin in being a slightly backward state with extremely modest expectations for its young people. That's been the guiding philosophy of our tightwad lawmakers for years, and the degree to which they've succeeded is illuminated annually in the FCAT charade.

If snubbing is to be done, Florida should be the snubber, not the snubbee. Keep your elite biotech payrolls up north and out west—we've got hundreds of thousands of low-paying, go-nowhere jobs that require little training and minimal education.

Should state officials vote this week to put evolution on the teaching agenda, it will be a small yet radical step out of Florida's backward-thinking past.

Resistance is not futile. We've worked hard to keep ourselves so far behind in education, and we must stay the course.

October 10, 2010
Running Scared over Amendment 4

Major homebuilders are uncorking a bombastic media blitz to scare Floridians away from voting yes to Amendment 4. The same people who helped ignite the housing crash and mortgage meltdown are absolutely terrified of giving citizens actual control over growth in their own communities.

The so-called Hometown Democracy Amendment would require local voters to approve any significant changes to a county or city "comprehensive land-use plan," the map by which municipalities evolve.

If the measure passes—and it needs the support of 60 percent of voters—no massive housing subdivision or commercial development could be built without the project first appearing on a ballot.

It's not exactly a radical concept, but the opposing special interests will do just about anything to kill it. They're scared because they know Floridians are fed up with lousy planning and overbuilding and the high taxes that always result.

They're scared because they know Floridians are sick of watching elected officials cave in again and again to developers, making a farce of land-use regulations.

But mostly they're scared because, if passed, Amendment 4

has the potential to disrupt the influence peddling and out-right corruption that have made it so easy to subvert the will of the public. As things stand now, development interests can thwart opposition to projects by simply buying off the politi-cians whose votes are needed to make it happen.

Typically, that's achieved by hiring connected lobbyists, who then approach a receptive county commissioner or city council member. In many cases, the lobbyist has raised money for the officeholder's election campaign, so a favor is perceived to be owed.

And a threat is implied, too: If you don't line up behind the project, don't expect any donations for your next cam-paign.

Occasionally, if the elected official is exceptionally greedy and dimwitted, a cash bribe or some other illicit benefit is arranged. Public hearings are often a formality, a minor road bump. Plenty of earnest folks show up to question the impact of a proposed subdivision or shopping mall upon their neigh-borhoods and lives, and the politicians pretend to listen. By that point, though, the deal is already sealed, the necessary majority of votes secured.

This cynical charade has been going on since the begin-ning of statehood. It's the reason so many Florida cities look like they were planned by chimpanzees on LSD. It's also the reason we now have an estimated 300,000 homes and condos sitting vacant statewide, while leading the nation in foreclo-sures as well as mortgage fraud. The term "growth manage-ment" is a joke.

Amendment 4 isn't a perfect solution. Much will depend on how the language is interpreted—for instance, determin-ing how large a project must be before it goes to a vote.

Many thoughtful people, including some professional planners, fear that the amendment will generate an endless spate of elections in fast-growing counties. They're also worried that deep-pocketed developers will be able to sway the outcomes with slick advertising campaigns.

Another issue is the wisdom of holding a countywide or citywide referendum on a building project that might affect only one neighborhood. At the very least, the amendment is bound to spawn lawsuits until the courts clarify its reach.

Despite such concerns, it's hard to imagine a system for managing growth that could possibly be more dishonest, or deaf to the public interest, than what we have now. Nobody with half a brain believes that development pays for itself. Study after study shows that residents are the ones who pay big-time for sprawl, which is why taxes are so brutal in Florida's most densely populated counties. So is the cost of living. Clogged highways, overcrowded schools and jails, water shortages—we pay for all of it.

Opponents claim that Amendment 4 will actually raise taxes, one of many straight-faced lies that will saturate the airwaves between now and Election Day. This is well-financed desperation. While the amendment's supporters have raised only about $2.4 million, the opposition had a war chest of $12 million by midsummer.

The biggest donor is the Florida Association of Realtors—what a shocker—followed by some of the biggest homebuilders on Wall Street.

Here's the killer: Many of the companies bankrolling the ad campaign against Amendment 4 are recipients of a congressional bailout, in the form of humongous tax refunds earlier this year.

According to an industry magazine (headline: "Builders Cash In on Tax Refunds"), Lennar Homes has already taken $251 million in taxpayer-funded relief. Yet somehow the firm scrounged up $367,000 to fight the Florida Hometown Democracy movement.

Pulte Homes accepted $800 million in federal bailout refunds while kicking in $567,000 to a political action committee opposed to Amendment 4.

So, when you see all those dire-sounding, fright-filled TV commercials, remember who's paying for them. You are.

These guys are using your money to keep your voice and your vote out of the neighborhood planning process. Think about that when you're standing in the voting booth on November 2.

Do the thing they dread the most: Read Amendment 4 and decide for yourself.

February 26, 2011
Pill Mills Thrive as Governor Scott Nixes Database

Last week, as drug agents secretly prepared to raid more than a dozen South Florida pill mills, Gov. Rick Scott reaffirmed his staunch opposition to a statewide computer database that would track prescriptions of Vicodin, Percocet, and other dangerous narcotics. Said Scott: "I don't support the database. I believe it's an invasion of privacy."

His statement raises numerous questions, none of them comforting.

Has Florida finally elected a certifiable wack job as governor?

Is Scott himself overmedicating? Undermedicating? Why would any sane or sober public official go out of his way—very publicly—to protect pill pushers and crooked doctors?

Thirty-eight states use databases to keep track of oxycodone and other painkillers that are now the most widely abused (and lethal) drugs in the country. Florida is the largest state without such a database, and the undisputed epicenter of the sleazy illegal pill trade.

In the first six months of 2010, doctors in Florida prescribed nine times more oxycodone than was sold in the entire United States during that same period. Pain mills here have prospered wildly and proliferated—in Broward County alone there are 130.

Two years ago, the Republican-controlled Legislature approved a painkiller database, which would be privately funded. Law enforcement officers say it's an absolutely essential tool for attacking storefront clinics and the drug dealers who flock to Florida from throughout the eastern United States.

The database should have been up and running by now, but bid disputes with private contractors have delayed implementation. Authorities were hoping to have the computerized system in place this spring, but then Scott took office and announced his intention to kill it, along with the state anti-drug office that conceived it.

No one can fathom why.

Top law enforcement officials, legislators, and even the governor of Kentucky (a state that has been saturated tragically with pills from Florida) have asked Scott to reconsider, but he won't budge.

Last week's raids, carried out from Miami to West Palm Beach, gave another squalid glimpse of the crisis. The clinics operate as high-volume dispensaries, sometimes with armed guards on patrol. Huge amounts of pills are prescribed by staff doctors to walk-in "patients" exhibiting few, if any, symptoms. Typically the buyers then go peddle the painkillers on the street for up to 10 times the amount they paid.

According to a federal indictment, seven clinics in Broward and Miami-Dade were controlled by a model citizen named Vincent Colangelo, a convicted heroin dealer. Apparently, pharmaceuticals now offer juicier profit margins than smack.

Over a two-year period, Colangelo allegedly distributed more than 660,000 oxycodone pills, enriching him and his partners to the tune of $150,000 a day.

Fortunately, the U.S. Drug Enforcement Administration has its own methods for tracking suspicious prescriptions, and the generous prescribing habits of several doctors attracted the agency's attention. One of them was Dr. Zvi Perper, who wrote scripts for 387,000 oxycodone tablets in six months at a Delray Beach pain clinic.

Ironically, Zvi Perper is the son of Dr. Joshua Perper, the Broward County medical examiner. Given the sky-high overdose statistics in South Florida, it's not farfetched to assume that the elder Perper has performed autopsies on some of the younger Perper's pill-popping customers.

One view of Gov. Scott's opposition to the drug database is that he's an ideological extremist who doesn't like any form of government snooping. Perhaps there are hard feelings left over from his days at Columbia/HCA, when the feds were nailing the company for massive Medicare fraud.

In any case, one can't help but wonder if Scott's concern for shielding the privacy of dope dealers will extend to other criminals. Perhaps next he'll suggest abolishing the Department of Highway Safety and Motor Vehicles, which maintains a fiendishly thorough computer list of every automobile, truck, and motorcycle registered in the state. Heck, does a police officer really need to know if the car he's pulling over at 4 A.M. on I-95 is stolen?

Among the many lawmakers in Tallahassee who are

unhappy with the governor's vision is Sen. Mike Fasano, a Republican from New Port Richey and an energetic supporter of the Prescription Drug Monitoring Program.

Fasano has vowed to do everything he can to get the database running and keep it in place, and he's got enough clout to do it. Senate President Mike Haridopolis says public funding will be used if necessary.

It would be crazy for Scott to veto the measure, but he seems determined to redefine crazy at least once a week.

Last week's raids on the pill mills provided some insight into whom and what the storefront dope peddlers fear. High on the list are big pharmacy chains, which have no qualms about using computers.

One undercover agent sat in a room full of pill buyers being coached by a clinic nurse on how to get their hefty prescriptions filled without attracting attention.

"Do not go to Walgreens," the nurse warned. "I can't say this enough. They are not your friend; they are the enemy."

Unlike a certain governor.

Note: Gov. Scott backed down, and a database was implemented allowing authorities to track storefront sales of painkillers.

April 2, 2011
The Best Legislature Money Can Buy

I once referred to a past Legislature as a festival of whores, which in retrospect was a vile insult to the world's oldest profession.

Today's lackluster assemblage in Tallahassee is possibly the worst in modern times, and it cannot fairly be compared to anything except a rodeo of phonies and pimps. It's impossible to remember a governor and lawmakers who were more virulently anti-consumer and more slavishly submissive to big business.

The list of who's getting screwed in the state budget battle is long and sadly familiar: the schools, college students, foster children, the poor, the elderly, the sick, and the jobless. The happiest faces, of course, belong to lobbyists for corporations, insurance companies, and utilities, who are getting almost everything they want.

It's astounding that so many voters were suckered into thinking that this new generation of Republicans was going to fight for the common man instead of for the fat cats and their special interests. What a joke. The so-called leadership was plainly bought and paid for by the time their shoes hit the steps of the Capitol.

The House is swiftly moving to deregulate 20 different types of business, including intrastate movers and telemarketers—two occupations that aren't exactly famous for being scrupulous and undeceptive. Deregulation is estimated to cost the state about $6 million in revenue (and who knows how much it will cost consumers in rip-offs), but just think of all the terrific new jobs it will create. That's what supporters claim. Seriously.

Just what Florida needs—more telemarketers!

Bills are also sailing through the House and Senate that will allow Florida Power & Light to raise your electric rates over the next five years while at the same time giving the utility a controlling grip on the state's future solar energy market.

GOP leaders who otherwise love to cheer free-market capitalism have already voiced support of the monopolistic bill, which gives FPL and four other major utilities exclusive rights to develop solar projects, eliminating pesky bids from smaller firms.

FPL achieved this coup the old-fashioned way, by hiring

30 lobbyists and donating about $4 million in campaign contributions to certain lawmakers and candidates for governor.

Renewable energy would be good for Florida, but competition among providers would actually hold down electric rates. Not happening.

More bad news: If your home is one of 1.3 million insured by Citizens—the state-run pool that was established after Hurricane Andrew—your premiums could soon rise by as much as 25 percent.

A Senate subcommittee last week voted to let Citizens jack up its rates and start dumping policies on homes valued at more than $1 million. The idea is to eventually close down Citizens and shunt all Floridians back into the private insurance market.

That would be a swell idea except for the many thousands of residents who live in coastal areas where private insurance companies will not offer coverage or will provide it only at outlandishly high rates. Citizens is indisputably a mess, but if the Senate bill becomes law, many Floridians could be facing a future hurricane season with no homeowners' insurance and with their mortgage companies breathing down their necks.

You might be wondering what the new Legislature has accomplished so far for the greater public good. The answer is not much. But to benefit themselves, lawmakers resurrected and decriminalized a scummy little gimmick called "leadership funds," which allow special-interest groups to give gobs of money to special campaign accounts controlled by the leaders of both political parties, who can spread it around as they see fit.

Outlawed by a long-ago Legislature, leadership funds are simply a sanitized way of buying votes, slightly less sleazy than taking cash in a paper bag.

This time around, donors to the politicians will be listed by name, which is supposed to make us all feel not quite so betrayed.

However, there has been at least one instance this spring when the issue of ethics raised its timid little head in Tallahassee.

Sen. Mike Fasano of New Port Richey introduced a bill that would have toughened penalties for crooked officeholders and public officials. However, the measure was quickly snuffed in the Rules Committee by Fasano's fellow Republicans and Democrat Gary Siplin of Orlando, who all felt that the current laws are quite stern enough to discourage corrupt behavior. It's hard to know whether to laugh or vomit.

On a faintly positive note, at least one terrible scheme that took seed in the Legislature will not become law, at least for now.

A few weeks ago, Sen. John Thrasher of St. Augustine and Rep. Pat Rooney of West Palm Beach launched legislation that would have let Jack Nicklaus build golf courses in several state parks, starting with the beautiful Jonathan Dickinson tract near Stuart. No one is a bigger Nicklaus fan than I am, but this truly was one of the nuttiest ideas of all time. Naturally, Gov. Rick Scott loved it.

Florida already has more than 1,000 golf courses, many of them losing business. Meanwhile, our state park system draws 16 million visitors annually and is recognized as one of the country's finest, a reputation that would disintegrate with the intrusion of driving ranges, fertilized fairways, and golf carts (not to mention hotels, which the bill idiotically allowed).

The outcry was loud and instant, and within days both Rooney and Thrasher bailed. The golf-in-the-parks bill got shelved.

In such dreary political times, it's good that Floridians can still come together and make themselves heard. The shocker is that they weren't ignored.

We Don't Need No Stinkin' U.S. Tax Dollars

Earlier this summer, a panel of low-wattage trolls known as the Legislative Budget Commission spurned $2.1 million of a federal grant designed to transition ill and elderly Floridians out of nursing facilities and back to their homes. The program, which started under President George W. Bush, is designed to save states millions in Medicaid costs because residential care for older citizens is less expensive than long-term institutional care. To that end, the feds offered Florida—which has one of the nation's largest populations of seniors—almost $36 million in phased grants. No thanks, said geniuses like Rep. Rob Schenck of Spring Hill and Rep. Denise Grimsley of Sebring.

Because the Bush program, Money Follows the Person, was renewed as part of the Obama administration's controversial health-care reform package, most GOP legislators on the panel declined to participate. This astoundingly stupid strategy of sending our U.S. tax dollars to other states is the hatchling of House Speaker Dean Cannon, cheered on by Gov. Rick Scott and other Republican zombies.

The money for moving sick and older residents back home was unnecessary, said Grimsley and Schenck, because state agencies already try to do that. That might come as a surprise to those with relatives in Florida nursing homes.

Even though no state funds were at stake, the members of the Legislative Budget Commission want you to believe that they rejected the $2.1 million seniors grant because of their staunch frugality. But guess what else they did at the same meeting?

They unanimously voted to hand out a total of $7.5 million to two business firms that were considering expanding operations in Florida or moving here. Here's the best part: The lawmakers weren't even given the names of the corporations—one was coded "Project Equis," the other "Project Christmas."

I'm totally serious. And these yahoos forked over the money anyway.

This is Florida's so-called leadership in the year 2011. Screw the sick, poor, and elderly, and grovel worshipfully before any half-assed company with a letterhead and a lobbyist.

To keep their punitive streak going, lawmakers also nixed more than $50 million in federal child-abuse prevention funds (because, gosh, we don't have a sickening problem with child abuse here, do we?). As before, the money was killed only because it was attached to the administration's health-care legislation, which many lawmakers say is unconstitutional. Yet the grants being rejected have no relation to the sections of the law being challenged in court.

One casualty of politics is a program in which nurses visit homes where there is a known risk of child abuse or neglect, and counsel young parents. The goal is not only to save lives but also to save the state tons of money. Victims of long-term child abuse often end up in hospitals, foster care, or eventually prison, at a perpetuating cost to Florida taxpayers.

Healthy Families Florida, whose work protecting children at risk has been much praised, would have run the visiting nurses program. After the $50 million from Uncle Sam was rebuffed, nobody in Tallahassee would stand up and take the blame. The House, the Senate, and the governor's office all claimed they had nothing to do with sabotaging the grant. It was just one of those mysterious things.

Not so easy to deny was the Legislature's whacking of $10 million from the Healthy Families state budget, which administrators estimate will cut services to about 6,000 children in 4,000 families.

Lawmakers also squashed a U.S. grant to enlarge two community health centers and build a third in Osceola County. State officials likewise turned their backs on a pilot Medicaid project that would have reimbursed medical providers up to $2 million for hospice services to children who are gravely ill.

Suck it up, kids. You don't need no stinking U.S. tax dollars.

With a $3.7 billion budget hole and the nation's second-highest rate of uninsured residents, Florida is rejecting more federal health-care funds than any other state. This is a matter of button-busting pride to Speaker Cannon and also to the governor, who continues to float through his own squirrelly parallel universe.

The same guy who made a fortune from overbilled Medicare payouts to his hospitals recently sat down with a *New York Times* reporter to reiterate his distaste for U.S. assistance. Said Scott: "There are a lot of programs that the federal government would like to give you that don't fit your state, don't fit your needs and ultimately create obligations that your taxpayers can't afford."

Sure. Why throw money away on abused children when you can spend it on something really important, like Project Equis?

Maybe someday, if we behave, they'll even tell us what it is.

August 13, 2011
ALFs' Foxes Guarding the Henhouses

Anyone who's been following this newspaper's investigation of the wretched conditions in some of Florida's assisted-living facilities might wonder how the state could have cruelly turned its back on so many sick and helpless people.

The answer is as simple as it is sickening: Money.

Florida doesn't spend enough of it enforcing the laws and regulations governing ALFs, while the industry spends a fortune buying off key state lawmakers with campaign donations.

One of them is Sen. Rene Garcia, a Republican from Hialeah who chairs the Health Regulation Committee. Remember this character's name, in case he ever dreams of running for statewide office.

Garcia's district includes more than 100 assisted-living facilities, including some of the worst and most heavily fined in Miami-Dade. Thanks to Garcia and others, it's not easy for one of these joints to get in trouble, no matter what horrors are taking place inside.

Statewide, more than 70 ALF residents are known to have perished from gangrene, starvation, narcotic overdoses, and burns. At least 200 others have died under suspicious circumstances, but the records have been sealed. In one case, caregivers at an ALF in Manatee County managed to overlook an 85-year-old man while nearly half of his face was consumed by a cancerous tumor. In another facility, three people died, including a senior who fell down 24 separate times.

Despite all this, legislators beholden to ALF lobbyists assiduously labored to gut the laws meant to keep these homes safe. Too many rules and regulations, they complained.

Heck, it's only human suffering we're talking about.

Even as the authorities found residents neglected, abused, and even dying, lawmakers like Garcia—who are rarely made to sleep in their own urine—were working aggressively on behalf of the ALFs. Their mission was to shrink state oversight, minimize the number of inspections, and make it harder to shut down rogue facilities.

This year in Tallahassee, 23 bills were introduced to weaken state supervision over ALFs. Most of them were written by the Florida Assisted Living Association, the industry lobby group. No one is more slavishly obedient to their wishes than Garcia, who collected $8,100 in campaign contributions from ALF corporate interests.

One of the bright ideas in Garcia's proposal would have removed the state's power to automatically shut down the most dangerous ALFs—the ones found to repeatedly put residents at risk of death—after two more Class I violations. Garcia also pushed to block the state from slapping additional fines on ALFs when inspectors catch workers breaking the law. Without that enforcement measure, operators wouldn't have much incentive to clean up their acts.

When questioned by reporters, Garcia said he didn't actually favor reducing legal protections for residents in assisted-living facilities. He said the legislation he sponsored was mostly initiated by FALA, the ALF lobby group—a pathetic excuse that tells you all you need to know about how things work at the Capitol.

Furthermore, Garcia said he wasn't aware of language in his own proposal that would have stripped regulators of the authority to revoke the licenses of ALFs with multiple critical violations. "I just don't recall that," he said.

People are dying under the most miserable conditions,

and this guy conveniently can't remember pimping a law that would have made things even worse.

He's not the only one who's foggy these days. Sen. Don Gaetz, a Destin Republican, said he couldn't recall language in one of his own cosponsored bills that stopped the state from bringing medical teams to ALFs to decide whether sick residents should be removed from the homes for their own safety. "I just don't remember," Gaetz said.

The legislation passed in 2009. Now the ALF operators, not doctors, decide when an ailing resident should be moved. No big deal, unless it happens to be your grandmother or grandfather who's in trouble.

To further deter nosy inspectors, lawmakers have kept on a shoestring budget the agency charged with overseeing ALFs. Over the last decade, investigations of serious incidents involving residents have declined radically even as the toll of deaths and abuse cases has risen.

Only seven homes were closed during a two-year period in which the state could have shut down 70, based on repeated violations that endangered residents, fatally in some cases. The *Herald*'s series temporarily stalled many of this year's worst bills, including Garcia's, but they'll be back the next session. Meanwhile, Gov. Rick Scott has put together a task force heavily weighted toward the ALF industry (big surprise), which began meeting last week.

In the fall, a group of state senators will convene to draw up new legislation that supposedly would increase inspections of ALFs and hike penalties for repeat offenders. The best choice to chair the panel would have been Ronda Storms, a Republican from Valrico who heads the Senate's Children, Families, and Elder Affairs Committee.

Storms has been a strong advocate for strengthening

supervision and cracking down on assisted-living facilities that neglect frail and sick residents. As leader of the reform committee, she would have brought some credibility and compassion to a debate that's been dominated by colleagues who sold out to the industry.

But Senate President Mike Haridopolos made sure that the ALF owners will have little to worry about this autumn. Instead of appointing Storms to run the committee, he appointed none other than Rene Garcia.

If it weren't so tragic, you'd almost have to laugh.

March 17, 2012
Surprise—Lawmakers Turn Down Free Drug Test

Among its dubious achievements this year, the Florida Legislature passed a law authorizing random drug tests for state workers.

Guess who's exempt? Lawmakers themselves.

So now the clerk down at the DMV gets to pee in a cup— but not the knuckleheads in Tallahassee who control $70 billion in public funds.

Who do you think is more dangerous to the future of Florida?

In the session that just ended, the Legislature jacked up tuition on state college students while creating a new university to placate one cranky senator. It threw more than 4,400 state workers out of their jobs while handing out more than $800 million in tax breaks to businesses.

Clearly, legislators are impaired. Is it meth? Coke? Mushrooms?

We'll never know.

A few months ago, I offered to pay for drug tests for all

160 state senators and representatives. The deal was that all of them had to do it. Not a penny of taxpayer money would be spent.

Shockingly, the Republican leadership showed zero interest in my proposal. However, they were very excited about Gov. Rick Scott's plan to impose mandatory urine testing on welfare applicants, who statistically use drugs at a lower rate than the public. That particular law is currently stalled in the courts because of serious constitutional questions, which is where the new statute will end up as well, if Scott signs it.

Meanwhile, let's hear from its proud sponsor, Rep. Jimmie Smith of Lecanto, which is near Inverness, which is sort of near Wildwood. Smith's Web page says he's a "security officer" who is retired from the army. He has been in the Legislature about 18 months. "This is not to do drug testing because they're state workers," he said. "This is to do drug testing for one problem: drugs in Florida."

The new law would allow state agencies to randomly test up to 10 percent of their workers every three months. Failing one test can get you fired; the present law requires treatment after the first positive urine screen.

An amendment that would have included drug-testing the governor and lawmakers was indignantly rejected. "Political theater," whined Rep. Smith. "It was found to be unconstitutional to drug-test elected officials because it prevents us, as citizens, from having that First Amendment right."

Based on that fog-headed explanation, which not even Cheech could explain to Chong, Smith's urine should be the first to get screened.

He was attempting to reference a 1997 U.S. Supreme Court decision that struck down a Georgia law requiring political candidates—not just elected officials—to take drug tests. The ruling wasn't based on the First Amendment but on the Fourth Amendment, which protects against unreasonable search and seizure.

It's the same constitutional provision at the core of multiple legal challenges to Scott's drug-testing initiatives. While private companies may screen employees whether or not there is cause or reasonable suspicion, the judiciary often takes a dim view when government tries that.

A few Florida lawmakers pointed out the hypocrisy of excluding themselves from a statewide drug-testing program. "I have to conclude that this is an elitist body not prepared or courageous [enough] to lead by example. Shame on you," Rep. Mark Pafford, a Democrat from West Palm Beach, told his colleagues.

Carlos Trujillo, a Republican from Miami, agreed that the governor and elected officeholders should be drug-tested with other state workers. Still he voted to ice the amendment, citing concerns over the Georgia ruling.

That decision, written for the majority by Justice Ruth Bader Ginsburg, criticized the Georgia law because it "diminishes personal privacy" and was mainly a symbolic remedy to a situation that hadn't even been documented—drug use among political candidates.

Ironically, the same argument can be made against random testing of Florida employees. Jimmie Smith and other supporters of the bill didn't produce any proof that drug abuse was rampant in the state work force. They just wanted to look like tough guys.

The high court has sanctioned government drug testing for certain professions in which public safety is at stake. For example, a train engineer may be ordered to submit a urine sample even if there's no indication of a substance problem.

You could make a strong case that lawmakers fall into the

same high-risk category, considering the damage they do in their annual train wreck known as the Legislative session.

The offer still stands. I'll pay for every one of them to pee in a cup.

The governor, too. In fact, we'll let him go first.

November 3, 2012
Florida Voters Won't Be Fooled Again—or Will We?

There are so many bad constitutional amendments on Florida's ballot that it's hard to know where to start.

The most deceptive is Amendment 8, which is fraudulently captioned "Religious Freedom." If passed, it would open the door to taxpayer funding of private religious schools and institutions, a dangerous mixing of church and state that has been prohibited here for 126 years. Amendment 8 used to be Amendment 7, which was derailed by a court challenge and then hastily rewritten. It would bar government from denying public funds to organizations or institutions based on "religious identity or belief." Specifically, it would eliminate the long-standing constitutional ban on using state money "directly or indirectly" to aid any "church, sect or religious denomination."

Amendment 8 was concocted by Republican lawmakers who support a student-voucher system that would benefit private schools and church schools while bleeding critical funds from state education revenues. This should anger you only if you've got children or grandchildren in public school.

Another terrible ballot measure is Amendment 6, an anti-abortion manifesto that would punch holes in the privacy clause in Florida's Constitution. If anything deserves a legal shield of privacy, it's a woman's personal and often difficult choices about birth planning.

Christian conservatives in the Legislature are exasperated because their attempts to restrict abortions have stalled in the courts because of the privacy issue. Their solution is to rewrite the Constitution to exclude abortion-related matters from that protection. By weakening privacy rights, Amendment 6 would set the stage for politicians to interfere in a broad range of medical and family decisions in which they should have no say, no influence, no presence whatsoever.

Who can forget their disgraceful theatrics during the Terri Schiavo case?

Partisan spittle is likewise all over Amendment 1, which is basically just a ham-handed attack on the federal health-care law. It declares that government can't make employers provide health insurance for their workers and that it can't force uninsured people to purchase insurance. Where were these bold libertarian voices when mandatory auto liability insurance got passed in Florida? You can be sure they carry their little State Farm cards tucked safely in their wallets.

The good thing about Amendment 1 is that it's all hot air, and it won't have any effect on health-care reform. That's because federal law supersedes state law, a somewhat substantial technicality that failed to deter the grandstanding boneheads in Tallahassee.

To demonstrate their contempt for taxes, lawmakers have also larded the ballot with several amendments that would amount to a mugging of city and county governments. Among them is Amendment 3, so dense and confusing that it might as well have been transcribed in Slovenian. It would change the equation for setting the state's revenue cap, potentially restricting the amount of funds available for some rather basic municipal needs.

Around the country, 20 other legislatures have rejected

versions of Amendment 3. Colorado voters passed one, and it proved to be such a mess that they hurried back to the polls and killed it. None of this served to discourage the GOP leadership in the Florida Legislature, whose appetite for doomed schemes seems boundless.

Amendment 4 is even worse than Amendment 3, a gift to wealthy owners of second homes in Florida. It would cut by half the cap on property-tax assessments for non-homesteaded properties, at a projected cost to city and county governments of between $600 million and $1 billion over the first three years. This should bother you only if you care about your local police and fire protection, ambulance service, city parks. You know, the little stuff.

Another amendment for which there's absolutely no public clamor is Amendment 5, which would give legislators unprecedented sway over Florida's judiciary. It's the pet project of House Speaker Dean Cannon, a Winter Park Republican who holds an actual law degree from the University of Florida. Presiding over a legislative body that cranks out one deficient statute after another, Cannon is miffed that the courts keep stomping on them.

His retort is Amendment 5, which would have the state Senate confirm all Supreme Court appointments. Stop laughing—the guy is serious. He thinks state senators should pick our Supreme Court justices. In addition, Cannon wants the entire Legislature to be able to change, by simple majority votes, procedural rules that govern the courts. Finally, his Amendment 5 allows the House Speaker (currently him) to see the confidential files of any Judicial Nominating Commission. He calls this "checks and balances," but it's really a flagrant dismantling of the constitutional boundaries between the Legislature and the justice system.

The result would be the total political pollution of our courts. Cannon's law professors at UF must be aghast. Lots of other Republicans are.

All these rotten amendments were written and captioned for the ballot in ways to appear harmless and even reformist, but they aren't.

And they won't pass unless 60 percent of Florida's voters are fooled.

MONEY SHOUTS

Island Justice, but Not for Lost Mangroves

Monroe County prosecutors are dropping all criminal charges related to a highly publicized slaughter of protected mangroves. The outcome is as pathetic as it was predictable, given the long, inglorious tradition of raping shoreline in the Keys.

This particular outrage occurred 18 months ago on North Key Largo, where the exclusive Ocean Reef Club abuts the John Pennekamp Coral Reef State Park. Here an estimated 12,000 red, white, and black mangrove trees—some of them five stories high—were illegally hacked, creating instant (and lucrative) oceanfront vistas for several planned home sites.

More than 90 percent of the large specimens that were cut then are either dead or dying today. Incredibly, about two-thirds of the trees are within the tidal boundaries of the park itself, a brazen incursion even by old-time Keys standards.

Chopping 12,000 mangroves is a noisy project, and the clamor went on for days. Oddly, not a soul at Ocean Reef seemed to notice—though it was the height of the winter season, and the clearing would have been visible to anybody taking off or landing at the club's busy airstrip. Cutting was halted only after the long raw gash in the tree line was spotted by a state biologist patrolling the waters of Pennekamp.

The lots benefiting from the crime belonged to O. R. Golf Partners Ltd. The firm's general partner, John Grunow, Jr., is a member and part-time resident of Ocean Reef. He called the mangrove episode a "terrible accident." He said his contractor had hired a landscaper to do some pruning, in accordance with a legal permit. However, the actual cutting, Grunow said, got assigned to a group of unemployed "surfers" who went blundering into the park with chain saws abuzz.

(Grunow said he didn't witness the event, as he was taking a Mexican vacation at the time.)

State environmental officers urged local prosecutors to do something. Last summer, Grunow and contractor Edward Sanders were charged with three misdemeanors and two felonies, including criminal mischief and pollution. They pleaded innocent.

The arrests were hailed by David Struhs, head of the state's Department of Environmental Protection, who said the prosecutions would send "a strong message" to would-be violators, no matter how wealthy. In this case, the message is obvious: Get yourself a big-time Miami defense attorney.

That's what Grunow did. His trial was postponed repeatedly while the lawyers did their thing. Finally, last week, Monroe State Attorney Mark Kohl threw in the towel, calling it the "case from hell." Kohl told the *Free Press* in Islamorada that obtaining convictions would have been difficult because the men hired to cut the trees changed their stories about what happened and who was there.

Granted, any prosecution that relies upon the testimony of surfers turned tree surgeons is probably in deep trouble.

Still, to those unfamiliar with Keys history, it must seem incredible that acres of mangroves in a state park can be mutilated in broad daylight, and nobody goes on trial.

Grunow isn't entirely out of the woods, or what's left of them. The DEP wants $644,600 in civil fines and expenses for wetland restoration—a gentle offer, considering that damage to North Key Largo's mangrove belt was estimated at $4 million to $6 million.

"Irreparable and irreversible" is the way county code-enforcement officials described the clearing. They're seeking another $20,000 from Grunow for filling wetlands on several other lots at Ocean Reef.

Prosecutors say he has agreed to new deed restrictions that won't let him sell the shorn lots for at least three years.

The plan is to allow the surviving mangroves to grow back high enough to obscure the ocean view. Ostensibly, that would eliminate any real-estate windfall that might have resulted from the hack job.

It's an interesting tactic, in lieu of a criminal prosecution, but there's one small problem: Mangroves don't grow like weeds. Replenishing a half-century-old stand will take a wee bit longer than three years.

But sometimes that's how island justice works. Goodbye, jailhouse. Hello, Miracle-Gro.

July 28, 2002
Arrest CEO, Buy Stocks, Watch Dow Jones Go Up

Last Wednesday, after the Dow Jones Industrial Average shot up 488 points, the TV news was crawling with Wall Street analysts eager to explain the phenomenal rebound.

Investor confidence was bolstered, they all said, because congressional leaders finally had agreed on legislation aimed at "cracking down" on corporate fraud and deceptive accounting practices.

Another reason for the burst of public optimism, they said, was the widely publicized arrest that very morning of a fellow named John J. Rigas.

Rigas, 78, is the founder of the now bankrupt Adelphia cable-television empire. He and two of his sons were hauled away by postal inspectors and charged with looting millions from Adelphia as it went down the tubes.

Those who have dealt with their local cable company couldn't be shocked to hear that there might be stealing and deceit at high levels. The surprise was that the feds actually had busted somebody for it. Apparently, the mere sight of a CEO in handcuffs was enough to help send the stock markets soaring. Americans are so infuriated by business scandals that they're aching to see crooked executives prosecuted and sent away like common bank robbers, or worse. The sentiment has not been lost on Congress, which is raising prison terms for certain corporate crimes to a maximum 20 years.

While the likelihood of any board chairman doing hard time is laughably remote, politicians are feeling pressure to act outraged and talk tough. This time they're in a particularly sticky situation. Big political campaigns are bankrolled heavily by corporations and business groups. Locking up too many CEOs could result in a precipitous decline of campaign contributions.

But with stock prices plummeting and midterm elections on the horizon, both Congress and the White House realized that something dramatic-looking had to be done.

Fortunately, of all the things that can go sour with the economy, the stock market is the most malleable, at least in the short term. Inflations and recessions last for years, spelling political doom for those in power (ask Jimmy Carter and George Bush Sr.). But the stock indexes tend to bounce up and down with the headlines. The Adelphia case is a good example.

Most people who engaged in last Wednesday's buying frenzy had likely never heard of John Rigas before he got pinched. Almost certainly, they had no idea whether or not the government's case was solid. Unless you were a disgruntled shareholder in Adelphia, there was truly no reason to get giddy over the arrests. Only a ninny would believe that the case will deter other corporate scoundrels from fictionalizing their annual reports.

The fact is, logic doesn't matter much on Wall Street. Regular working folks tend to buy stocks when they're feeling good about things, and the arrest of an allegedly sleazy tycoon obviously made them feel pretty good—at least for a day.

Now, say you're President Bush, and you're worried about the mood of the country and the possibility of losing your Republican majority in the House in November. The last thing you need is a sickly stock market.

What you do now is play the Adelphia card. Whenever the Dow starts to dive, you simply call the Justice Department and tell it to go out and bust a Fortune 500 big shot. Make sure CNN is alerted in advance, of course.

If the market was so rejuvenated by the Rigas arrest, imagine the heights to which it would climb if, say, a SWAT team snatched Martha Stewart midcasserole. That's bound to boost the NASDAQ up 75 points, at least.

Want more? Imagine if the entire board of Arthur Andersen were rounded up, blindfolded, and flown to Guantánamo Bay for interrogation. While you're at it, save a tent for the top dogs at WorldCom, Tyco, and AOL Time Warner. And if all that still fails to launch the Dow back to 10,000–plus before the elections, there's always the big enchilada: Enron.

That's right, Mr. President. You personally take down your old pal Kenneth "Kenny Boy" Lay on a special Wall Street edition of *COPS*.

Yank him out of his Houston mansion while he's still in his pajamas, frog-march him to a squad car, and read him his rights. Then rush home and call your broker, Mr. President, because the blue chips will be going through the roof. Guaranteed.

October 13, 2002
A Sweet Setup at MIA

Next time you're trying to find your way out of the lunatic rat maze called Miami International Airport, remember the story of Linda Forrest: She's one of eight partners in Dade Aviation Consultants, the consortium of so-called experts being paid to oversee the $5 billion construction spectacle at MIA.

Every month, Forrest receives nearly $50,000 for essentially having a pulse. This is a sweet setup, and not many people knew about it until *Herald* reporters Ronnie Greene and Joe Mozingo put it in the newspaper last week.

Forrest was brought into the DAC group a decade ago as a minority participant. At the time, she'd had her contractor's license less than two years, causing some folks to marvel at her sudden good fortune. In retrospect, it wasn't such a mystery. Whenever huge public-works contracts are being bid, the white guys trying to win the project scramble around looking for minority "partners."

They do this to curry favor with the politicians who are awarding the contracts, and also to make themselves appear as if they honestly care about utilizing non-white contractors. This is called a minority set-aside program, and in South Florida it works like this: You recruit minorities, put their names on the letterhead, then set them aside.

Soon after the MIA deal was done, Linda Forrest agreed to pay 7 percent of all her airport revenues to a white guy named Richard Clark, in return for "consulting" and public relations services. Richard Clark just happened to be the brother of the late Steve Clark, who was mayor of both Dade County and the city of Miami.

That would be the same Steve Clark who seconded the motion to give the airport deal to DAC; the same Steve Clark whose buddy, lobbyist Rodney Barreto, was a key player in convincing the County Commission to approve Forrest's company.

What a wacky coincidence, huh?

At first the mayor's brother, being so shy and modest, kept his name off the paperwork detailing the payments from Forrest's company. Now he's suing her to collect money he says she owes.

Unfortunately, her firm is in bankruptcy. The state won't let her hire anybody until she pays $17,086 in past unemployment taxes, while an insurance company has accused her in a $145,000 embezzlement scheme. Forrest's plight is puzzling considering the torrent of public funds her company continues to receive—$5.8 million over the last 10 years.

And what did she do at MIA to deserve such a windfall? Not much. She wasn't even required to provide her own employees; all she had to do was pay the ones sent to her by DAC managers. Even that didn't go smoothly. Some workers complained about paychecks that arrived late or bounced and insurance premiums that were deducted but never paid. In response, Forrest has said that her company occasionally wrestles with "cash-flow problems" and that she is working to resolve all pending legal issues.

It's now embarrassingly obvious that her inclusion in the DAC airport-management contract was a charade. The big shots needed a black contractor on board in order to win the necessary votes, and Forrest was in the right place with the right connections.

Once the bid was approved, she was basically expected to take the dough and stay out of the way. Nobody would have been the wiser if only she'd kept up her side payments to the late mayor's brother.

The arrangement between Forrest and Richard Clark

ended in 1997. Clark's lawsuit says Forrest still owes him $163,968; she says he didn't do anything to earn it. In any event, Clark seems to be doing just fine. Now retired in the Blue Ridge Mountains, he's still profiting from his associations at MIA—as a lobbyist for the group that runs the duty-free shops.

You can understand why politicians and their pals don't want to give up their stranglehold on the airport. It's a place where ridiculous sums of money seem to fall from the sky, and all you've got to do is hold out your arms and catch it.

Every month, nearly $50,000 lands on Linda Forrest. Nobody in authority asks where it goes, because they don't care. In this way, $5.8 million has evaporated in a single stinking deal.

Plenty of experienced, qualified black contractors would have been thrilled to get a piece of the airport project—and would have actually put in the work. That isn't what the deal makers wanted. They wanted a front.

Given what we know about MIA, it's harrowing to think how many millions of dollars have been squandered, funneled off, or diverted to friends and relatives of elected officials. One day MIA's expansion might be finished, but in the meantime it's enriching too many people who haven't lifted a finger except to count the cash.

September 7, 2003
For Some, Indentured Misery Is a Way of Life

"They're not worth killing anyhow."

With those compassionate words, North Florida farmer Thomas R. Lee summed up his view of many of the laborers who sweat and toil in his potato plant.

"They are not much more than a damn animal, to be honest with you," he told *Herald* reporter Ronnie Greene. "The good people that you do hire, you are going to treat them right, and do them right. A lot of these type of people, if you give them $25, they are going to drink it up and dope it up."

It would be nice to report that Thomas R. Lee is an anachronism in 21st-century American agriculture, but he's not. He might be more blunt-spoken than the folks at Tropicana and Taco Bell, but they're all in essentially the same business: exploiting the poor and the pathetic for profit.

Generations pass, but the story of the farmworker never changes, as Greene and photographer Nuri Vallbona graphically documented in a recent *Herald* series. The men and women who pick the fruit and vegetables that we eat live too often in indentured misery. Efforts to improve abominable working conditions are regularly thwarted by elected officials with family and financial ties to Big Agriculture.

To avoid lawsuits and ugly publicity, corporate farm operators take great pains to try to buffer themselves from the sickening abuses that occur daily in the fields and work camps.

Potato farmer Lee, for example, does not directly hire or pay his workers. For that, he employs a fine upstanding citizen named Ronald M. "Too Tall" Jones.

Jones is an independent crew-chief contractor, otherwise known as a crew boss. It's not an occupation that tends to attract sensitive, big-hearted souls.

According to those who have worked for him, Jones recruits primarily homeless persons, many with crack and alcohol addictions that make them vulnerable to intimidation. In a plain work van or his own Cadillac Escalade, Jones trolls public parks and shelters in the greater Jacksonville area, rolling up with fat wads of cash and promises of other recreational enticements.

By no mere coincidence, he also owns several grubby

housing camps for farmworkers. There you can purchase marked-up food, beer, liquor, and cigarettes. According to at least five laborers, Jones is also glad to extend cash loans— at 100 percent interest.

One potato worker who had calculated his week's pay at $300 was crestfallen to end up with only $35, Jones having voluminously deducted for rent and other "expenses."

As you might expect, Jones was not available to be interviewed about his employment practices. One of his camps was recently shut down as unfit for human habitation.

Crew bosses get away with ripping off laborers because they purposely select those who, for a variety of personal reasons, are reluctant to complain. Said Gregory S. Schell, a lawyer representing migrant workers: "You've made a job so bad that the only people who are going to do farmwork are undocumented aliens or crack addicts."

As a major agricultural state, Florida is home territory for some of the industry's sleaziest and most brutal crew chiefs. More than 200 have been barred for offenses such as cheating workers, while a dozen bosses and migrant smugglers have been imprisoned for slavery, assault, sexual exploitation, and other crimes against farmworkers.

Naturally, the people on the high end of the profit chain claim to deplore the predatory treatment of laborers. They will also hastily add that the problem is out of their hands, since many deal strictly with the independent contractors supplying the crews.

The immorality of that dodge did not escape U.S. District Judge K. Michael Moore, who, during the recent trial of several crew bosses, suggested that the blanket of guilt and shame also belongs upon those at the top of the corporate ladder.

Efforts to improve working conditions for farmworkers are regularly thwarted.

Every executive at Lykes Bros. or Consolidated Citrus is well aware of what life is like for the farm crews who make those companies rich. The big shots know all about the rip-offs, the slum housing, the loan sharking, the beatings and rapes—yet they continue to do business with the same thug bosses.

Why? Because the system works fabulously. The crops get picked, the money rolls in, and if anybody gets in trouble, it's the crew chief. The rich white guys running the farm are safe.

Hefty campaign donations guarantee a smooth ride in the Legislature, where two bills that would have helped Florida farmworkers in a modest way were dead on arrival this year. One bill would have enabled those who get cheated on their pay to sue the growers. The other measure would have provided laborers with information about the pesticides being sprayed on the crops. Both measures were deemed too burdensome for farmers, proving once again that the lawmakers' regard for those who work the fields is really no different from that of Thomas R. Lee.

It's easier on the conscience to think of them as animals when you treat them that way.

January 23, 2005
Getting Rich in the Newspaper Business

As President Bush took the oath of office Thursday, it was hard not to be swept along in the tide of hope and optimism.

That's because this administration is obviously working to forge a new, more mutually beneficial relationship with the press. The next four years could be lucrative indeed for those of us in the Fourth Estate.

Look at Armstrong Williams, the conservative talk-show commentator and newspaper columnist. During the 2004 election campaign, the U.S. government paid Williams $240,000 to say and write wonderful things about the president's No Child Left Behind education program. This arrangement, exposed by *USA Today*, was a revelation to many working stiffs in the media. While every administration attempts to manipulate the news, the outright purchase of journalists is an audacious and clever approach—using taxpayer dollars, to boot!

If Bill Clinton had tried something like that, they would have impeached him again.

Bush's fixers simply shrugged and said that the Williams payola, funneled through the Department of Education, was a straight "public relations" contract. Williams himself insists that he didn't realize it was wrong to cash the government's check and not tell his readers or viewers that he was being paid to praise the president's policies.

Most reporters don't make a lot of money, and $240,000 is a windfall. It's impossible to believe that Williams was the first journalist to have been bought by the Bush administration or that he'll be the last.

Therefore, in the spirit of the administration's new No Scum Left Behind initiative, I humbly offer my services.

In exchange for a modest fee (a bargain compared to Williams), I promise to write glowing commentary about any policy, no matter how radical or half-baked, that Bush's gang cooks up.

But, unlike Williams, I promise to dutifully inform my readers (by a small footnote or perhaps a secret code) on those occasions when I'm being bribed.

For starters, I could do a bang-up job helping to convince Americans that the Social Security system is shot, and that they'd be better off handing over their hard-earned retirement savings to Dick Cheney's pals on Wall Street.

For the right sum, I'd be happy to overlook the fact that there's currently a humongous surplus in the Social Security trust fund, and that a true budget shortfall is almost 40 years away (and possibly much longer).

Bush and Cheney have been trying their best to scare people into believing that Social Security is verging on flat broke, the same way they successfully scared people into believing that Saddam Hussein actually had weapons of mass destruction. This time around, though, Americans seem more skeptical. That's why the president needs columnists like me, to sway public opinion.

Admittedly, the last time I swayed public opinion was . . . well, I can't recall the last time. Anyway, here's my fee schedule, which is based on an escalating level of fake enthusiasm:

For a mere $25, I'll drop a line into my next column that says: "Privatizing Social Security isn't nearly as reckless or goofy as the president's critics would have you believe."

For $50, the line would be: "Privatizing Social Security is an intriguing concept and one that should be seriously explored."

For $99, I'd do two sentences, including a bonus exclamation mark: "Privatizing Social Security is a bold idea whose time has come. Kudos to President Bush!"

For $199.99, a fully punctuated paragraph:

"Here's food for thought. If, instead of dull old Treasury bonds, you'd been allowed to invest your Social Security deductions in Enron stock (and then dumped it when Kenny Lay dumped his, before the company turned turtle), you might have doubled your earnings. Hey, if privatization is such a 'risky gamble,' then deal me in!"

For a flat $500, I'd give them a whole scary column, beginning with:

"If Congress doesn't get behind our president and privatize Social Security, we hardworking 'baby boomers' are doomed to a hellhole retirement straight out of a Dickens novel—impoverished, miserable, bleak. Those puny monthly checks from Uncle Sam (assuming they don't bounce!) won't be enough to fill our cupboards with stale cat food and Sterno. . . ."

And finally, for $999, the big enchilada—the screamer to end all screamers:

"If those wimps in Congress don't wake up and privatize Social Security now—I mean this week!—President Bush will be forced to invade Nassau, the Caymans, and possibly Liechtenstein in search of tax-sheltered assets to replenish the soon-to-be-bankrupt Social Security coffers.

"My own mother has burned her AARP card and rushed off to Washington, D.C., to demonstrate in support of the president's innovative private-investment plan. She can't wait to cash out her T-bills and sink her retirement savings into Halliburton. . . ."

That's baloney, of course, and if Mom gives me any grief, I'll offer to cut her in on the action—but no more than 10 percent, tops.

Who said you can't get rich in the newspaper business?

July 27, 2008
Loan Scandal: Maybe It Was Just Job Rehab

The revelation that more than 10,000 convicted criminals have been welcomed with open arms into Florida's mortgage industry is shocking, even in light of the state's sleazy anything-goes history.

At first blush, things look bad for the Office of Financial Regulation and its commissioner, Don Saxon, whose long nap was harshly interrupted by last week's headlines. And although it's tempting to view this story as just another embarrassing validation of Florida's reputation as the most crooked, screwed-up place in America, there might be an upside to the scandal.

Granted, a *Miami Herald* investigation revealed that just about any scumbag with an arm's-length rap sheet can get work as a mortgage broker or so-called loan originator.

From 2000 to 2007, the OFR allowed at least 10,529 persons with criminal records to begin arranging and selling Florida mortgages. Of that motley throng, 4,065 somehow cleared background checks, even though most had previously committed serious crimes—including bank robbery, racketeering, extortion, and fraud—that by law should have kept them out of the mortgage business. Other crimes of "moral turpitude" found on the records of newly approved mortgage peddlers: assaults, dope deals, sex offenses, and at least 15 homicides.

As it turned out, some of those felons failed to become model citizens upon entering Florida's then-booming real-estate market. They went on to commit at least $85 million in mortgage frauds, fleecing both lenders and borrowers, according to the newspaper's findings. Some people might look at such alarming facts and see a colossal failure by regulators to protect home buyers from known scammers and thieves. No wonder Florida has the highest rate of mortgage fraud in the country, you might say.

But let's look at it another way—not as horrendous bureaucratic incompetence but, rather, as a daring, innovative way of diverting and retraining Florida's inexhaustible supply of felons.

Take Donald Lewis Smith, for example. In 2003 he was licensed to sell mortgages in Kissimmee despite lying about his criminal record—a 17-year sentence for strangling his wife and dumping her body into Tampa Bay. It should be noted, however, that in five years as a broker, Smith hasn't murdered a single customer.

Then there's Scott Almeida, who forthrightly informed mortgage regulators about his federal drug-trafficking conviction. In 1998 he'd been busted with two kilos of coke, two assault rifles, a stolen pistol, and a drug-packaging device. Not long after Almeida got out of prison, the state gave him a broker's license and told him to behave. He promptly went out and racked up $3 million in fraudulent loans, choosing as his victims disabled and elderly persons.

What Almeida did was truly rotten, but on the bright side, at least he gave up the cocaine trade.

Consider also the case of Anthony Hollis, an Orlando felon who was given a license to own a mortgage brokerage despite having been convicted of passing bad checks and auto theft. Hollis used his new access to private credit histories to steal more than $200,000 from customers before he was nailed for racketeering.

Sure, it was a slimy scam, but give Hollis credit for showing ambition. Some car thieves are content to stay car thieves their whole lives. Thanks to the great state of Florida, Hollis got an opportunity to advance up the felonious ladder from street crime to white-collar crime.

Same for Richard Crowder of Miami Beach, one of 23 convicted burglars who successfully transitioned into the mortgage field. Eventually, Crowder masterminded one of the state's worst frauds, setting up $37 million in bad loans by falsifying documents, lying on applications, and staging phony property appraisals.

Crowder, of course, is a lowlife who richly deserves the nine-year prison hitch that awaits him. Yet, without our forgiving state regulators, he'd never have graduated from burglar to swindler. And wouldn't you rather have a creep like that tricking your grandmother out of her life savings than breaking into her house in the dead of night?

Likewise, the OFR might have been doing us a favor by not screening aspiring loan originators such as Ronald D. Collins. He was convicted 37 times between 1983 and 2000 of assorted low-rent money crimes, including forgery and grand theft.

Yet had Collins been banned from the lucrative world of mortgages, he might have turned to more dangerous endeavors such as bank robbery or carjacking.

See, after you live in Florida long enough, you learn to look philosophically for the silver lining in every storm cloud.

That will be Don Saxon's mission as he tries to explain his agency's chronic inattentiveness to Gov. Charlie Crist and other members of the Financial Services Commission, which is scheduled to meet this week.

Maybe Saxon's been asleep at the switch, or maybe he was simply trying to keep known criminals off the streets by putting them behind desks instead.

Isn't it better to be robbed over the phone than at gunpoint?

October 5, 2008
Cindy to Blame for Woes on Wall Street

The collapse of Wall Street and the freeze of credit markets can be traced to one unlikely culprit: Cindy Crawford.

I'm sure she didn't mean to cripple the economy. Most supermodels avoid meddling in global monetary markets, and it's unlikely that Cindy realized how much influence she commanded.

Tragically, however, the crash of 2008 can be connected

to that fateful day, a few short years ago, when Cindy got into the business of designing furniture for a popular retail firm.

It wasn't long before the Crawford brand caught fire. Every time you turned on the television, there she was, languidly sprawling across one of her microfiber plush sofas, or carefully arranging the pastel placemats on one of her cherry-veneer dining tables. She looked great. She had style. She was also much taller than most interior designers.

And, amazingly, you could buy a whole roomful of Cindy's furniture with no down payment. Unbelievable!

More amazingly, you didn't have to start paying off the stuff for a whole year or even longer. As a result, thousands of Americans who could barely afford their car payments eagerly started purchasing Cindy's terrific furniture—although it wasn't technically purchasing, because not much actual money was involved.

As bankers watched the Cindy phenomenon grow, they realized that the customers who were snapping up all this accessible furniture might want larger homes to put it in. The bankers also understood that special mortgages would be necessary when dealing with folks who already needed at least a year to pay for a headboard and a nightstand. Thus was born the concept of subprime loans, a financing ploy very similar to the one used so successfully by Cindy Crawford's furniture company.

Subprimes allowed Americans to get homes with a minimal down payment. Interest rates were extremely low and extremely temporary. The mortgages were structured so that those rates—and the customers' monthly nut—would shoot up radically after a few years, yet nobody seemed worried about that.

Bankers were just tickled to be selling so many loans,

real-estate agents were thrilled to be selling so many houses, and home buyers were elated to have more rooms in which to arrange all their new (and still-unpaid-for) Cindy Crawford furnishings.

The economy was booming, or so we were told. Unfortunately, at no point in this brainless orgy of lending was it required for the folks who were borrowing all that easy money to show they had the means to repay it.

Inevitably, Wall Street was smitten by the Cindy factor. Venerable institutions like Lehman Brothers bought up billions of dollars' worth of bundled subprime mortgages, on the theory that the price of real estate would keep rising insanely until the end of time. If some poor sucker had to default, so what? Repossess his house and sell it for a profit to some other sucker, who could then fill it with more unpaid-for furniture by Cindy Crawford.

But the Wall Street wizards who control the credit flow made a disastrous blunder. The Cindy Model of friendly finance doesn't work very well when the stakes are high.

Selling a roomful of furniture to a family that can't afford to put any cash on the table is different from selling them a house. Thousands of subprime and adjustable-rate mortgages went plummeting into default, and the rest is history.

As Congress and the White House scramble to stanch the bleeding, investor confidence remains shaky. It might be helpful if Cindy stepped forward in some dramatic way, as fellow icon Warren Buffett has done. Here's what she should say to reassure worried Americans: "Please don't buy any more of my elegant yet comfortable furniture unless you actually have the money to pay for it. Before coming to the store, take a close look at your bank statements to make sure you're not making an incredibly foolish mistake.

"Hey, if you can't write a personal check for that five-piece king bedroom set, then you probably shouldn't buy it. Be stylish, America, but be smart. Tomorrow will be a brighter day."

Who knows what impact such a bold speech would have on the stock markets, but I wouldn't be surprised to see an instant rebound. The financial titans who followed Cindy Crawford down the path of carefree lending will just as faithfully follow her back to the realm of fiscal prudence.

There are encouraging signs from the furniture empire for which Cindy is the marquee draw. If you ordered that five-piece king bedroom set today, you wouldn't get to wait years before making the first payment. You'd only get six months.

It looks like Cindy's getting tough.

Take heed, Mr. Treasury Secretary. The handwriting is on the wallpaper.

November 23, 2008
The Beggars in Their Corporate Jets

If you're like most Americans, you probably weren't dabbing tears from your eyes while listening to the woeful pleas of Richard Wagoner, Alan Mulally, and Robert Nardelli.

They are the chiefs of the Big Three automakers, who last week traveled in high style to our nation's capital and begged for $25 billion to save their companies—and, by dire inference, the whole American economy—from ruin.

Interestingly, none of these gentlemen took much blame for leading the U.S. car industry into this terrible abyss, citing instead the global credit crunch, unfavorable trade policies, and other factors out of their control. And while it's probably true that the automobiles being made today by GM, Ford, and Chrysler are safer, more reliable, and more fuel-efficient than ever, that's only because they're scrambling to catch up with Japanese competitors, who've been kicking their butts for the last 30 years.

Toyota and Honda aren't asking Congress to bail them out, because they don't need it. But if they ever do, they probably won't be so foolish as to send their top executives on a public money-grubbing mission in a private luxury aircraft. Wagoner, Mulally, and Nardelli all flew to Washington on separate corporate jets, which provoked lacerating commentary from the legislators whose sympathy they sought.

Said Rep. Gary Ackerman of New York: "It's almost like seeing a guy show up at the soup kitchen in high-hat and tuxedo. . . . I mean, couldn't you all have downgraded to first class or jet-pooled or something to get here?" The response to that inquiry was a blank stare from the pampered auto chiefs, for whom the idea of flying commercial is inconceivable, worse than standing in the deli line at the grocery.

You'd be hard pressed to find three guys more disconnected from Main Street and less qualified to talk about the plight of the average autoworker. According to *The Washington Post*, Wagoner's total compensation from GM last year was $15.7 million. Mulally collected $21.7 million from Ford.

When asked by Rep. Peter Roskam of Illinois if he'd be willing to cut his salary to $1 a year, as Chrysler's Nardelli has said he would do, Mulally replied: "I think I'm okay where I am."

Spoken like a true capitalist. Now give that man a big fat government bailout! As for Nardelli's benevolent offer to accept only a buck a year in compensation, he could surely afford it. In January 2007, he quit abruptly after six years as CEO of Home Depot, Inc., where he'd been paid as much as $38 million annually. Before leaving the company, Nardelli negotiated a "retirement" package worth $210 million, a stunningly obscene sum even in the surreal realm of corporate parachutes.

The amazing thing is that GM, Ford, and Chrysler all have sophisticated public relations departments that their executives obviously failed to consult before hopping in their Gulfstreams and Lears and zooming off to Washington. Nobody was asking that the CEOs apologize for their personal wealth and career successes. But when the corporation that rewards you so extravagantly is going down the toilet, a little humility and sensitivity is in order.

If one or more of the Big Three should collapse, the impact on the economic markets will be massive, the ripple extending far beyond Detroit. Labor experts estimate that as many as 2.5 million people could be thrown out of work nationwide. Nobody wants that to happen, but we also don't want to throw our money at an industry that stupidly continued to crank out SUVs even as gasoline was hitting $4 per gallon.

When the Big Three belatedly decided to "retool" and go green, what did they do? They asked for, and have been promised, a $25 billion loan from Uncle Sam. Then the companies announced they needed *another* $25 billion as a cash float, to get through these rocky times. Boy, did they send the wrong bunch to make their pitch. The generosity of Americans doesn't—and shouldn't—extend to sustaining the ethereal lifestyles of multimillionaires. Lots of executives fly private, but not to their own pity parties.

Bailouts are meant to save jobs, not corporate chariots. The CEOs went back to Detroit rejected, if not chastened. While Congress is mulling a compromise loan package, the attitude toward the automakers remains deeply skeptical.

If the companies were smart, they would have benched

the Fab Three and instead sent some Main Street faces to Washington—an assembly-line worker from a Ford plant, a transmission mechanic from a Chrysler dealership, an upholstery cutter from a GM parts supplier. In other words, men and women who would truly suffer if those companies folded; folks who might not be able to pay their mortgages, or keep their kids in college . . . or even fly Jet Blue, much less on a Gulfstream.

February 8, 2009
Bernie Madoff, the Prisoner of Park Avenue

Private reflections of Bernard L. Madoff, a prisoner on Park Avenue.

> *Dear Diary,*
>
> *For hours I stand at the vast impact-resistant windows of this lonely penthouse and gaze down at the city that never sleeps. I don't sleep much, either—not because I've ripped off and ruined thousands of people but because my electronic ankle bracelet has given me a beast of a rash that itches all night long.*
>
> *Ruth? She has no sympathy. My whining drives her crazy, she says. Last night I caught her writing a letter to the judge, begging him to revoke my bail.*
>
> *Nobody calls these days except for my lawyers and a few very angry investors, to whom I was once foolish enough to offer our home number. Consequently, I am now careful to answer the phone with an impenetrable French accent, like Inspector Clouseau.*
>
>

Your miserable correspondent,
Mssr. B. Madoff
>

Dear Diary,

Unbelievable! A gang of hooligans has defaced my Palm Beach estate with miles of toilet paper!

The news is all over the television, and everyone seems to be getting quite a chuckle out of this senseless act of vandalism. Shockingly, the local authorities show no interest in pursuing the barbarians who did this.

To make things worse, I've now lost my permanent lunch table at the Palm Beach Country Club to Donald Trump's son.

This is America, people! What happened to "innocent until proven guilty"?

> Your persecuted Ponzi,
> Bernard

Dear Diary,

The walls of this $7 million penthouse are closing in on me day by day, and I feel trapped like a rat. No, make that a chinchilla.

At breakfast this morning, it's Ruth—again with the pocket calculator!

"How many zeros are in $50 billion?" she asks with that sly glint in her eye. "And tell me again, honey, where did it all go?" As if she doesn't know!

Today my lawyers are petitioning the court so that I may spend one hour a week at the driving range in East Hampton. I sure hope the judge is a golfer.

> Your 9-handicap detainee,
> Bernie "Tiger" Madoff

Dear Diary,

Finally, some good news! Temporarily, I'm no longer the most despised human being in the United States.

Some knucklehead named John Thain at Merrill Lynch spent $1.2 million redecorating his office while he was failing to save the firm from financial ruin.

Among his many expenditures were $68,000 for a 19th-century credenza and $35,000 for a "commode on legs," which actually sounds kind of nifty.

Maybe I could order one with wheels, so I could roll away from Ruth whenever she goes off on one of her rants.

Your humble Imodium addict,
B.L.M.

Dear Diary,

Don't believe what you see in the media—"house arrest" is brutal. Every day I feel more and more like a walking zombie.

I get up early, eat my imported Norwegian lox, and mail out a few gold Rolexes and Tiffany tennis bracelets to distant family members.

Then I watch The View while I faithfully Tivo Ellen, and of course I never miss the new half-hour version of Deal or No Deal. (I really love that show—what a bunch of suckers!)

Nights are the hardest time, as I lie awake trembling in fear of another vicious toilet-paper attack. I suppose this is what prison will be like, except without my silk kimono and lamb's-wool slippers and chamomile tea and $50 foot massages . . .

Ruth promises she'll wait for me, although I notice she's spending lots of time uptown with some forensic accountant. I'm bracing for the worst.

For inspiration in my darkest hours, I think of all those men who emerged from unjust incarcerations with

strength and dignity to embrace full, vibrant futures—
Solzhenitsyn, Mandela, Robert Downey, Jr.

At the very least, one helluva book contract should be
waiting for me when I get out. As for the movie rights, can
you say Slimedog Billionaire?

Your future bestseller,
"Papa" Madoff

February 15, 2009
Reaping the Fruit Planted by Greed

It wasn't surprising that President Barack Obama came to
Florida to push his economic stimulus package, because no
place in the United States has fallen so hard, so fast.

And when the mega-recession finally ends, Florida will
be one of the last places in the country to turn itself around.
That's because other states have actual industry, while our
employment base depends fatally on double-digit population
growth and, to a lesser extent, tourism.

Everything was going gangbusters when a thousand people a day were moving here, but now the stampede is over,
and the jig's up. Without fresh meat for the housing market,
Florida basically hasn't got an economy. Developers have
controlled state and county governments for so long that no
Plan B exists. Lost and clueless, lawmakers desperately hack
away at public budgets while clinging to the hope that boom
times will return.

For good reason, Florida has become the poster child
for America's fiscal disintegration. We stand at the top of the
leaderboard in rising unemployment, foreclosures, and, of
course, mortgage fraud. Where else could a man step out of
prison and straight into a job peddling adjustable-rate home
loans to buyers with virtually no credit?

As has been documented, more than 10,000 convicted felons were welcomed into the mortgage business under the unwatchful eye of the state's Office of Financial Regulation. Believe it or not, many of those felons went on to perpetrate dishonest deeds and victimize gullible citizens.

The banks grabbed their piece of the action, too. Every major institution now standing in line for a taxpayer handout was an eager player in Florida's real-estate frenzy, throwing money at just about anybody who asked for a loan. If you had a pulse and a checking account, you could find a mortgage.

For a while it seemed like everyone caught the fever. Couples who could barely afford one house rushed out and bought two or three more, planning to flip the properties for a quick windfall. Rabid speculation warped the market, and by 2005, the price of most homes bore no credible relation to their true value.

A few experts voiced alarm, but nobody listened. The history of Florida is that of greed run amok, and old habits die hard.

The most recent issue of *The New Yorker* features a scathingly accurate article about Florida called "The Ponzi State." As one investment fund operator explained to journalist George Packer: "The Florida economy has been based on selling Florida. Our growth is all about population growth. When you take that away, what have you got?"

Today there's a new wave of growth in the Sunshine State: Ghost suburbs. They're springing up from one coast to the other—block after block of vacant, foreclosed homes, or houses that were built but never sold.

Obama's visit to Fort Myers was meaningful for many who attended the town rally, but the president didn't address the unique uphill challenges facing Florida's path to recovery. For a state with 18 million residents, there are relatively few large factories or assembly plants and not much high-tech enterprise. Agriculture—the one major sector that's not tied to population growth—has been waning for years, as vast tracts of groves and farm fields have been bought up by developers.

Yet besides orange juice, veggies, and cattle, we don't produce much of anything that the rest of the country wants. The state never made an effort to diversify because it didn't have to. As long as people kept pouring in, nobody worried. For the most part, those who migrated here wound up with jobs that directly or indirectly depended on more people coming.

It was, in fact, a Ponzi scheme of phenomenal proportions.

Now, lacking that daily fix of a thousand new warm bodies, Florida's in deep trouble. This is inevitable when the mechanism of your economy is modeled on that of a cancer cell.

Who knows when, or if, all those ghost suburbs will become neighborhoods again, all those empty condo towers and boarded-up shopping centers will bustle to life. One thing is certain: Government can't make it happen.

The state stands to receive billions in recovery funds from Uncle Sam, some of which might actually trickle down to people who need it. Still, the money will do nothing for the long-range dead-end plight of a place where growth isn't the product of prosperous industry; it *is* the industry.

Nothing about Florida's frantic real-estate boom turned out to be enduring or real, except the suffering of those now losing their homes and their jobs.

They bought in to a dream and wound up in a nightmare.

February 21, 2010
"All the Free Speech Big Money Can Buy"

Despite the public's epidemic disgust with politicians, now would be a splendid time to run for office in this country.

That's because the U.S. Supreme Court has made it infinitely easier for candidates to sell themselves to special interests, who in return will peddle those candidates to voters.

The court's controversial decision allowing unions and corporations to spend as much as they want on political races essentially trashed a century of campaign-finance laws, saying they violated the constitutional right to free speech.

Of course, the five justices who signed the majority ruling have lifetime appointments to the high court and will never have to run for office. That means they won't get to experience the challenge of trying to campaign against an opponent whose media attacks are anonymously funded by the telecommunications industry or the banking lobby or the AFL-CIO.

Here in Florida, where oil companies are pushing hard for offshore drilling, the Supreme Court's decision opens bountiful opportunities to incumbent officeholders and newcomers alike. Although coastal drilling remains an unpopular concept in most beachside communities, any candidate for federal office who supports it could probably count on Exxon-Mobil or Shell to come up with some slick and persuasive commercials, which would be blared over and over and over . . .

The old campaign-finance laws had holes as wide as the Holland Tunnel, but there were limits. Now it's a free-for-all.

Candidates who take a stand in favor of industry regulation are certain to become targets of those industries in election years. More significantly, special interests will be able to pick their own candidates and spend whatever their shareholders can afford.

For instance, now would be a great year to run as a pro–Wall Street candidate. Think about it. The whole nation is fuming about the federal bailouts, and the Obama administration is seeking to reinstate tough regulations on big banks and trading firms. Just last week, a group of senior and well-respected figures from the financial industry told *The New York Times* that strict reforms were necessary to prevent another crippling economic crisis.

Firms like Goldman Sachs, whose executives don't like the idea, are eager to kill it. They have literally a fortune at their disposal during this election cycle, and would surely embrace any candidate who had nice, positive things to say about Wall Street.

A number of Republicans have already spoken out against the proposed banking regulations and are well positioned to receive boundless gobs of campaign money from Goldman and other "toobigtofail" companies. The only possible hurdle is public sentiment.

A new *Washington Post*–ABC News survey reports that a lopsided majority of Americans are seriously ticked off by the Supreme Court's decision on election financing. The opposition cuts almost evenly across party lines. Of those polled, 85 percent of Democrats, 81 percent of independents, and 76 percent of Republicans think it was a bad move to remove campaign spending restrictions for companies and unions.

That's an impressive consensus for a nation that's supposedly divided.

Interestingly, on the issue of election funding, the Republican leadership appears to be orbiting a different planet than its conservative base. Senate Minority Leader Mitch McConnell of Kentucky and other GOP big shots have cheered the

Supreme Court ruling, and they've made it clear that they would try to block any new legislation that would curtail corporate donations to political candidates. The reason is no mystery—the Republicans have traditionally been the party that snuggles up to Big Business, and they stand to gain the most from this opening of the floodgates.

Two Democrats, Sen. Charles Schumer of New York and Rep. Chris Van Hollen of Maryland, are leading an effort to pass a new campaign-finance law in advance of the November elections. They want to make corporations tell shareholders what they're spending on political races, and they also want top executives to appear in campaign ads being funded by their companies.

Knowing who paid for political commercials would definitely make them more informative, but neither the corporations nor their stooge candidates will be eager to advertise the cozy relationship.

Neutralizing the Supreme Court decision is practically impossible without bipartisan cooperation, which no longer exists in Congress. If nothing happens soon, special-interest windfalls will shape the upcoming elections as never before.

If you thought the airwaves were polluted during the 2008 campaign, just wait until the fall. Political ads will be even more deceptive, nasty, insulting, and abundant—all the free speech that big money can buy.

That's dreary news for voters but good news for a certain breed of politician.

September 26, 2010

Someone Give These Guys Memory Pills

The myth of Republican frugality is graphically exemplified by an ornate new state courthouse, about six miles from downtown Tallahassee.

It will soon house the First District Court of Appeal, and it was financed primarily with a $35 million bond issue that was slipped into the 2007–2008 budget at the last minute.

Originally (before a splatter of bad publicity), plans called for the new courthouse to provide each of the 15 appellate judges with their own 60-inch mahogany-trimmed flat-screen televisions. Architectural features included individual bathrooms and kitchens, as well as a fitness room. A grand dome was installed, modeled on a Michigan courthouse that some of the Florida judges had toured, traveling there on a private jet paid for by the builder.

The $48 million judicial palace—now derisively dubbed the "Taj Mahal"—was constructed at $425 per square foot, compared with $250 per square foot for most state buildings.

To make matters worse, the new First DCA courthouse will cost the badly strapped state court system about $1.7 million a year in rent. The old court building was rent-free.

How could this happen?

It started with now–Chief Judge Paul Hawkes, a former GOP House member, and Judge Brad Thomas, who worked for years as a Senate staffer. Both men, who were appointed to the First DCA by then-Governor Jeb Bush, aggressively worked the halls of the Capitol, lobbying former colleagues to build them a swanky new courthouse.

The boondoggle was a Republican operation from start to finish, and election-year amnesia has afflicted almost everyone involved.

Marco Rubio, for example, was the House speaker at the time the courthouse bond issue got tacked on to a 142-page transportation bill. For such a young fellow, Rubio has frequent memory lapses. Just as he supposedly couldn't remember all those personal expenses he put on his GOP American Express card, he now says he can't remember the hefty courthouse appropriation. Rubio insists the project was a state Senate priority and that he had nothing to do with it.

Unfortunately, his version of events is disputed by his old buddy and former House budget chief, Ray Sansom, now awaiting trial for allegedly steering $6 million in public funds to build a jet hangar for a rich crony (another suspect budget item that Rubio cannot recall). Sansom says Rubio personally assured him that the new First DCA courthouse was a top priority, and that Hawkes repeatedly reminded him of Rubio's interest.

Also at odds with Rubio's claim of noninvolvement is an e-mail circulated among the judges on the building committee for the new district courthouse. The e-mail, obtained by Lucy Morgan of *The St. Petersburg Times*, identified the "heroes" in the Legislature who helped secure money for the opulent new structure. Among four who were lauded as "especially helpful" was "House Speaker Marco Rubio."

Now running for the U.S. Senate on a platform of cost-cutting and fiscal responsibility, Rubio doesn't wish to be outed as a helpful "hero" behind Tallahassee's new Taj Mahal. "I never heard of this list," he said.

Numerous fellow Republicans wish they'd never heard of it, either. Sen. Victor Crist of Tampa (no relation to the governor) is named in the e-mail. So is former Senate President Jeff Pruitt. Likewise for Representatives Dean Cannon and Will Weatherford, both future House speakers.

All these guys present themselves as vigilant guardians

against wasteful spending, so it's no surprise that they now claim memory loss about the courthouse splurge. Sen. Crist said he added the amendment to the Senate bill at the request of Pruitt, who of course says he doesn't remember.

Gov. Charlie Crist, then a loyal Republican, signed the legislative package despite a plea from Florida Supreme Court Justice R. Fred Lewis for him to veto the courthouse funding. The governor, now an independent candidate for the Senate, said he can't recall Lewis's concern.

Somebody please feed these stooges some ginkgo.

And God forbid they should actually read an appropriations bill before approving it. Evidently, $35 million is chump change to the GOP lawmakers who controlled (and still control) the flow of public money in Tallahassee.

The I-know-nothing defense presented by Rubio and other party leaders was expanded by Weatherford, the House member from Wesley Chapel, who, despite being named to the courthouse heroes list, now condemns the project as "a monstrosity." Said he: "I doubt that people in the Legislature had any idea what they were doing."

If only that were true.

April 7, 2012
Stimulus Spending for Party Animals

In a new twist on stimulus spending, the government's General Services Administration laid out more than $822,000 for a rocking mega-party at a gambling resort near Las Vegas. It was fabulous for the economy of Nevada; not so good for U.S. taxpayers.

The idiot who came up with this boondoggle still hasn't been publicly identified, but the supposed mission was to reward 300 federal workers with an over-the-top conference in October 2010 at the M Resort and Casino.

Apparently, six advance scouting trips were necessary, costing a mere $130,000. Here are some of the other items paid for by you and me:

* A $31,208 "networking" reception that offered a thousand sushi rolls bought for $7 apiece, and morsels of gourmet cheese for which Uncle Sam paid about $19 per attendee.

* Commemorative coins, delivered in velvet-lined boxes to all participants at a tab of $6,325.

* Breakfast every day at $44 per head.

* "Team-building" conferences that included an inspiring $75,000 presentation on how to screw together a bicycle.

* The professional services of a clown (who probably felt right at home) and a mind reader, whose bold fee of $3,200 suggests that he also performed some hypnotism.

A powerful and far-reaching agency, the GSA is in charge of major government purchases such as office buildings and fleet vehicles. Why not reward its workers for efficiency and frugality by sending them to a Vegas casino at taxpayer expense? Brilliant.

The scandal is the talk of Washington, fueling as it does a widespread national sentiment that government is wasteful, arrogant, and clueless. As the economy claws back from a near-paralyzing recession, it's boggling that anyone in a position of authority could dream up such a junket for federal bureaucrats and that their knuckleheaded bosses would approve.

On the eve of a critical inspector general's report, the White House moved quickly to douse the flames. GSA Administrator Martha Johnson resigned last week, and two of her top people were fired. Four other managers were put on leave.

Congress plans to hold hearings about the Vegas extravaganza, and it would be nice to think that those responsible will be hauled forward to answer the question: "What on earth were you thinking?"

Next question: "Did you at least learn how to build a bicycle?"

We know that one of the high-ranking GSA folks on the trip was Robert A. Peck, head of the agency's Public Buildings Service. He threw a $2,000 bash in his top-floor suite at the M. Peck no longer has a job with GSA, but he'll always have those memories. And if he got his picture taken with a fake Elvis, we probably paid for that, too.

It's easy to flog the Obama administration for lax management, but the truth is that the GSA has been roaring out of control for a long time. Imagine a humongous stoned octopus that has no idea what all its legs are doing.

One embarrassing GSA headline after another plagued the second Bush administration. The agency's chief of staff resigned and was convicted of lying to Congress during the investigation of scumbag lobbyist Jack Abramoff, who later went to prison.

And Bush's choice for GSA administrator, Lurita Doan, departed under pressure after a series of controversies. Among other things, she was accused of trying to steer government contracts to her pals, which she denied, and had sought to slash the budget of investigators looking at gross overspending within the agency.

The most infamous of GSA extravagances surfaced during the Reagan years, when it was revealed that the Pentagon had been paying $535 each for hammers and a bowel-churning $640 for toilet seats. It turned out there was nothing special about those toilet seats, either. They weren't made of titanium or even skid-proof Kevlar, and they served no function other than to prevent the user from falling into the commode.

The tradition of hog-wild excess continues, now with the Las Vegas excursion. As this is being written, reporters are intrepidly searching for the clown and the mind reader who were brought in to entertain the partiers.

It goes without saying that the GSA wasn't smart enough to hire a mime, who might keep his mouth shut, or a psychic, who could have warned of the furor to come.

This time, what happened in Vegas didn't stay in Vegas.

Only our tax money did.

LIBERTY AND JUSTICE FOR ALL

Human Desperation Fuels Greed on the High Seas

The indictment of two alleged alien smugglers gives hope that the U.S. government is serious about cracking down on a dangerous and cold-blooded commerce.

Three children and three adults drowned off Key West on a blustery night in July when a smuggling run turned to disaster. What happened was beyond the realm of nightmares. Roberto Montero-Domínguez and Osvaldo Fernández-Marrero have been charged with conspiracy, attempted smuggling for financial gain, and attempted smuggling resulting in death. If convicted, the Miami-Dade men could be sentenced to die.

Prosecutors are making a big show out of the case because indictments are so rare. Refugees often are reluctant to testify, as are the family members who paid for the illicit passage. This time, though, some of the survivors went before a grand jury. It has been speculated that the government offered not to repatriate them to Cuba in exchange for their testimony.

That would give defense attorneys something to chew on. Still, it's a breakthrough for prosecutors to get willing eyewitnesses in an alien-smuggling case.

The outlaw trade is booming, thanks partly to the dry-foot immigration policy that allows Cuban migrants to remain here if they make it ashore by any means.

That was the prayer of those 26 people who were met on a beach east of Havana and crammed on a 27-foot speedboat that had come from Florida to get them.

The trip back was calamitous. According to authorities, the passengers became frantic as the waves grew to eight feet and the boat began to wallow. At that point, one of the two alleged smugglers pulled a gun and ordered everyone to calm down.

When the migrants rushed to the back of the boat, it pitched bow over stern and sank. The shouts of the survivors were heard by the crew of a passing freighter. As a bleak irony, the wife and two daughters of one of the alleged smugglers were among those who perished.

Both men have pleaded innocent and have yet to present their accounts of the voyage. Don't be surprised if they cast themselves in heroic roles, claiming they didn't do it for money but, rather, to rescue others from communist oppression.

Whatever their story might be, the crossing from Cuba was no casual pleasure cruise. Ask yourself what kind of a captain sets out across rough seas in the dead of night on a grossly overloaded vessel with only two or three life jackets. It's a textbook smuggler scenario. They're paid thousands of dollars per head, so they pack as many bodies on board as possible. Only greed breeds that kind of recklessness.

Ask yourself who would get on such a precariously crowded craft, and the answer is obvious: anyone desperate and determined enough to get to the United States. Sadly, that hunger of the heart is where the profit lies for the alien smuggler. What makes the trade so repugnant is its exploitation of human longing.

Whether a migrant is Cuban or Haitian, he or she usually has relatives waiting in Florida and always the promise of a brighter future. The stronger a person's desire to come here, the more they're willing to pay—and the greater the chance they're willing to take.

Cashing in on the immigrant dream is a scummy tradition as old as the high seas. Twenty years ago, plenty of freelance captains made a killing off the Mariel exodus, gouging big bucks from anxious families trying to get relatives out of Cuba before Castro slammed the door.

Today's profiteers do so with no invitation from Fidel Castro. The trips usually are made at night with fast boats that deliver their human cargo to the Bahamas or, increasingly, to the Keys. Nobody knows how many refugees have died on these crossings or under what dreadful circumstances. There are known instances of panicky smugglers ordering all their passengers into the water, whether the passengers could swim or not.

That was the scene a few years ago when a group of terrified Haitians was forced overboard off a Broward beach. Tragically, several drowned.

More recently, suspicious trauma injuries have been observed on bodies of Cuban refugees that were found floating in the Keys. Who knows what happened.

As long as there's money in it, there'll always be smugglers. However, a successful prosecution of Montero and Fernández would introduce a serious new element of risk for those who traffic in human desperation.

May 5, 2002
One Little Lost Girl, One Bureaucratic Mess

Three feet tall. Forty pounds. No wonder Rilya Wilson got lost. She's way too small for a place as big and crowded as Florida.

There are 16 million people here, mostly grown-ups busy with their own lives and their own grown-up problems. For a little 5-year-old who doesn't say much and who has no mother or father speaking up for her, it's not easy to get noticed.

For 15 months, Florida's child welfare agency failed to notice that Rilya Wilson wasn't where she was supposed to be, at the home of a woman who says she is Rilya's grandmother.

Geralyn Graham said somebody who claimed to be from the state had taken the child away. Graham said she wasn't suspicious because she'd been calling authorities to report that Rilya was having behavioral problems and needed professional help.

As young as she was, Rilya already had led a hard and confusing life. Her mother was a cocaine addict. Her father might or might not be Geralyn Graham's often arrested son. Graham says that Rilya is definitely her granddaughter and that she had planned to adopt her. Not long after the girl was taken away, Graham phoned Rilya's caseworker to ask when Rilya would be returned.

Graham says she was told not to worry, everything would be fine. That was in early 2001.

Last week, out of the blue, somebody else from the Department of Children and Families showed up at Graham's house in Kendall. They asked to visit with Rilya. Geralyn Graham said she was stunned. Those who she thought were treating her granddaughter didn't have her after all.

With well-practiced chagrin, Florida child-care authorities admit that there was an awful lapse in supervision. They don't know where Rilya Wilson is, who has her, or what in the world happened. They don't know if she's healthy or sick. They don't know if she's well fed or hungry. They don't know if she's being loved or ignored or worse. They don't even know if she's dead or alive.

Three feet tall, 40 pounds—and lost by a bureaucracy that remains a teetering monument to the incompetence of grown-ups.

This despite the fact that the state had hastily retooled the laws meant to protect at-risk children from abuse and neglect. It happened after a 6-year-old girl named Kayla McKean was viciously murdered by her own father on the day before Thanksgiving in 1998.

The following year, the Legislature made it a crime for police officers, teachers, and others who work with kids not to report suspected instances of abuse. A special hotline was swamped with phone tips, and the backlog of cases exploded from 4,000 to more than 50,000 in only two years. Meanwhile, more children under state supervision were dying than ever—a total of 60 in 1999 and 2000. The stories are excruciatingly familiar, as are the DCF's dismal apologies.

Despite the tragedies, Florida still spends too little to protect its youngest and most vulnerable citizens. Caseworkers, many of whom are fiercely dedicated, remain underpaid and overloaded. Inevitably, a few are also lazy bunglers.

The caseworker assigned to Rilya Wilson, Deborah Muskelly, quit a few months ago after an audit revealed that she had falsified records and wasn't making the required monthly visits to some of the children assigned to her. Evidently, no one checked on Rilya Wilson for a long time. The best-case scenario is that she was taken from Graham's house by someone who truly cared about her, and that today she is leading a happy, settled life somewhere safe. The worst-case scenario needs no delineation.

So chaotic and haphazard is the child-care infrastructure that it's possible Rilya was picked up by DFC workers and placed in a foster home, and the information simply wasn't put in her file. Whatever really happened, one fact is indisputable: Rilya went missing because the state stopped paying attention.

As of this writing, the child hasn't yet been located. However, she's no longer just another name and number in the data bank. Rilya is newly famous, her photo televised all over the country. Missouri police thought she might be the girl of similar age and size, known only as "Precious Doe," who was found savagely killed near Kansas City. Palm prints thought to be Rilya's didn't match those of the dead child in Missouri, but authorities are seeking a DNA test to make sure.

Meanwhile, Rilya's mother has surfaced in Cleveland, Ohio, where she is tearfully denouncing Florida officials for misplacing the daughter that she herself gave up in favor of dope.

Finally, Rilya Wilson has been noticed, and she didn't have to make a sound.

All she had to do was disappear.

Note: Rilya has never been found, but she is presumed dead. On February 12, 2013, Geralyn Graham was sentenced to 55 years in prison for kidnapping and child abuse in the case. Graham was Rilya's foster parent, not her grandmother, as she first claimed.

February 1, 2004
"Utter Lack of Humanity" Killed Paisley

The prolonged, pain-racked death of young Omar Paisley is like a tale from the old Soviet gulags. That it happened only last year at the Miami-Dade Regional Juvenile Detention Center is an atrocity and a heinous stain on Florida's justice system.

Grand jurors proclaimed themselves "united in our outrage," and last week they indicted two nurses for manslaughter and third-degree murder. Yet the panel's 50-page report, alternately chilling and sickening, goes far beyond the gruesome account of Paisley's final days. It describes a facility in borderline chaos, crippled by an inept bureaucracy and indifferent workers.

"At every turn in our investigation," the grand jury wrote, "we were confronted with incompetence, ambivalence and negligence on the part of the administration and the staff of the M-DRJDC as well as the nurses employed by Miami Children's Hospital [which provided medical staff for the detention center]."

Paisley, 17, had been charged with aggravated battery after a fight. He'd taken a plea agreement and was staying at M-DRJDC until he could move to Bay Point Schools, a live-in program where he would receive counseling.

On the morning of June 7, 2003, Paisley told staff members and other inmates that he felt ill. As required, he filled out a "Youth Request for Sick Call" form. "My stomach hurts really bad," he wrote. "I don't know what to do. I cand [*sic*] sleep."

Paisley didn't know it, but he was dying from a ruptured appendix. He would spend the next and final two days of his life in slow torture—vomiting, soiling himself, and begging for help. The licensed practical nurses who were supposed to treat him were Gaile Loperfido and Dianne Demeritte. The grand jury found their conduct "so outrageous as to rise to the level of criminal negligence," and it indicted them.

The nurses say they're innocent. Grand jurors say they are but two of "numerous individuals" who played roles in Paisley's death.

To appreciate the prevailing culture at M-DRJDC, consider this: Rules forbade workers from calling 911 without the approval of a supervisor. Worse, when grand jurors toured the facility, they found that the phones in the housing modules were programmed to block even detention officers from dialing 911. If somebody had tried to help Paisley, they would have needed to use a cell phone—violating yet another regulation.

The true situation at the Miami-Dade lockup contrasted sharply with that portrayed by Larry Lumpee, the assistant secretary of the Department of Juvenile Justice. He told a legislative hearing that any detention officer can call 911 from any facility, whenever it's necessary. Grand jurors were unimpressed by Lumpee's testimony, which they said "failed to accurately portray the reality" at M-DRJDC.

Either the state was blind to the disarray at the jail or committed to whitewashing the crisis. In any case, the juvenile agency's response to Paisley's needless death has been little more than a shrug.

Last week's grand jury report set forth 20 recommendations for M-DRJDC, many of them based on procedures successfully implemented in Broward.

None of the ideas are radical or frivolous. Among them:

* More staff, better supervision.

* An intercom system so that guards and staff members can communicate instantly in emergencies.

* Direct employee access to 911. (There's a concept!)

* A video surveillance system with cameras and recorders that actually function.

* Twenty-four-hour on-site medical care.

* Rules requiring nurses to see an inmate on the same day that he or she gets sick, to keep complete charts, and to have those records reviewed by an actual physician.

Grand jurors also urged "immediate sanctions" against any jail worker who fails to give CPR or administer emergency first aid. Who would do such a thing, you ask?

Every detention worker in Omar Paisley's unit was trained

in CPR, but not one tried to revive him when he was found without a pulse, collapsed over a chair outside Room 13.

It was the chair to which Paisley had dragged himself to wait for the help that never came. And that's how the kid died, waiting.

Declared the grand jurors: "We were appalled at the utter lack of humanity demonstrated by many of the detention workers charged with the safety and care of our youth." Such a searing censure kindled no obvious shame at the state's Department of Juvenile Justice. Instead came a flat, written response from Secretary William G. Bankhead, displaying his customary reluctance to take action.

Bankhead said that an investigation of "administrative issues" has commenced and that the M-DRJDC workers have been "retrained" in emergency medical protocol. He also said he would enact the grand jury recommendations where "appropriate," coldly implying that some were not.

It was a decidedly indecisive response to a homicidal act of negligence. You've got to wonder if that "utter lack of humanity" lamented by the grand jurors is leaking down from the top of the bureaucracy.

May 30, 2004
New Rules Trap Immigrants with Old Secrets

Sleep soundly, America.

Our government has finally tracked down Fidencio Resendiz and is diligently taking action to boot him back to Mexico.

Not that Resendiz, who came here 20 years ago, was terribly hard to find. He's been living in Homestead, working construction jobs, and raising a family. In fact, he'd be a model candidate for President Bush's recent proposal to grant legal status to thousands of illegal immigrants now employed in the United States—except for one dark secret.

No, Fidencio Resendiz isn't an agent of Al Qaeda. As far as authorities can tell, he's never plotted a single act of terror or advocated overthrowing our government or even littered in a national park.

But 10 years ago, at age 23, he got caught with a single marijuana joint in his pocket. It was the first and last time he was ever arrested. This happened in Missouri, coincidentally, the home state of Attorney General John Ashcroft. Under his vigilant eye, the Bureau of Immigration and Customs Enforcement is avidly deporting noncitizens with criminal convictions, no matter how minor.

Interestingly, Missouri considers Fidencio Resendiz never to have been convicted at all. He pleaded guilty to a misdemeanor possession charge and received a suspended sentence. After a year on probation, his record was expunged by the state. However, by the time Resendiz applied for permanent U.S. residency, Congress had passed tough new immigration rules that made him and thousands of others retroactively eligible for deportation.

It is the same controversial law that ensnared Kari Rein, an Oregon woman whose outlandish case I wrote about in April. A Norwegian citizen, Rein has lived in the United States legally for 15 years. But last December, she was detained and then jailed by immigration agents as she returned home from Europe with her husband and two children.

The reason: A computer check had turned up a 1993 arrest for growing six marijuana plants. She and her husband had pleaded guilty, paid a fine, and served out their probations. The judge in that case had said there was no reason to put Rein in jail because she was a productive member of the community and had no prior arrests.

Eleven law-abiding years later, the Department of Homeland Security decided Rein was a threat and that she should be sent back to Norway. She and her family were stunned. After three weeks, she got out on bail and began a legal battle that seems to have ended with a victory for sanity and common sense.

Last Monday, Oregon Gov. Ted Kulongoski pardoned Rein for the 1993 pot conviction, wiping her record clean. Kulongoski made the decision after meeting with Rein and her family. A spokesperson for the governor told *The Oregonian:* "He was very impressed by her and the fact that she feels absolute remorse for the whole thing. He believes that she's a very good citizen of Oregon." The very next day, U.S. immigration officials said they would "terminate" their efforts to deport Rein to Norway. Because her conviction has been nullified, she's finally free to apply for U.S. citizenship, which she intends to do.

Here in Florida, Fidencio Resendiz is fighting deportation by trying to point out the government's own maddeningly inconsistent policies. In federal court, first offenders found guilty of simple possession of small amounts of marijuana may have their charge dismissed after a year's probation, leaving no record. By law, the case cannot be considered a criminal conviction "for any other purpose"—including deportation proceedings. But, like most first-timers caught with a joint, Resendiz was prosecuted in a state court. At the time, though, U.S. officials didn't typically go after illegal immigrants for small-time dope offenses.

Unfortunately, Resendiz didn't apply for permanent residency until after 1996, when the new immigration rules were enacted. A heavy crackdown began after 9/11, and since then, even first offenders in state drug cases have become targets for deportation.

Resendiz says he deserves the same break offered to first offenders in federal court. Immigration officials say he doesn't qualify because he wasn't prosecuted by the feds. In other words, not everybody in the same fix gets the same second chance. It all depends on your luck. When the ruling comes, it will impact many deportation cases.

If, back in 1994, Resendiz had been busted by a DEA agent instead of a Missouri cop, the immigration service wouldn't be hassling him today. He could've had a clean pass as a federal first offender, and gotten a green card with no problem. His case was argued last week in Miami before a panel of the 11th U.S. Circuit Court of Appeals. When the ruling comes, it will impact many pending deportation cases.

Whether it will stop the bumbling excesses of the so-called war on terror is doubtful.

At a time when we're warned that more Al Qaeda fanatics are loose within our borders and planning another bloodbath, it's idiotic to be spending a single penny of the federal budget—or a single minute of an immigration prosecutor's time—pursuing the harmless likes of Kari Rein or Fidencio Resendiz.

Such cases will seem worse than foolish if the latest Al Qaeda threat proves real. They will seem tragic, for what was wasted.

August 15, 2004
State Fought to Keep Innocent Man in Prison

At 3 A.M. Thursday, Wilton Dedge and his father took a walk. It was warm outside, but the air smelled glorious, and Dedge couldn't stop staring up at the crystal Florida sky. "It was just unreal," he said, "just to go out at night and see the stars."

Dedge hadn't taken a walk with his dad in 22 years. Since May 3, 1982, every night had been spent under a prison roof, locked up for a crime he didn't commit. He went away at 20 and came out as a middle-aged man, robbed of his youth by a colossal injustice.

Last week, the state of Florida admitted what Dedge has been claiming all along: He is completely innocent of the violent rape for which he was convicted.

His story is one of tragically mistaken identity, made worse by cold prosecutorial obstinacy. It's awful enough that he spent more than half his life behind bars for something he didn't do. More outrageous is the fact that prosecutors have known for more than three years of a DNA test pointing to Dedge's innocence. Yet they tenaciously battled to keep that evidence out of court—and to keep Dedge imprisoned.

Dedge wrote to me in June, after I'd done a column about him: "Had you told me 22 years ago that our justice system would do what it has done to me, I would have laughed in your face. . . . But I can no longer do this and it truly saddens and angers me that I can't."

The case was shaky from the start. The 17-year-old victim initially described her attacker as six feet tall, balding, and 200 pounds. Dedge weighed 130 pounds dripping wet, stood five feet six, and had all his hair. Unaccountably, the victim picked him from a photo shown to her by police. Today she is said to be "devastated" to know that she made a mistake.

At the first trial, six of Dedge's coworkers at an auto body shop testified that he was working there at the time the rape occurred. But a technician from the Florida Department of Law Enforcement took the witness stand to say that a pubic hair found in the victim's bed was "microscopically identical" to Dedge's. Brevard prosecutor Robert Wayne Holmes told jurors that the hair "proves that Mr. Dedge was the rapist." A special crime-scene dog was also said to have detected Dedge's scent in the victim's room.

The jury convicted Dedge, though he was later given a new trial after the reputed talents of the crime-sniffing canine were embarrassingly discredited.

At the second trial, prosecutors produced a sleazeball prison informant who claimed that Dedge casually admitted to the rape. In exchange for his testimony, the informant had 120 years lopped off his own sentence. Dedge was convicted again and received 30 years to life. He served his time stoically, though he simmered on the inside.

As DNA testing evolved into an accepted forensic technique, Dedge saw hope for exoneration. In 1996, he asked that his DNA be matched against that of the pubic hair found at the rape scene. Prosecutor Holmes opposed his request and, for eight long years, would not yield.

In the meantime, the case caught the attention of attorney Barry Scheck, a DNA defense specialist and one of the founders of the Innocence Project. He, Nina Morrison, and Miami defense lawyer Milt Hirsch took up Dedge's cause pro bono.

The DNA test was finally done in late 2000. The results were sobering and unequivocal: The hair from the rape victim's bed belonged to someone other than Dedge.

Prosecutor Holmes didn't challenge the findings but, astoundingly, shrugged them off. He insisted that Dedge had committed the crime, even if the telltale hair wasn't his.

The same physical evidence that Holmes once trumpeted as decisive was suddenly of "little significance." Moreover, the state said that Dedge's test should be ignored because it had been conducted a few months before Florida finalized its rules on DNA procedure.

Assistant Attorney General Bonnie Jean Parrish carried that argument to the Fifth District Court of Appeal. The judges seemed incredulous when she said that the issue was not Dedge's guilt or innocence but the premature timing of his DNA test.

The panel bluntly rejected that position, so prosecutors launched a startling new tactic. After years of trying to block Dedge's DNA evidence, they abruptly embraced the science. They asked a judge for a new test—not on the hair but on a semen sample taken from the victim. The sample had degraded during the two decades, but new technical advancements enabled experts to check for a genetic match.

The result was the same as before: The semen, like the pubic hair, belonged to someone other than Wilton Dedge. He could not possibly be the rapist, and prosecutors could no longer duck the truth.

Holmes finally agreed to drop all charges. A judge signed the paper, and at 1 A.M. Thursday Wilton Dedge stepped out of the Brevard County Jail into the summer night and freedom. The first thing he did was hug his mother and father. "I'm just trying to soak it all in right now," he said.

Seminole-Brevard State Attorney Norm Wolfinger called a press conference. "It is truly tragic," he intoned, "to have an innocent person spend time behind bars, not to mention as much time as Wilton Dedge." As for the new DNA test, Wolfinger said, "Frankly, we anticipated different results."

Unbelievable. His office had seen similar exculpatory results three years earlier and wouldn't give Dedge a new day in court. It's worse than disgraceful; it's an abomination.

Dedge is a free man only because he and his lawyers never gave up. Prosecutors did everything in their power to keep him in prison, and he'd be rotting there still if they'd had their way.

Although Dedge is richly entitled to bitterness, there's no trace in his voice. "Right now I'm not even thinking about that. I kind of blocked it out. I'm just enjoying being with my family."

I asked if he always thought that someday he'd be free.

"I believed it," he said, "but I was beginning to have doubts."

Robert Wayne Holmes hasn't apologized to Dedge for taking 22 years of his life, and it wouldn't matter much if he did. The damage is done, the time is lost, and nothing can give it back.

Nothing under the stars.

Note: The Florida Legislature eventually awarded Wilton Dedge a compensation package of $2 million.

March 27, 2005
Easy Prey for Exploiting Politicians

As this is being written, Terri Schiavo is still barely alive and still easy prey for the politicians who have so despicably exploited her tragedy. They will exploit her in death, too. You can bet on it.

Rebuffed again by the courts, Gov. Jeb Bush hit a new personal low last week. He called a press conference to declare that a "renowned neurologist" had raised doubts about whether Schiavo was really in a "persistent vegetative state." The doctor, William Cheshire, turns out to be a conservative evangelical who is renowned mainly to close friends and immediate family.

In addition to working at the Jacksonville branch of the Mayo Clinic, Cheshire is "director of biotech ethics" for an outfit called the Center of Bioethics and Human Dignity. He has expounded against stem-cell research and other issues of interest dear to the Christian right.

Cheshire offered up his wisdom about Schiavo's condition after spending 90 minutes at her bedside and watching tapes provided by her parents, who've opposed removing her feeding tube. He did not perform a medical examination of Schiavo, which makes his report all the more suspect.

Dr. Ronald Cranford is a University of Minnesota neurologist who did examine Terri for the state of Florida. Here's what he told *The New York Times*: "You'll not find any credible neurologist or neurosurgeon to get involved at this point and say she's not vegetative. Her CAT scan shows massive shrinking of the brain. Her EEG is flat-flat. There's no electrical activity coming from her brain."

That's consistently been the medical finding, and one reason the courts have ruled repeatedly in favor of Michael Schiavo's efforts to remove his wife's feeding tube.

Even if Gov. Bush sincerely believes all those judges were wrong, it's reprehensible that he would at the eleventh hour scrounge up a sympathetic physician and try to pass him off as an expert on the vegetative condition. Cheshire hasn't published a single paper on the subject in any known medical journal. Most of his articles focus on headache pain, which was never Terri Schiavo's problem.

But the governor wasn't finished posturing. He said the state Department of Children and Families might physically take custody of Schiavo because of anonymous allegations of abuse in the hospice.

Pinellas Circuit Judge George Greer promptly said he would tolerate no such theatrics. Still, Floridians had to marvel at the absurdity of Jeb seeking DCF "protection" for Schiavo. Under his watch, the agency has been a disaster, marked by contract scandals, ineptitude, and horror stories of children left to die or even disappear while under state supervision.

Given a choice between DCF care and a hospice, take the hospice. At least you won't get misplaced there.

Speaking of lost, that's where some sober-minded Republicans find themselves after this debacle. The party that preaches state's rights and individual freedom has now given us the biggest, most intrusive federal government of all time.

That the Congress basically climbed into Terri Schiavo's private deathbed is not only disgraceful, it's scary. This was a family matter and nobody else's business. Five years ago, in the midst of their guardianship battle with her husband, Schiavo's parents conceded that their daughter was in a persistent vegetative state.

Then they went national, and that's when the circus started—the wailing Bible-thumpers, the goofballs with their homemade crucifixes, the pious anti-abortion lobby and their rabidly misinformed bloggers.

Close behind were politicians on the scent of votes and money. "This is an important moral issue and the pro-life base will be excited that the Senate is debating [it]," said a memo sent last weekend to Senate Republicans, who then passed the bill that recycled the Schiavo case once more through the courts.

Topping the list of shameless exploiters is House Speaker and shakedown king Tom DeLay, who's already touting the Schiavo crusade to raise legal funds in advance of a possible unrelated indictment by Texas prosecutors.

DeLay is highly selective with his compassion. He recently voted to slash Medicaid by $15 billion, which would adversely affect millions of needy patients who, unlike Schiavo, actually have a chance to recover.

Next among the hypocrites is Senate Majority Leader Bill Frist, a doctor who knows better. But he so badly wants to be president that he couldn't pass up a chance to ingratiate himself with evangelical church leaders.

As a lawyer, our own freshman Sen. Mel Martinez also knew the inevitable outcome. Yet he had no qualms about floating false hope for Schiavo's parents in exchange for scoring a few brownie points with the right-to-lifers.

All this was staged with blithe disdain for the judicial process, which isn't surprising. The Bush administration loves to bad-mouth judges. How fitting that some of those who ruled in Michael Schiavo's favor were appointed by the president's own father.

The whole thing was one of the most cynical charades in memory. From the Congress to the White House to the statehouse, they all got their piece of Terri Schiavo.

By the time this column appears, she might be gone, but you can be sure that the politicians and the zealots they're courting will never let this poor woman die.

Even when she's dead.

June 12, 2005
In Gitmo, Diet Rich in Carbs, Lean on Rights

To rebuff accusations that the United States is running a "gulag" at its Guantánamo Bay naval base, the Pentagon last week revealed that it's spending $12.68 per day to feed each of the 520 detainees at the controversial Camp Delta prison.

The Gitmo Diet includes whole-wheat bagels, fresh fruit, baklava, yams, veggie patties, and nearly 10 pounds of halal-certified meat every month for the Muslim inmates. The menu was made public to reassure the Islamic world and concerned Americans that the Guantánamo facility isn't such a bad place, compared to other lockups.

Nutritionally, that certainly seems true. The $12.68 spent on each detainee's daily meals at Camp Delta is about five times what it costs to feed a prisoner in Florida. On the other hand, all prisoners in Florida get a few things that the Guantánamo inmates do not. For starters, they get charged with an actual crime.

Then they get a lawyer.

Then they get a day in court and an opportunity to defend themselves.

In lieu of indictments, the Camp Delta detainees are served bagels and fruit salad. There's reason to believe that many would gladly trade their healthy breakfast for a good old-fashioned American trial.

Most were rounded up during the U.S. military incursion into Afghanistan following the 9/11 attacks. Classified as "enemy combatants," they've been sitting behind razor wire in Cuba for more than three years. Few, if any, have been charged with a crime.

That—not dietary issues—was the main reason that former President Jimmy Carter, Sen. Joseph Biden, and the respected columnist Thomas Friedman all recently urged President Bush to close down Camp Delta. Its existence has become an incendiary propaganda weapon for radical Muslim factions—a symbol for what is seen as American harshness and hypocrisy.

Recent allegations that the Koran was being desecrated by military personnel at the prison ignited deadly riots abroad. Only five incidents of "mishandling" of the holy text by Guantánamo staff were confirmed by the Pentagon, but the report has done little to quell emotions in the Mideast.

The administration reacted sharply when Amnesty International described the Gitmo detention facility as "the gulag of our times." While living conditions are infinitely better than those of the old Soviet labor camps, there's one ugly similarity: the indefinite and distant imprisonment of persons with no legal recourse.

Siberia is a lot closer to Moscow than Cuba is to Kabul. The Guantánamo prison, said Amnesty's Irene Khan, "is a disgrace to American values and international law."

Preposterously, Secretary of Defense Donald Rumsfeld says our justice system—the most advanced in the world—can't handle the sort of cases to be found at Guantánamo and other secret military prisons established since 9/11.

It's all part of the administration's ongoing efforts to white-out parts of the Constitution in the name of fighting terror. Even the U.S. Supreme Court couldn't stomach the Pentagon's position that Camp Delta, being in Cuba, was exempt from judicial review. Last summer the justices ruled that Gitmo inmates can legally challenge their detentions. Since then, more than 550 military tribunals have been held.

Many detainees are denying having terrorist sympathies, and some have complained of abuse by American guards. The Pentagon says that the prisoners, from 40 countries, are mostly Taliban or Al Qaeda supporters. It would be comforting to believe that everyone was a dangerous terrorist whose jailing has made the world safer, but that's not true. Innocent persons have languished at Camp Delta, evidenced by the fact that the United States has started shipping home inmates who it has finally decided didn't belong there. And if those guys didn't hate our guts before we put them in a cell, they probably do now.

The Pentagon's assertion that the detainees are providing valuable intelligence is increasingly shaky. Somebody who's been locked away for three years isn't likely to know Osama bin Laden's cellular number or much else that's currently going on in the Al Qaeda underground. It's ludicrous for the United States to present itself as the model of a free and fair society while maintaining internment camps where foreign prisoners are presumed guilty without trial.

This is an instance where the moral thing to do is also the smart thing, if our goal truly is to lead by example. The bad guys at Camp Delta should be swiftly charged and prosecuted. The others should be freed. Then the prison ought to be shut down, before anything else occurs that will further inspire the fanatic bombers who are picking off our soldiers in Iraq and Afghanistan.

The longer that Camp Delta stays open, the more claims of injustice and wrongful imprisonment will come out of the tribunals. For the United States, there's no upside to that scenario.

Democracies aren't supposed to lock up people for years on a hunch, no matter how well you feed them. The Gitmo Diet is heavy on carbs but lean on basic human rights.

February 5, 2006
Policy Is "White Foot, Black Foot"

When the U.S. Coast Guard recently repatriated a group of Cuban migrants who'd landed at an old bridge in the Keys, lawmakers from South Florida implored the White House to reconsider its bizarre "wet foot, dry foot" policy.

Under current rules, Cubans who make landfall in the United States usually are allowed to stay, while those intercepted before they reach shore are typically sent home. Haitian migrants must have been discouraged by the public outcry that followed the Seven Mile Bridge incident, knowing that a Haitian landing would have drawn no such attention in Washington, D.C.

Like those before it, the Bush administration doesn't care whether the feet of arriving Haitians are wet or dry. They're going back, one way or another.

It's no secret that U.S. immigration policy is a farce—irrational, inconsistent, ineffective, and discriminatory. And no nationality has been more consistently singled out for exclusion than the Haitians. A prime example is the Department of Homeland Security's continuing refusal to grant temporary protected status (TPS) to Haitian migrants awaiting deportation hearings.

The TPS program was designed to provide an interim safe haven for undocumented immigrants who would otherwise be sent home to dangerous conditions caused by armed conflict, natural disasters, or other extraordinary circumstances. Haiti is a textbook case for TPS. Lashed by hurricanes, the desperately impoverished nation is again being ravaged by political violence, daily kidnappings, and marauding street gangs.

The situation is so perilous that U.S. travelers have been warned to stay away. American Embassy workers are forbidden from going out at night, and their children under age 21 are supposed to return to the United States. A bloody snapshot of life in Haiti: Last summer, a U.S.-sponsored soccer match in Port-au-Prince ended with approximately 10 deaths when gang members and riot police attacked the Haitian crowd. Incredibly, Bush officials insist that migrants from Haiti don't need protected status. The place is too deadly for tourists and diplomats—but not for the Haitians we're sending home.

The TPS program was meant to be humanitarian but also

impartial. In the past, undocumented aliens from war-torn Liberia, Sudan, and Somalia have been given temporary protected status. After Hurricane Mitch devastated Central America in 1998, TPS was granted to thousands of undocumented Hondurans and Nicaraguans here. It was offered again to Salvadorans fighting deportation after a series of killer earthquakes racked their homeland in 2001.

TPS isn't an amnesty; it's an 18-month window of safe haven, which is then reviewed periodically. Those immigrants allowed to remain here must register with Homeland Security and pay income taxes during their stay. More than 300,000 Central American TPS designates are still working in the United States and sending money home. Some immigration reformists want the TPS program scuttled or absorbed into guest-worker legislation backed by President Bush.

Whatever form the new rules might take, it's unrealistic to hope that Haitians will be treated as equals with other migrants. The disparity is painfully glaring here in South Florida, where immigration policy plays out as "white foot, black foot." Boatloads of Cuban migrants are joyously welcomed if they reach shore, but Haitians are quietly processed and shipped back.

Officially, the U.S. government has explained the double standard by saying that the Cubans are political refugees while the Haitians are fleeing here purely for economic reasons. The two issues are patently inseparable, so the distinction is a sham. Almost everyone who sneaks into this country is seeking the opportunity to make a decent living. Often that requires escaping from inept, crooked, or oppressive governments. Every year an estimated 700,000 immigrants from all over the world illegally cross the U.S. borders, and few are true political refugees. By far the largest single group is from an ally nation and established democracy—Mexico.

The schizoid actions of our own leaders helped cause the current disaster in Haiti. After a coup, we sent troops to reinstall its first elected president, Jean-Bertrand Aristide; then we sat on our hands while his government unraveled in corruption and rebellion. Much of the violence throttling Haiti is between supporters and enemies of the exiled Aristide and is pegged to the long-delayed elections now set for this Tuesday. More bedlam and bloodshed are certain.

Immigration lawyers around the United States have filed motions to halt all deportation proceedings against Haitians because of chaotic, life-threatening conditions there. It remains to be seen whether any judges will acknowledge the hypocrisy of the present policy.

It makes no sense to offer a haven to Somalians and Sudanese and turn our backs on a human calamity unfolding in our own hemisphere. Tragically, there isn't much common sense or decency to be found in the history of how Haitian boat people have been treated.

It doesn't matter whether they land at a bridge or a beach or the steps of the Statue of Liberty. They still can't get in.

March 5, 2006
Autopsy: At Least Doc Got Gender Right

The good folks of Panama City can rest easy, as long as they don't die. Dr. Charles Siebert has renewed his license to practice medicine.

He's the medical examiner who recently ruled that 14-year-old Martin Lee Anderson expired of "natural causes" after being kneed, choked, and punched by guards at the Bay County Boot Camp.

Previously, Siebert had signed an autopsy report on a woman named Donna Reed in which he described her appendix, gallbladder, ovaries, and uterus—organs that had been surgically removed years earlier, according to her mother. As a bonus, Dr. Siebert also awarded Ms. Reed a prostate gland and two testicles, a mistake he attributed to conducting the autopsy during a storm-related power outage.

Apparently, the lights were working fine when Siebert examined Martin's body.

On the plus side, he correctly identified the gender of the victim. On the negative side, he flubbed the case.

Instead of focusing on the boot-camp beating, Siebert concluded that Martin died of complications from sickle-cell trait, a genetic blood disorder. He later speculated that the condition was exacerbated by strenuous exercise at the camp.

The ruling has baffled sickle-cell experts, not to mention legislators, Martin's family, and millions of TV viewers who've seen the disturbing videotape of the boy being kneed and shoved to the ground by a group of seven to nine guards on January 5. He was rushed to a hospital and died the next day.

Incredibly, seven weeks afterward, Gov. Jeb Bush was saying he still hadn't seen the video. Maybe the VCR at the mansion was on the fritz, or maybe he got swept up watching the Olympic curling competition. Regardless, it's a fairly serious event when a young teen dies under chaotic circumstances in state custody. Bush, a big fan of boot camps, has been slow to criticize anybody.

Of the five such facilities in Florida, Bay County's is one of the worst performing, according to the Department of Juvenile Justice. In four of the years between 1999 and 2004, more than half the camp's graduates were rearrested or convicted of another crime within 12 months of their release.

Martin was sent there after taking his grandmother's car

for a joyride. A spokesman for the boot camp said the guards got physical with the teen because he was being "uncooperative," although there was no indication that he was unruly or violent. The Bay County Boot Camp's manual says that force should be a "last resort," but evidently, the rule was often ignored.

Martin's death was handled suspiciously from day one. His body wasn't autopsied at the hospital in Escambia County where he was pronounced dead. Instead, it was flown back to Panama City and sent to Dr. Siebert. A DJJ official said Siebert told her that shifting the autopsy venue was "highly unusual" and was done at the request of Bay County Sheriff Frank McKeithen. His office runs the boot camp where Martin was roughed up. Later, Siebert denied saying there was anything extraordinary about how the youth's autopsy was assigned.

The outlandish sickle-cell explanation for Martin's death would have been difficult to challenge were it not for the 20-minute videotape of the guards' actions, during which the teen appears limp and unresisting.

And the tape itself wouldn't have been made public if *The Miami Herald* and CNN hadn't sued the Florida Department of Law Enforcement to get it.

We are assured that the agency's reluctance to cough up the video had nothing to do with the fact that FDLE Commissioner Guy Tunnell is the former Bay County sheriff and founder of the boot camp. Several of the guards now under investigation were hired on his watch. Sheriff McKeithen says he's shutting down the facility in May because of the controversy. In the past, other kids have come forward to complain of being choked and struck.

Bush expressed surprise at the camp's closing, but it couldn't come soon enough for Rep. Gus Barreiro, the

Miami Beach Republican who chairs the House criminal-justice appropriations committee.

Unlike the governor, Barreiro demanded a prompt screening of the boot-camp videotape. He was so outraged by what he saw that he wanted all juvenile boot-camp inmates transferred elsewhere until strict use-of-force rules and other safety measures were emplaced.

Another Republican, Rep. J. C. Planas of Miami, has called for the state to close down all juvenile boot-camp facilities.

Bush recently asked sheriffs running the camps to come up with tighter guidelines. Meanwhile, a special prosecutor from Tampa has been appointed to investigate the Martin Lee Anderson case, and a second autopsy will be done by a different medical examiner.

Dr. Siebert's license to practice expired on January 31, though he kept working until he got it renewed in late February.

The doctor has said he didn't see the boot-camp video before finishing Martin's autopsy. After viewing the tape, he now acknowledges the possibility that the clobbering by guards "played a bit of a role" in the teen's death.

Right. In the same small way that John Wilkes Booth contributed to Abe Lincoln's headache.

May 7, 2006
Killing Animals for Profit

If your kids asked to bury a small animal alive, you'd be horrified. You'd tell them that's an awful thing and that they ought to be ashamed. Most children wouldn't dream of doing it, of course, because they know what's wrong and what's right. Unfortunately, they don't make the rules.

Consider Florida's poor, pokey gopher tortoise. Since 1991, the state has allowed grown-ups to bury 74,000 of them because their burrows stood in the path of future subdivisions, highways, golf courses, and supermarkets.

Officials prefer the word "entomb" instead of "bury," but it's the same dirty deed. Even on his most fleet-footed day, the average tortoise cannot outrace earthmoving machinery. Some are able to tunnel to freedom, but most suffocate slowly over a period of weeks.

Gopher tortoises have been around for 60 million years, but the last few decades have been murder. The Florida Fish and Wildlife Conservation Commission classifies these ancient land turtles as a "species of special concern," though obviously not special enough to be left in peace. A child can't legally keep one as a pet, yet a big company or even a school district can obtain permits to snuff them by the hundreds.

Dwindling in numbers, the animals live in dry hammocks, coastal dunes, and pine scrub. There they dig elaborate dens that provide shelter to more than 300 other species, including rabbits, burrowing owls, and the endangered indigo snake.

As luck would have it, prime tortoise habitat is often prime real estate, which means the tortoises get the boot or, more typically, the bulldozer. The state calls this "incidental taking," which is a bureaucratically sanitized way of saying "smothering to death."

The permit process is straightforward. Developers seeking to build on land colonized by tortoises typically agree to contribute to a habitat fund or set aside a relatively small parcel. It's called mitigation, a lame charade intended to make the state appear vigilant and to make developers appear caring. In the past 10 months, Florida has granted 345 permits to bury tortoises. The *Sun-Sentinel* recently published a sampling:

The Tuscano golf course development near Sarasota got permission to kill 260 of the reptiles in exchange for preserving 138 acres.

In Duval County, the Young Land Group was told it could destroy 190 tortoises if it paid $169,442 for 29 acres of habitat.

The Orange County Public Schools received permission to kill 110 tortoises on the future site of a high school in exchange for preserving 12 acres at a cost of $92,037.

Vikings LLC in Marion County was approved to wipe out 470 tortoises for a 542-home golf-course development, in exchange for preserving 136 acres.

In Palm Beach County, Walmart got permission to bury five tortoises in exchange for a whopping 1.49 acres of habitat.

Mitigation is always meager. A pending project in the Tampa Bay area would obliterate 2,573 acres of tortoise habitat, yet under current rules, the developer is required to set aside only 168 acres. That's a net loss to the tortoises of 93 percent of their home territory.

News accounts about the tortoise-burying permits have angered many Floridians and discomfited wildlife officials, who admit that not enough is being done to save the reptiles. The state now wants to expand tortoise preserves in the Panhandle, which sounds like a plan except that moving the critters hasn't worked. Studies have shown that most of the relocated newcomers have died from respiratory disease or other ailments.

Four years ago, the FWCC staff proposed elevating the status of the gopher tortoise to a "threatened species," which theoretically would offer more protection from habitat loss. No action was taken, and the sanctioned killings continued. Several local governments decided there was no time to lose.

Lee, Collier, Martin, and Hillsborough counties adopted ordinances that made it more difficult to destroy the species, even with a permit.

On June 7, the state wildlife commission convenes in West Palm Beach, a public meeting at which the plight of the gopher tortoise finally will be addressed. A key factor will be the "risk of extinction," which grows worse with every mass burial.

If commissioners agree that the species should be reclassified as threatened, biologists and administrators will begin drafting a management plan. It's a process as slow and lumbering as the tortoise itself.

In the meantime, officials say they're working with developers and landowners to deal with the "entombment issue," which has turned into a serious public relations headache.

There's nothing "incidental" about burying an animal alive. Just ask your kids. They'll know better.

April 8, 2007
Haiti Migrants: If Only They Had a Golden Arm

U.S. immigration policy is a sporting proposition.

Some boat people get locked up. Some boat people get to play ball.

Jean-Ferdinand Monestime, who landed on Hallandale Beach on March 28, is in government custody, awaiting an asylum hearing that will likely result in his deportation.

Francisely Bueno, who landed on Big Pine Key in August 2004, is pitching for the Atlanta Braves' AA farm team in Pearl, Mississippi. The lefty is here to stay.

Monestime arrived on a dilapidated sailboat after weeks at sea with 100 other weary and hungry Haitians, including 13 children and teenagers. Bueno arrived from Cuba on a speedboat with four other ballplayers, 13 other migrants, and a smuggler at the helm.

Monestime and Bueno came to America for the same reason: to find a good job.

In order to stay, Monestime must prove to a judge that he faces political persecution if he returns to Haiti. Bueno didn't spend a day behind bars, and he didn't have to prove anything. That's because the United States awards political asylum to almost all Cubans who reach the shores of Florida. Those who are intercepted at sea are usually returned to the island.

Bueno and his friends didn't reach the Keys the first time they tried. The speedboat was stopped by the Coast Guard, the athletes shipped home. A month later, they launched again and made it.

No other boat people are permitted to stay here simply because they reach dry land. Cubans are treated differently because politicians of both parties covet the exile vote in South Florida.

There are many other dictators in the world besides Fidel Castro, yet our government doesn't open its arms to all who have fled those countries in search of freedom. The "wet foot, dry foot" rule is a farce. Illogical, unfair, and racist in practice, it's also been a boon to people-smugglers with fast boats, and to other profiteers.

Last week, in a Key West courtroom, sports agent Gustavo Dominguez was on trial for allegedly masterminding the smuggling voyage that brought Bueno and the other ballplayers to Florida. Prosecutors said Dominguez hired a convicted drug trafficker to help him plan and execute the trip. Once the players landed safely in the Keys, they were driven to California. There, according to the government, Dominguez got apartments for the men and began lining up professional baseball contracts. Defense attorneys for the sports agent said he's innocent. They said he was acting out of compassion, not greed.

Unfortunately for Jean-Ferdinand Monestime, he can't throw a 95 mph fastball or hit a slider out of the park. No American rich guys sent a go-fast to whisk him to Florida in the dark of night. Monestime paid for his own passage, boarded the overcrowded sailboat, and endured a rough, treacherous crossing that has claimed hundreds—probably thousands—of Haitian lives during the past three decades. Those who've made it to U.S. shores have mixed luck, depending on the judge reviewing their case. Some have been allowed to stay in the United States, but many, many more have been deported.

Haiti isn't ruled by a dictatorship; it has a shaky government crippled by poverty, corruption, and chaos. Despite the presence of UN troops, roving armed gangs terrorize the cities; in the countryside, the deadly threats are disease and hunger. There is no place in the hemisphere more wretched or dangerous, and it's perfectly understandable why so many Haitians set out for Florida. They are not alone in this dream.

The U.S. Census Bureau says that 409,426 immigrants settled in Miami-Dade, Broward, and Palm Beach counties between April 2000 and July 2006. That means that nine out of every 10 newcomers were from other countries, an astonishing statistic.

South Florida needs more people like the Sahara needs more sand, but our economy obviously has become reliant on foreign-born labor. No less plain is the fact that many builders, farmers, and company owners will never turn down an immigrant work force. Consequently, the government has no hope whatsoever of controlling the borders. The least we should demand, though, is an immigration policy that's humane, fair, and free of favoritism.

Unaccountably, the Department of Homeland Security won't give temporary protected status to Haitians awaiting deportation hearings. The TPS program was created specifically to provide haven for undocumented migrants who would face perilous conditions if sent home. Haiti is such a violent place that the State Department advises Americans not to travel there, yet somehow it's all right to send Haitians back into the bloody chaos.

Church leaders and Cuban-American organizations have called on the government to grant temporary status to Jean-Ferdinand Monestime and the 100 others who scrambled ashore last month in Hallandale Beach, but all the migrants remain in detention.

Meanwhile, it's springtime, and in America that means baseball. Francisely Bueno will be taking the mound for the Mississippi Braves as a free man, hoping for a shot at the big leagues.

He's a very lucky young fellow.

Lucky to have a golden arm.

Luckier still not to have been born in Haiti.

April 11, 2010
Criminals or "Confused Souls"?

On Easter Sunday, Pope Benedict XVI stood before a sea of Catholic worshippers in St. Peter's Square and—in grand papal tradition—said nothing about the latest sex-abuse scandal that is shaking the church. Instead, the pontiff jabbed at his critics, asserting that faith in God can lead one "towards the courage of not allowing oneself to be intimidated by the petty gossip of dominant opinion."

The "petty gossip" to which Pope Benedict obviously referred is the uproar over new revelations of serial molestation of children by Catholic priests and the ignoring of those terrible crimes by church officials.

If the pope seems defensive, there's a reason. From 1981 to 2005, it was he—then known as Cardinal Joseph Ratzinger—who headed the Congregation for the Doctrine of Faith, the Vatican office to which complaints of unpriestly behavior are routed.

One among thousands was the nauseating case of Father Lawrence Murphy, who molested as many as 200 boys at a Wisconsin school for deaf children between 1950 and 1974. According to documents obtained through lawsuits, three consecutive archbishops in Wisconsin were informed that Father Murphy was abusing children, and yet they never told authorities. When victims complained directly to police, nothing happened. Eventually, the priest was moved to another diocese, though he spent the final 24 years of his life working with kids in other schools and parishes.

As usual, the church chose to treat Father Murphy as a confused soul and not a dangerous criminal, which he was. In a 1993 session with a social worker, he admitted to frequently victimizing the deaf youngsters. Three years later, an archbishop in charge of the diocese wrote twice to Cardinal Ratzinger, the future pope, seeking to have Father Murphy defrocked. He got no reply.

So in 1997 the archbishop reached out to another church official in Rome, warning that grown victims were getting ready to file lawsuits that could lead to a "true scandal."

Hoping to avoid a canonical trial, Father Murphy, who was in fading health, appealed directly to Cardinal Ratzinger: "I simply want to live out the time I have left in the dignity of priesthood."

While the file contained no response from the future pope, efforts to defrock Father Murphy were soon dropped. He was buried in church vestments with his dignity intact, having robbed the same from scores of innocent children.

He should have died in prison—and he might have, if he hadn't been a priest.

A church spokesman told *The New York Times* that the Vatican didn't learn of Father Murphy's crimes until 1996, even though victims had been complaining since the 1950s.

The spokesman said he hadn't discussed the Wisconsin abuse case, or any other, with Pope Benedict. He surmised that Father Murphy's illness, and the absence of more recent accusations, were factors in the decision to not remove him from the priesthood.

Meanwhile, the pope himself isn't saying what he knew about the Murphy case or if he personally halted the canonical trial. He is likewise mum about an incident that occurred while he was an archbishop in Munich, where a pedophile priest was allowed to resume interacting with young parishioners. The Vatican says that a subordinate made the decision and that the future pope had complete "nonresponsibility" in the matter. Still, it would be useful to know his reaction to a memo he received at the time about the predatory priest, who later went on to assault other kids.

In Ireland, disclosures of a long, widespread cover-up of sex-abuse cases have prompted the resignation of two bishops and a rare reaction from Benedict. In a letter to the country's Roman Catholics, he admitted that "grave errors of judgment were made and failures of leadership occurred."

No kidding. In this country, it's called obstruction of justice, and rosary beads won't get you off the hook. To cover up is the first bureaucratic impulse in a covert culture as smothering as the Vatican's. Benedict flourished in that culture and rose to power in its shadows. "A plague" is what the church now calls pedophilia by its priests, but for decades it was just a dirty secret to be guarded at all costs. Bad priests were shuffled from place to place until they finally were exposed. Lawsuits were filed, settlement checks were written, and every so often, one of these monsters actually got locked up.

If they hadn't been wearing priests' collars, none would have gotten away with what they did for as long as they did.

For nearly 25 years, the man now called pope sat in the Vatican office where these sordid cases piled up. That is a fact, not "petty gossip."

What did he know? What did he do about it?

The answers won't be offered in St. Peter's Square.

April 22, 2012
Zimmerman Charge Will Be Hard to Prove

It will be astonishing if George Zimmerman is convicted of second-degree murder for shooting 17-year-old Trayvon Martin.

Not that Zimmerman was right to pull the trigger, but that particular charge will be extremely difficult to prove. Why Special Prosecutor Angela Corey didn't file for manslaughter instead has lots of smart lawyers scratching their heads.

Perhaps it's a strategic move aimed at nudging Zimmerman toward a plea bargain, but in the meantime, her decision only serves to raise expectations among the many—outraged and grieving—who'd been calling for Zimmerman's arrest.

True, the lethal confrontation between the neighborhood

crime-watch patroller and the Miami Gardens teen would never have occurred if Zimmerman hadn't been tailing Martin through that gated townhouse community in Sanford. There's no law against walking at night while black or running at night while black. Or wearing a hoodie at night while black.

But Zimmerman was sure the kid was up to "no good," and he made a 911 call that stands as a tragic foreshadowing of what was to come. "These a——— always get away," he said at one point, an edge of exasperation in his tone.

He ignored the police operator's advice to stop following Martin, and on the tape, he can clearly be heard hastening his pursuit. It turned out that the teen was merely returning to the home of his father's girlfriend after a trip to a nearby store.

To win a conviction for second-degree murder, however, prosecutors must convince a six-member jury that Zimmerman acted in a manner that was "evincing a depraved mind." Suspicion, unfounded or not, isn't inherently malicious. Nor is reckless judgment a sure sign of mental depravity.

A judge has sealed the file on this case, over the protests of this newspaper and other media outlets, so it's possible that Corey has evidence about Zimmerman's state of mind that we don't know about. So far, the 911 tape of his phone call offers the best glimpse of what was going through his head. When you listen to the whole thing, there's no hint of violent intent, no overt racial slurs. What you hear is a guy playing the role of cop without a badge, a guy who perceives himself as a protector of his home territory. He wants the police to come investigate a black kid in a hoodie.

Would Zimmerman have chased a white kid in a hoodie? There's no way to know.

Would a white kid have approached Zimmerman, as

Martin apparently did, to demand to know why he was being followed? It's very possible. Would the exchange have ended in a homicide? Again, there's no way to know.

Two things are certain: If Trayvon Martin had shot an unarmed George Zimmerman and claimed a "stand your ground" defense, Martin would have been put in jail that night. A black man shooting a white or a Hispanic man seldom gets the benefit of the doubt. And if both Zimmerman and Martin were black, the country wouldn't know a thing about this case. Probably nobody outside Sanford would. One black man killing another rarely makes the headlines.

Long before the trial begins, the media fibrillation is under way, with no shortage of gasbags on both sides. Predictably, some gun nuts and racist droolers are trying to make a hero of Zimmerman and a street thug of Martin (who had no criminal record). From extreme factions in the other camp, you may hear Zimmerman portrayed as a trigger-happy stalker of black youths, a view disputed by one of his African-American friends.

We'll probably never know what really happened when Martin and Zimmerman spoke face-to-face, since one is dead and the other is trying to avoid prison. The few witnesses will probably give conflicting accounts of what they saw and heard.

Still, a trial is vital because Martin's death was so wrong and so avoidable, and it took place purely because Zimmerman foolishly propelled events in that direction. It's a classic case for manslaughter, not second-degree murder.

Jurors will be able to vote for that lesser charge of manslaughter, which might be why prosecutors overreached. A compromise manslaughter verdict is bound to stir less public reaction than an acquittal or a murder conviction. Zimmerman's attorney will try to bypass a jury through asking the judge for a dismissal, based on Florida's brilliant "stand your ground" law—now a favored legal defense for gang members and dope dealers who plug each other on the streets.

Given the national spotlight on the Martin shooting, it seems unlikely that Zimmerman will be able to dodge a trial. Trayvon isn't around to tell his side of the story or to hear his killer's, but his family deserves a day in court.

Because in the end, a young man carrying a bag of Skittles and a can of iced tea lay dead in the grass, a young man who was being followed by a stranger and didn't know why.

Note: George Zimmerman was acquitted by a Sanford jury in July 2013.

May 5, 2012
A Violent Homicide Isn't Hazing

Eleven of the 13 people who allegedly participated in killing Florida A&M drum major Robert Champion have been charged with "a hazing resulting in death," a low-grade felony. The two others are accused of misdemeanors.

You can't blame Champion's family for being disappointed and a bit confused.

Champion was singled out for an attack, then beaten until he died. That it occurred during a hazing doesn't mean it should be handled differently from any other violent homicide, yet it *is* being handled differently. Way differently.

Not one of the 13 suspects was booked for murder or even plain old manslaughter, a second-degree felony that can bring up to 15 years in prison. By contrast, causing a death by hazing is only a third-degree felony for which the maximum term is six years.

In other words, a gang-style lethal assault in Florida is more leniently appraised when it's a moronic college ritual gone awry. Six years behind bars isn't light time, but it's much better than the high end of a manslaughter conviction.

What do you think would have happened if Champion had been killed by a mob of strangers in a barroom or on a street corner? For starters, authorities wouldn't have taken more than five months to make an arrest, especially if they had the names of everyone involved. You can also be sure that the defendants in such a case wouldn't be charged with "hazing"—they'd be facing much heavier felonies.

Here's how Champion died. The 26-year-old man was made to walk down the aisle of a chartered bus that was parked outside an Orlando hotel, while fellow band members (and possibly others) repeatedly kicked and punched him. Evidently, this is what passed for dear tradition within the famed A&M Marching 100, now in disciplinary limbo.

Eventually, Champion collapsed. Later somebody dialed 911: "One of our drum majors is on the bus, and he's not breathing. . . . He's in my hands, ma'am. He's cold."

If Champion was cold to the touch, it was likely he'd been down for a while.

Dying among his own bandmates after a football-game performance.

In December, less than a month after the incident, the Orange-Osceola Medical Examiner's Office ruled Champion's death was a homicide, the autopsy showing "extensive contusions of his chest, arms, shoulder and back with extensive hemorrhage."

Although coroners found no bone fractures or damage to Champion's internal organs, there was "significant rapid blood loss" from the injuries he'd received. The cause of death was reported as "hemorrhagic shock due to soft tissue hemorrhage, incurred by blunt force trauma sustained during a hazing incident."

So it was manifest from the beginning that Champion hadn't fallen down the steps of the bus 20 or 30 times. He'd been battered—and not by teenagers gone wild. Most of the suspects are men in their 20s.

The state of Florida didn't need a special anti-hazing law in order to prosecute. Long-standing criminal statutes specifically address assaults that end in death. Nowhere in this country is it legal for 13 persons—or six, or two, or one—to strike another person if he or she isn't a threat. Theoretically, it shouldn't matter to prosecutors whether the assailants are wearing band uniforms, fraternity jerseys, or the do-rag of a street gang. Orange-Osceola State Attorney Lawson Lamar said the Champion case is complicated, and investigators didn't find sufficient evidence for a murder charge.

Then how about manslaughter, at least?

Said Lamar: "We do not have a blow or a shot or a knife thrust that killed Mr. Champion. It is an aggregation of things. . . ."

In fact, Champion suffered repeated blows. Identifying which of the band members delivered the most—or the most damaging—won't be easy. It seldom is when multiple participants are involved. But Lamar said the killing fits Florida's statute against hazing, a widely banned practice that he described as "bullying with a tradition—a tradition that we cannot bear in America."

It would be nice to think that the publicity about the attack on Champion will deter future hazing in high schools, colleges, and the military. So far, the prospects aren't so good. Two months after the FAMU killing, two male students seeking to join the Kappa Alpha Psi fraternity at Youngstown State University in Ohio were "initiated" by being beaten with fists, a paddle, and a wire laundry hanger. The abuse continued over a period of 12 days, after which one of the victims required a ventilator to breathe. Nine men, only one a current YSU student, were indicted.

Here's the difference: The Ohio defendants aren't being charged with hazing but, rather, with felony assault.

A grown-up charge for a grown-up crime, as it should be.

And they'd be facing far worse if one of their victims had died, the way Robert Champion did.

READY, AIM, FIRE

December 9, 2001
Gun Lobby's Interests Before Public Safety

This is some wacky war on terrorism.

Incredibly, the U.S. Justice Department has forbidden the FBI from checking its own records to see whether any of the 1,200 persons detained since September 11 had bought guns.

The information is sitting in computer files, and FBI agents are eager to examine them. But Attorney General John Ashcroft, a hard-line critic of firearms laws and background checks, opposes using gun-purchase records to investigate potential terrorists in the United States.

He's the same guy who advocated detaining hundreds of foreign nationals without criminal charges; the same guy who pushed for peremptory authority to wiretap individuals without court approval; the same guy who, after the slaughter of September 11, solemnly vowed that the government would do everything in its power to protect Americans from future attacks.

Everything, apparently, except offend the National Rifle Association.

In a move that has exasperated FBI officials and angered law-enforcement organizations, the Justice Department has decided that federal gun records cannot be used to investigate individuals, even in terrorism cases. "Absurd and unconscionable" was the reaction of Larry Todd, a California police chief who serves on the firearms committee of the International Association of the Chiefs of Police. The group has formally objected to Ashcroft's closing the files to investigators.

Currently, firearms dealers fax applications from prospective buyers to the FBI or state police agencies. Computers search to find out whether the applicant is a convicted felon or fits into another category of persons prohibited to buy guns. Those include illegal immigrants and foreigners who have been in the United States less than 90 days. The FBI says that many detainees fall into those two groups.

In past criminal probes, the agency has used its gun-purchase data to determine whether someone was mistakenly allowed to buy a weapon when he or she should have been denied permission. Five days after the terrorist attacks on New York and Washington, D.C., the Bureau of Alcohol, Tobacco, and Firearms sent the names of 186 detainees to the FBI. Two of them, it turned out, had received approval to buy guns. The very next day, however, the FBI was informed that reviews of gun records no longer would be allowed. The Justice Department said that the policy reversal was based on a narrow new interpretation of the law.

FBI officials believed the law gave clear authority and immediately asked to have the ban reconsidered. They failed.

According to *The New York Times*, the Justice Department's trigger man was Assistant Attorney General Viet Dinh, a political appointee and a pal of Ashcroft. Dinh's ruling was a masterpiece of hypocrisy. He stated that the background checks being sought by terrorism investigators would violate the privacy rights of foreigners, including those being detained.

In other words, we'll lock you up with no trial, interrogate you with no lawyer present, secretly wiretap your friends and relatives—but heaven forbid we invade your privacy by checking to see whether you've bought any guns during your stay in the United States.

That stupefying contradiction is merely Ashcroft playing politics. As a senator, he staunchly fronted for the gun lobby, which reciprocated generously. According to the Violence

Policy Center, National Rifle Association sources contributed nearly $340,000 to his last campaign.

Among Ashcroft's favorite targets was the Brady Law, which gave authorities the power to screen firearms buyers for past crimes. The legislation was welcomed by police and has blocked thousands of felons from purchasing handguns and other deadly weapons.

Ashcroft remains unpersuaded. Now the country's top cop, he's seizing the opportunity to impose his pro-NRA agenda on the Justice Department. His timing couldn't be worse. These days, the sight of a box cutter makes people jumpy. Extending gun-toting rights to visiting foreigners isn't likely to be a popular idea.

Notwithstanding Ashcroft's sudden concern for their privacy, the detainees remain central to the September 11 investigation. If some turn out to have Al Qaeda connections, it would be helpful to know whether they've been building an arsenal while they're here.

The attorney general might say it's being nosy to check, but most Americans will think it's crazy not to.

November 23, 2003
Legislators' Attempt to Block Police from Ownership Records Absurd

If you're a prosecutor or a police officer in Florida, here are some names to remember:

Juan-Carlos Planas of Westchester; Carl Domino of Jupiter; Ken Sorensen of Key Largo; Mark Mahon, John Quinones, and Mike Davis of Jacksonville; Curtis Richardson and Lorraine Ausley of Tallahassee; Don Davis of Naples; Dennis Ross of Lakeland; Jeffrey Kottkamp of Cape Coral; Kevin Ambler of Lutz; and Gaton Catens of Miami.

These are not friends of law enforcement.

These are state legislators who are trying to make it as difficult as possible to trace the ownership of guns found at crime scenes. Every pistol-packing felon in Florida should write these knuckleheads a thank-you note.

Last week, the House Judiciary Committee—on which the above-named politicians serve—okayed a bill that would ban police from maintaining computerized lists of gun sales and owners for more than 30 days. If passed by the Legislature next spring, the law will strip authorities of an important crime-solving tool for no other reason but politics.

Currently, Florida police keep databases of firearm-sales records from pawnshops and some gun dealers. When one turns up at a crime scene or in a suspect's possession, its origin can be traced by typing the serial number into a computer.

The paranoid droolers at the National Rifle Association have long opposed police efforts to computerize gun records, saying it's an iron-fisted step toward totalitarianism. According to the NRA's propaganda, which reads like the *National Lampoon*, the same government that can't locate thousands of visa violators (including terrorists) is somehow capable of tracking down and confiscating every lawfully owned firearm in America.

To peddle this loony Orwellian fantasy, NRA lobbyists in Florida dredged up a couple of goobers named Dennis Baxley and Lindsay Harrington, Republican legislators from Ocala and Punta Gorda, respectively. Baxley and Harrington "cosponsored" the anti-cop bill that went to the House panel. As originally penned by the NRA, the legislation invoked the names of Adolf Hitler and Fidel Castro as examples of despots who espoused gun controls.

Get a load of Baxley: "We're at a point in our history

where the government is trying to slowly take away our rights, piece by piece, and I'm trying to stop that. By accumulating all this [gun] data, it could fall into the wrong hands. And that could be a treacherous thing."

Don't bother to ask him in what way a sales receipt for a .38 Special might be put to nefarious use and into whose evil hands it might fall. And don't ask if he can name a single instance when it's happened, because he can't. Not even Marion Hammer, the NRA's hatchet woman in Tallahassee, provided lawmakers with one example of a law-abiding citizen being "harassed" or "abused" because of computerized sales data. Police, however, can tell lots of stories about crimes being solved because they were able to swiftly track the ownership of a weapon. One recent example: Pawnshop sales records helped detectives connect a Miami Beach man accused of shooting three of his neighbors with the gun used in the attack.

The notion that firearms buyers have a constitutional right to anonymity is a fiction promoted by the NRA, and one consistently not embraced by the courts. The government already keeps track of the land we own, the people we marry, the children we have, and the money we make. Most reasonable citizens don't have a problem providing their names when pawning or purchasing a handgun. But the NRA fuels its recruiting with rabid fear, not facts, and there's no shortage of hayseed politicians who are eager to take its money and go rant for the cause.

It's impossible to overstate the brainless lunacy of the proposed law, which would penalize police departments up to $5 million for keeping computerized gun lists.

Yet, at the same time, law-enforcement agencies would be allowed to obtain the very same firearm-sales and ownership information—but only on paper. What is now a 30-second piece of keyboard detective work would become an all-day chore, requiring manual reviews of thousands of records.

Obviously, the intent of the law is to discourage gun tracking by police, especially in busy, understaffed departments. The result will be more unsolved crimes, less evidence upon which to prosecute violent criminals, and more acquittals in court.

And Republicans claim to be the law-and-order party?

Every armed robber, carjacker, and gangbanger in Florida will sleep easier, if Rep. Baxley and the others get their way.

May 8, 2005
With New Law, Shooters May Beat the Rap

If you're a defense attorney in Florida, you've got to be excited by the new Protection of Persons and Property bill passed by the Legislature and signed by Gov. Jeb Bush.

This is the bogus "stand your ground" law that allows people to start shooting wherever they happen to be, whenever they happen to feel threatened. The measure was written by the National Rifle Association, but the National Association of Criminal Defense Lawyers couldn't have done a slicker job.

Starting October 1, any person who is confronted has no "duty to retreat" and "has the right to stand his or her ground and meet force with force, including deadly force if he or she reasonably believes it is necessary to do so to prevent death or great bodily harm. . . ."

Every gangbanger in the state should write a thank-you note to the NRA. For years, street thugs have tried without much luck to use self-defense as an excuse for their bloody shoot-outs—and now it's right there in the statute books: If you get fired at, dawg, you can fire back.

Better yet, the law is so purposefully slack that if you even imagine you're going to be fired at, you can pull out your legally purchased AK-47 and open up. Your attorney will say you had a "reasonable belief" that you were in danger, and it's hard to dispute. Being a gangster is a full-time dangerous gig.

Thanks to the nitwits in Tallahassee, the courts could be seeing a lot more cases in which self-defense is creatively invoked. "You don't even have to be that creative," quips Richard Sharpstein, a top Miami trial lawyer. He predicts "an enormous swell" in assault and homicide cases in which the main defense is self-defense.

Except for generating more political contributions from the NRA, passing the law was utterly pointless. Floridians have never been too shy about shooting each other. The motivation is more often an insult than a threat.

We've got one of the worst murder rates in the country, and the vast majority of those killings are committed by family members or acquaintances of the victims. In the relatively few cases where citizens have killed a menacing criminal, the justice system has been solid in its support. The head of the state prosecutors' association said that he knows of no instance when a law-abiding person has been hauled to court for using deadly force to protect himself or his family—at home or elsewhere. Even the main sponsor of the new law, Rep. Dennis Baxley of Ocala, couldn't cite a single case of a lawful firearm owner being locked up for shooting someone in self-defense. But Florida lawmakers seldom let the facts deter them from sucking up to rich special-interest lobbies such as the NRA.

By broadly expanding the so-called castle doctrine to public places—whether it's the Publix, Dolphins stadium, or the neighborhood pub—the Legislature has opened what Sharpstein calls a "Pandora's box of excuses and justifications" for violent assault.

Deterrent? Yeah, right.

Long ago I interviewed a member of the infamous Outlaws motorcycle gang who was doing a prison stretch for fatally stabbing a man during a bar fight. Naturally, the Outlaw said he'd acted in self-defense, an argument that didn't fly in court. "Today he probably wouldn't even be charged," says Fred Haddad, a prominent Broward defense attorney involved in the case.

Like Sharpstein, Haddad thinks the Legislature has made it easier to try the "self-defense" defense. "Where it's really going to help is the cases of those who act first" and claim they feared for their safety, he says.

In the absence of any demonstrable need for broadening the self-defense provisions, Rep. Baxley and others were left to argue that it would be a powerful deterrent to criminals, who would henceforth be reluctant to accost potentially armed citizens in public places.

Oh, sure. The death penalty doesn't deter these creeps. Mandatory hard time for using a gun doesn't discourage them. They aren't overly worried about the cops. But the remote possibility of being winged by a little old lady on her way to the ATM—that's supposed to scare a hard-core badass into giving up his predatory ways and going straight.

Only in the inverted universe of Tallahassee would such laughable nonsense carry the day.

Implicitly encouraging armed citizens to "stand their ground" when they could get away doesn't make the streets safer. It invites tragedy for the crime victims as well as bystanders. The bad guys surely aren't scared. Ironically, more of them could be out on the streets because of the new law, which will make it easier for shooters to beat the rap in court.

It was self-defense, Your Honor.

Honest.

April 22, 2007
Focus on the Victims, Not Their Disturbed Killer

Somewhere in the bowels of hell, Seung-Hui Cho must be smiling. He's getting what he wanted: global infamy.

Now everybody with a TV set knows his name and his face. That sick little ditty bag that he sent to NBC did the trick.

Look at me, world! I'm the Virginia Tech killer!

In the news business, it's unusual to receive a publicity packet from a dead person, much less a dead mass murderer. To help craft his legacy, Cho put together an ambitious multimedia presentation: photos, videos, and writings compiled in the six days before he murdered 32 students and faculty members and then shot himself.

NBC quickly turned over the material to investigators, but not before copying it. The contents are pretty much what you'd expect from a paranoid, homicidal, narcissistic nut job.

There's the tediously hateful, vague, and meandering scribblings; the predictably rambling video loops in which the killer portrays himself as a long-suffering victim of unspecified injustices; and finally, the personal photo gallery complete with vainglorious self-portraits and the obligatory macho gun poses.

Certainly it's shocking stuff, but it's also a premeditated performance. Cho was still sane enough to know that because most of us could not fathom such a monstrous crime, we'd be frantic to learn every possible detail about him. He was also sane enough to know that the media would go wild over his posthumously delivered press kit, which was mailed during a break in the shooting spree. Cho is not the first mass killer to have craved recognition, but he's the first to successfully exploit DVD technology.

Back in the summer of 1966, Charlie Whitman had only a typewriter with which to attempt to explain what he was about to do. "I don't really understand myself these days," he wrote. "I am supposed to be an average reasonable and intelligent man. However, lately (I can't recall when it started) I have been a victim of many unusual and irrational thoughts."

Hours later, Whitman murdered his mother and then his wife. The next morning, the Florida-born former Marine took a high-powered arsenal to the top of the University of Texas Tower and shot 45 innocent people, killing 16.

Those of us old enough to remember that terrible day also remember the stunned bafflement pervading the nation. "Why?" was the question everybody was asking. Why in the world did Whitman do it?

In the typed suicide note, he complained of severe headaches and even requested that an autopsy be performed on his body to see if something was wrong. Medical examiners did find a brain tumor, although experts disagreed about whether that could have caused him to snap so violently.

Unlike Cho's suicide messages, Whitman's final notes were neither seething with anger nor laced with fantasies of persecution. He hinted at a difficult relationship with his father, yet he wrote adoringly of both his mother and his wife. In the end, the reason for Whitman's sniping rampage remained a mystery. This is what was known beyond any doubt: He was a seriously screwed-up guy.

Which is ultimately all that will ever be known—and

all that really matters—about Seung-Hui Cho. He was demented, he was deluded, he was dangerous. End of story. I don't care if he had a brain tumor or an impacted wisdom tooth. I don't care if he had an adverse reaction to his medicines. I don't particularly care about his childhood, his dorm life, or what songs he played on his iPod.

After all is said and done—and that day cannot come soon enough—Cho will go into the history books as another troubled loner with documented mental problems who walked into a gun shop and bought himself a headline.

As in the Whitman case, the incalculable misery inflicted by Cho has generated an almost desperate hunger for answers. NBC had no choice but to broadcast his disturbing photos and video rants; sketchy insight into the murderous mind is better than none at all. Cho surely was aware that once his self-promotional package hit the airwaves, his face would be everywhere, indelible and inescapable. As crazy as he was, he knew exactly what to feed the media beast.

So we sit through replay after replay of his toxic tirades on television. We pick up a newspaper or a magazine, and there's the ubiquitous faux Rambo picture, a glowering Cho with his arms extended, a gun in each black-gloved hand. We get it, already. He was an angry and unwell young man who cracked up. He was also an evil publicity freak. Now that we know what we do about Cho, the choice falls to us. Mine is to change the channel whenever his face appears. Let him be infamous on someone else's time.

Among the many who deserve more attention in death are those he executed for no reason: Ross Alameddine, Christopher Bishop, Brian Bluhm, Ryan Clark, Austin Cloyd, Jocelyne Couture-Nowak, Daniel Perez Cueva, Kevin Granata, Mathew Gwaltney, Caitlin Hammaren, Jeremy Herbstritt, Rachel Hill, Emily Hilscher, Jarrett Lane, Matt La Porte,

Henry J. Lee, Liviu Librescu, G. V. Loganathan, Partahi Lumbantoruan, Lauren McCain, Daniel O'Neill, Juan Ortiz, Minal Panchal, Erin Peterson, Michael Pohle, Julia Pryde, Mary Karen Read, Reema Samaha, Waleed Mohammed Shaalan, Leslie Sherman, Maxine Turner, and Nicole White.

These are names worth remembering, lives worth examining.

That other guy? Just another sicko in a long bloody line.

April 13, 2008
Firearm Law Adds Danger to Workplace

Happiness is a warm gun in a steaming-hot car.

After years of wimping around, Florida lawmakers finally passed a law that will allow you to bring your favorite firearm to work, providing you leave it locked in your vehicle.

Last week, the Legislature approved the Preservation and Protection of the Right to Keep and Bear Arms in Motor Vehicles Act, otherwise known as the Disgruntled Workers' Speedy Revenge and Retaliation Law.

In the past, deranged employees who wanted to mow down their boss and colleagues had to drive all the way home to fetch their guns. It was a waste of a perfectly good lunch hour, not to mention the gasoline.

Soon, however, any simmering paranoid with a concealed-weapons permit will legally be able to take his firearms to work. If a supervisor rebukes him for surfing porn sites, or a coworker makes fun of his mismatched socks, he can simply stroll out to the parking lot and retrieve his Glock or AK-47 (or both) to settle the grievance.

There will be no long ride home during which he might reconsider what he's about to do, no time lost rummaging through closets in search of ammunition and clean camo

fatigues. Everything he needs for instant revenge will be waiting right there in his car, whenever the urge might arise.

Sissy liberals and even conservative business leaders
say the new law is a recipe for mayhem, but they have no
faith in the competence or judgment of Florida's gun owners. Concealed-weapons permits have been issued to about
490,000 residents, not one of whom could possibly be vola-
tile, schizoid, or even slightly unreliable. The standards are
too exclusive, requiring a gun-safety course, a pulse, and a rap
sheet free of nasty felonies.

The business lobby and state Chamber of Commerce successfully fought the new gun bill for three years, citing many
violent workplace shootings committed by unhinged employees around the country. At last, though, the Republican-led
Legislature and Gov. Charlie Crist have bowed to the wisdom
of the National Rifle Association. While there was no public demand for bringing firearms to office buildings, malls,
and other workplaces, the gun lobby recognized the urgent
need—not to mention the obvious convenience—of having
loaded weapons in the parking lot.

The bill was sponsored in the Senate by Durell Peaden, a
Republican from the Panhandle town of Crestview, located
on Route 90 between DeFuniak Springs and Milton. This
must be a perilous stretch of highway, with robbers and thugs
lurking behind every billboard—why else would Sen. Peaden
have taken up the cause for putting more guns on the road?

It's true that, statewide, crime statistics show that few
motorists are randomly assaulted on the way to or from
their jobs. And it's also true that you're far more likely to be
accosted by someone who disapproves of the way you change
lanes than by someone who wants to steal your BlackBerry.

But don't be confused by facts, and don't be afraid to
be afraid. Millions of Floridians innocently drive to work

unarmed every day. If there's terror in their eyes, it's only because our highways are crawling with maniacs who don't know how to drive. Fortunately, the Legislature and the NRA are here to remind us of a larger, unseen menace. Without a firearm in the vehicle, commuters are easy prey for marauding dope fiends, muggers, and carjackers.

The new law isn't perfect because of the aforementioned requirement that you can't take your gun to work unless you have a concealed-weapons permit. Not to worry. The law prohibits your employer from inquiring about your gun permit — and the list of Floridians who have one is secret. In other words, feel free to lie to your boss, because there's no way he or she can check it out. The NRA thinks of everything.

Business lobbyists are threatening to go to court and challenge the law, which they say will make the workplace atmosphere more dangerous. They might be right, but danger cuts both ways.

Say a discontented employee runs out to his truck and gets a pistol. Once he stalks back into the stockroom and begins shooting, what do you think is going to happen next? His coworkers will dash out to their own vehicles, grab their own guns, and start firing, too. Somebody's bound to hit the crazy bastard eventually — and then problem solved!

So, the new gun law was written with built-in checks and balances. It fiercely protects the Second Amendment rights of potential snipers, and also of those unlucky souls who work side by side with them.

May the best shot win.

May 31, 2009
Camping? Don't Forget to Bring Your Gun

Like many other Americans, every time I take my family to a national park, I find myself thinking: *Wow! If I only had a gun . . .*

Now, thanks to Congress and President Obama, all of us will soon be able to carry loaded firearms into national parks and wildlife refuges. Even concealed weapons will be allowed for those who have state permits.

It's about time. The one element that's been missing from the outdoor experience in Yellowstone and Yosemite was the adventurous possibility that the drunks at the next campsite might be fooling around with a loaded .357.

Now the thrill is back, and the man to praise is Sen. Tom Coburn, a Republican from Oklahoma and a proud warrior for the National Rifle Association. Even though Oklahoma isn't famous for its national parks—you're probably not planning your summer around a trip to the Chickasaw National Recreation Area—Coburn took up the battle on behalf of armed tourists everywhere.

It was those yellow-bellied liberals in the Reagan administration who imposed the current restrictions on guns in federal parklands. Ever since the '80s, owners have been required to lock or store their weapons in car trunks or glove boxes. That meant everyone entering a national park was essentially stripped of his or her Second Amendment rights for the duration of their visit. (Despite this punitive constraint, attendance mysteriously soared at parks from coast to coast.)

The battle to put loaded guns back in the hands of American vacationers wasn't easy. Efforts to revoke the Reagan rules fell short even when Congress was controlled by the Republicans and George W. Bush was president. But Coburn and the NRA saw a golden opportunity two weeks ago, as Congress was rushing to rein in credit-card companies that were jacking up interest rates on debt-ridden customers.

The senator slyly attached the controversial parks measure as an amendment to the credit-card reform bill, which he knew was certain to be passed and sent to Obama. The president was pushing to sign it by Memorial Day. Said Coburn, "Timing is everything in politics." Democratic leaders couldn't figure out how to separate the gun issue from the credit-card issue and again found themselves outfoxed and outmaneuvered.

Unfortunately, the new firearm rules won't be in effect this summer, so campers and hikers in national parks still can't arm themselves with anything stronger than pepper spray or barbecue tongs. That will make domestic disputes a bit more difficult to settle.

However, beginning in February, two great American traditions will return: Not only can park visitors pack heat, they can purchase all the guns and ammo they want on multiple credit cards, without fear of being gouged when they fall behind on the payments.

Critics of the new law, including wildlife officers, say that since hunting is still illegal in national parks, there's no reason to be roaming around with a loaded weapon unless you're a poacher. Admittedly, poachers might cheer the Coburn rules because they'll no longer have to hassle with unlocking their car trunks to grab their rifles, an activity that tends to alert the elk. Instead, poachers can keep their guns handy in the backseat or, more conveniently, on their laps.

Law-abiding citizens have even more compelling reasons to bring firearms to a park. Statistically, you're far more likely to die from a bee sting than be attacked by a bear or moose, but that doesn't mean the woods are safe.

Don't forget the raccoons. Wilderness regions like the Rocky Mountain National Park and Grand Teton produce some gimongous raccoons, and those mothers are absolutely fearless. Given the chance, they'll swipe every darn Oreo in your backpack. Finally, thanks to Congress, such brazen intruders will soon be staring down the business end of a 20-gauge Remington. Go ahead, varmint, make my day.

Tourists planning a stop at Everglades National Park would likewise be smart to come prepared, because the place is crawling with huge pythons. It's a veritable infestation, and the new gun law couldn't have come at a better time.

The problem with shooting at a 20-foot-long snake is that the odds of hitting its tiny brainpan are about 200-to-1. And if you do miss the brain, you risk infuriating the snake. Luckily, no humans have been devoured by any Everglades pythons so far. In fact, there hasn't been a single attack—but what does that really prove?

All it takes is one rogue reptile that develops a fondness for sunblock, Tevas, and pale human flesh.

Listen to the NRA. There's no place for naive complacency in the great outdoors, so lock and load, America.

Next summer we can pack our MAC-10s with the marshmallows.

December 10, 2011
Why Some Lawmakers Are in Panic

An absolutely true news item: Having passed a law allowing gun owners to bring their weapons inside the state Capitol building, the Florida Senate has hastily installed panic buttons on the office phone of every senator and staff member.

This is an open letter from concerned members of the Florida House of Representatives to the sergeant of arms:

We couldn't help but notice that our colleagues in the Senate were provided with enhanced security measures as a result of our controversial—but patriotic!—decision to allow licensed owners of concealed weapons to carry their loaded guns through the corridors of the Capitol.

As everybody knows, the legislation wasn't our idea. It was written by lobbyists for the National Rifle Association, a fine organization that isn't nearly as crazed and paranoid as some people make it out to be. Also, the NRA contributes generously to most of our political campaigns, which is why we blindly do whatever it tells us to do.

Up until a few months ago, law-enforcement officers asked all pistol-packing constituents to leave their weapons in a lockbox before entering the Capitol. That system worked pretty darn well, in our humble opinion, but then we learned of the NRA's desire to further broaden the Second Amendment rights of law-abiding Americans.

So we went ahead and passed this new law that prevents local governments from regulating firearms, except in a few places where the state specifically says guns don't belong— hospitals, schools, and courthouses.

We'd be fibbing if we said every single member of the House actually read this bill and comprehended all its ramifications. Basically, we took the NRA's word that it was no biggie. Ever since October 1, anybody with a concealed-weapons permit can bring their favorite pistol to beaches, parks, even public libraries. Most legislators weren't too worried because, seriously, who the heck still goes to a library? Not us!

Beaches didn't seem like a problem area, either. Everybody's wearing bathing suits, so where would you even conceal a weapon? If some guy's got a .357 sticking out of his *Speedo,* little kids should have enough common sense not to mess with his sand castle. Right?

Then we come to find out that the new law also allows loaded handguns inside government buildings such as school board headquarters, city halls, county halls, and even the venerable state Capitol here in Tallahassee, where we the undersigned happened to work.

Bearing in mind that citizens occasionally get angry at their politicians, and also bearing in mind that even a normally sober firearms owner can have a bad day, the NRA kindly allowed us to bar gun toters from the legislative chambers and committee rooms, where we conduct the important business of selling out to special interests.

However, the law doesn't prevent armed voters from freely walking the hallways of the Capitol or visiting the offices of we the undersigned. Consequently, we were intrigued by media reports about the so-called panic buttons that have been given to members of the Senate, even the Democrats who voted against the darn law. Not that we have an inferiority complex, but we who serve in the House are curious to know why our phones weren't also equipped with emergency devices.

It's true that there are only 40 state senators while there are 120 representatives. And it's also true that Florida is in a severe budget crisis and that government needs to shave expenses wherever possible. But seriously, how much money can these stupid little gizmos possibly cost? Don't we have any pull at Radio Shack?

After consulting the House leadership, we've decided to take the high road and assume that the absence of panic buttons isn't a snub but, rather, the result of clerical oversight or perhaps assembly-line problems at the panic-button factory in Taiwan. This temporary disparity in the level of safety precautions doesn't mean that the life of a House member is somehow less valued than that of a senator. In truth, all of us in the legislative branch stand equal in the eyes of those who are seeking to buy our favor.

Therefore, as sergeant of arms, you are hereby instructed to promptly obtain and install the proper quantity of panic buttons in the offices of the House of Representatives. Said buttons should be connected to an emergency command center and should ring at an earsplitting pitch when activated by the user.

Upon hearing such an alarm, Capitol police should assume that a House member is facing a gun-wielding Floridian who is disgruntled, deranged, or possibly both. At this point, Second Amendment concerns should be set aside and all diligent efforts should be aimed at stopping this nut job by whatever means necessary (and we're not talking about Tasering his butt, okay?).

Also, we wish to formally inquire about the availability of body armor. Does it come with pockets?

July 7, 2012
Florida Loses Another Ridiculous Legal Battle

Another one bites the dust.

A Miami federal judge has struck down the new law prohibiting Florida doctors from discussing gun ownership with their patients. The ruling extends the legal losing streak of Gov. Rick Scott and right-wing lawmakers, who have set a pathetic record for unconstitutional bills.

Written by the National Rifle Association, the so-called Firearm Owners' Privacy Act would have prevented concerned physicians from asking patients about guns kept in their houses. It's a reasonable query in domestic situations where children might be at risk.

But the GOP-controlled Legislature wants doctors to shut up about guns and stick to lecturing women about their abortion decisions. So much for privacy.

By necessity, doctors ask lots of personal questions. Are you using any illegal drugs? How much alcohol do you drink in a week? Do you smoke cigarettes? Do you suffer from depression? We've all filled out the checklists while sitting in the waiting room. And on the examination table, we've all heard doctors and nurses ask things we wouldn't post on Facebook.

Say, have you noticed if your urine is changing color?

Uh, no.

Most of us have never been asked by our health-care providers whether we have a gun or where on the premises we keep it. However, most of us don't have bullet scars, needle tracks, or booze on our breath when showing up for a medical appointment. Some people do, and too often they have kids. Doctors who ask questions are usually just doctors who care, and the best doctors have more questions than others.

The ban on asking about gun habits originated after an Ocala couple reportedly claimed their physician wouldn't treat them anymore because they refused to talk about it. Cue the NRA, which had no trouble finding a stooge in the Legislature to sponsor a bill that effectively prohibited physicians from raising the subject.

Republican supporters claimed that merely by inquiring about firearms in the house, doctors are infringing on a patient's Second Amendment rights. The argument is embarrassingly lame. Suggesting that someone put a trigger lock on their handgun is not quite the same as confiscating it. Extending the Legislature's knothead logic, a doctor who promotes the safe use of condoms is violating your constitutional right to accidentally impregnate whomever you want.

The gun law was doomed in the courts from the day the NRA hacks delivered it. Still, it passed last year and was proudly signed by Scott, generating a swift legal challenge from the Florida Pediatric Society, the Florida Academy of Family Physicians, and other groups.

In the media, the battle became known as "Docs vs. Glocks," and on June 29 the docs won.

U.S. District Judge Marcia Cooke made permanent an order blocking the law, saying it violated the free-speech rights of physicians. She said the wording of the legislation was "vague" and offered no guidelines for health-care practitioners. For instance, the statute allowed doctors to ask about firearms only if they believed in "good faith" that the information was relevant to a patient's care and safety. Yet no specific standards were laid out in the law. The judge said it had a "chilling" effect on medical providers who feared heavy fines or even losing their licenses if they spoke to families about gun safety—a rather serious health issue in Florida, judging by the number of emergency-room admissions.

Increasingly, doctors around the country are putting firearm ownership on their checklists of questions for patients. That's because, according to the American Academy of Pediatrics, one out of every 25 children delivered to pediatric trauma centers has a gunshot wound.

It's likely that Florida will appeal Judge Cooke's decision and try to reinstate the doctor-muzzling law. The governor thinks it's a dandy piece of legislation and totally constitutional. His hapless scorecard in that area speaks for itself.

Tom Julin, a prominent First Amendment lawyer involved in challenging the statute, recently wrote in the *Sun-Sentinel*: "The fact of the matter is the NRA asked the Legislature to pass this law to censor doctors who might advocate gun control the NRA opposes. Doctors who see children bearing bullet holes on a regular basis can be very powerful advocates."

To do their jobs right, doctors are obligated to ask about anything that might affect the health of you and your family.

You certainly can't be forced to answer those questions, just as your doctor can't be forced to keep you as a patient. Take your funny-colored pee and move on.

January 12, 2013
Appropriate Job for Big NRA Backer

It's only fitting that the NRA's biggest tool in Florida is a funeral director.

He is Rep. Dennis Baxley, an Ocala Republican who does whatever the gun lobby wants.

Three days after the slaughter of first-graders in Newtown, Connecticut, Baxley made national headlines by suggesting that weapons should be carried by employees at public schools. Said he: "In our zealousness to protect people from harm, we've created all these gun-free zones, and what we've inadvertently done is we've made them a target. A helpless target is exactly what a deranged person is looking for where they cannot be stopped."

So that's the problem. It's not crackpots with Bushmasters, it's those darn gun-free zones.

And since a brain-free zone usually encircles Florida's Legislature, count on some eager-beaver lawmaker to follow up on Baxley's idea of arming teachers, coaches, maybe even cafeteria workers.

You might be wondering what kind of a person would advocate saturating our schools with loaded firearms. How about a grandfather of eight who lists his hobbies as fishing, reading, and "listening to Gospel music"? Rock on, Dennis. Nearer my Glock to thee!

Although Baxley has been on the boards of child-protection groups in Marion County, the massacre of those innocent children in Connecticut failed to shake his faith in a guns-for-all philosophy. He's been a longtime darling of the NRA. In 2004 the group gave him an A-plus rating and a Defender of Freedom Award, and four years later, it pumped $35,000 into his election campaign, according to *Mother Jones* magazine.

In return, Baxley has been obedient and loyal as a puppy. He's responsible for Florida's half-baked "stand your ground" law, now a go-to legal defense for any dope dealer or gang-banger who shoots down a rival on the street. The law has been so problematic for prosecutors that Gov. Rick Scott last year formed a task force to review it.

Baxley, of course, was given a prime seat. As head of the House Judiciary Committee, he's in position to snuff proposed changes to the "stand your ground" statute. Similarly, any sane legislation that might limit access to weapons and mass ammo clips of the sort used at Sandy Hook Elementary would have to get Baxley's approval, which will never happen. He's way too tight with Marion Hammer, Florida's top gun lobbyist and a cloud-mate of that jibbering NRA wing nut Wayne LaPierre. Both Hammer and LaPierre trade on the myth that they speak for America's gun owners when they don't even speak for the group's membership.

A conservative pollster reported that more than 70 percent of NRA members surveyed support certain reforms that are rabidly opposed by the leadership—requiring criminal background checks on all gun buyers, for example, and banning firearm ownership by anyone on the FBI's terrorist watch list.

Another fact that the NRA doesn't brag about: Its funding increasingly depends on gun manufacturers, not gun owners. According to the Violence Policy Center, 22 firearms manufacturers, including Beretta USA and Smith & Wesson, gave almost $39 million to the NRA between 2005 and 2011. So it's basically a corporate shill promoting itself as a grassroots defender of the Constitution.

In many states, the NRA has used campaign contributions and threats of retribution to secure political puppets such as Baxley. The successful tactic has given the lobby a clout that far outweighs the true size of its constituency. The NRA claims 4.3 million members. If you charitably assume it's not padding the numbers, the total still represents just a tiny fraction of American gun owners, of whom there are at least 146 million. In other words, more than 97 percent of legal gun owners in this country—hunters, target shooters, people who keep or carry a firearm for protection—don't belong to the NRA.

Many gun owners have multiple weapons (I own two, a shotgun and a rifle), but the vast majority don't keep assault rifles or military-style semi-automatics of the type used on the moviegoers in Aurora, Colorado, the children in Newtown, or, more recently, four firefighters and an off-duty policeman in Webster, New York.

The latest wave of attacks has shaken up a few pro-NRA stalwarts like Sen. Joe Manchin, a West Virginia Democrat, who said: "I don't know anybody in the sporting or hunting arena that goes out with an assault rifle. I don't know anybody who needs 30 rounds in a clip to go hunting."

Tragically, nothing so sensible is being heard from lawmakers such as Baxley, though he undoubtedly has embalmed enough young gunshot victims to realize that something needs to change.

April 7, 2013
A Stylish Tote for Your Ammo Clips

The National Rifle Association wants to give me a "heavy-duty" duffel bag.

It's a nice one, too—roomy enough for an AR-15 and maybe a half-dozen 30-round clips. Stitched on the side is a bold-looking NRA patch. The bag is mine if I pay $25 and join up.

Like most gun owners in this country, I'm not an NRA member. It's possible that Wayne LaPierre got my name off a mailing list from catalogs that sell hunting gear. LaPierre is the NRA's perpetually apoplectic executive vice president. You see him on TV preaching against gun control, practically levitating with paranoia. He signed the letter that arrived with the nifty duffel-bag offer.

One thing about Wayne, he likes to underline. He's also fond of boldface type and of capitalizing important words. This rises to a fever pitch when he's writing about "anti-gun members of Congress":

> And they will not stop until they BAN hundreds of commonly owned firearms, PROHIBIT private transfers of firearms, CLOSE gun shops and shows, and DESTROY your freedom to defend yourself, your home and your loved ones.

Here's another beauty:

> Remember, gun ban politicians and their media allies are on the attack. And the future of your freedom is at stake.

LaPierre might seem like an undermedicated wack job, but he's just acting. His job is to frighten people and to sell more guns.

Major firearms manufacturers such as Smith & Wesson and Beretta have given millions of dollars to the NRA. Sturm, Ruger & Co. donated a dollar from every gun sale to the organization from May 2011 to May 2012, raising $1.25 million. This isn't mentioned in Wayne's letter. He calls the NRA a "grassroots membership organization," when in reality it's a coldhearted lobby for the gun industry.

And the industry definitely gets its money's worth. The push in Congress to revive the ban on assault rifles is dead, and other modest reforms are in trouble, in spite of the nation's horror at the massacres in Aurora, Colorado, and Newtown, Connecticut. The NRA scares politicians far more than it scares the average citizen. The senators who are now wimping out on broader background checks for gun buyers aren't afraid for our Second Amendment rights; they're afraid the NRA will bankroll their opponents in the next election.

Republicans cower most reliably, but spineless Democrats are in no short supply. A push to federally limit the capacity of ammo magazines to a mere 10 bullets is foundering strictly because the NRA opposes it.

Hunters and sport shooters don't need 30 rounds to hit what they're aiming at, but mass murderers, gangbangers, and cop killers love those big macho clips.

Buying bullets online is another convenience that the NRA is fighting to preserve. It's how a disturbed University of Central Florida student, James Seevakumaran, compiled the arsenal that he intended to use against fellow dorm residents last month. (He killed himself during preparations, after his roommate called the police.)

The NRA wasn't always quite so loony. It once supported comprehensive background checks on gun purchases and even took a position against guns being carried in public schools.

Now the group has swung 180 degrees, in sneering opposition to public sentiment. Polls show 90 percent of Americans favor background checks on all firearms sales, including those at local gun shows, which are currently unregulated.

LaPierre insists that background checks will lead to a "national gun registry," which will then lead to mass confiscation of firearms by the government. Oh, sure. The same government that can't afford to deliver mail on Saturdays is poised to send armed agents to every single house in the country to search for weapons.

The notion is ridiculous, and Wayne's well aware of it. The NRA isn't aiming for the mainstream support. The fringe is what they're after—the spooked-out guys who were lining up to buy assault rifles after the mass shooting in Newtown.

By the way, those 20 murdered children and six murdered adults aren't mentioned anywhere in LaPierre's rousing membership letter. I double-checked all the underlined sentences and boldfaced paragraphs.

Not a single word, capitalized or otherwise, about how some nutcase with a Bushmaster fired 154 rounds in less than five minutes, turning a schoolhouse into a slaughterhouse.

His name was Adam Lanza, and he already owned a duffel bag. Investigators who opened it found 50 .22-caliber bullets, ear protection, binoculars, paper targets, and two NRA certificates, one each for the killer and his mother.

The organization says they were not card-carrying members. Lanza shot his mom before he drove to Sandy Hook Elementary.

His duffel bag didn't have an NRA logo, but maybe next time.

There's always a next time.

SHOCK, AWE, AND SWAGGER

June 15, 2003
And the Hunt Goes On

Rough draft of hastily canceled presidential address regarding the effort to locate weapons of mass destruction in Iraq.

My fellow Americans,

Lots of people at home and abroad are increasingly skeptical about the existence of chemical, biological, and nuclear weapons in Iraq. Perhaps this is because, after three months of looking, we haven't found diddly.

However, I am urging you to be more patient with our search effort than we were with the United Nations' search effort.

While it's true that there's nobody left in Saddam Hussein's regime to "delay and deceive" us—as they did to those pushovers from the UN—the weapons hunt is still mighty challenging. Let me remind you for about the twenty-seventh time that Iraq is as big as California and is mostly desert.

Deserts are vast arid flatlands made up predominantly of sand. Sand is loose granular matter that is produced by the disintegration of rock. Rock is a formation of stony minerals . . . well, you get the picture.

According to our most current intelligence estimates, the Iraqi desert is made up of "jillions and kazillions" of grains of sand. One particle of anthrax the size of a single grain could infect thousands of innocent people. Therefore, it is our intention to search Iraq one grain of sand at a time until we're absolutely sure that Saddam did not disguise any biological agent as desert cover.

How long will this take? I can't answer that question. But now that we've occupied Iraq, what's the big darn hurry? Heck, we basically own the joint.

I've been disturbed by the mounting accusations in Europe and elsewhere that the United States invaded on false pretenses. This is completely untrue. Granted, in the weeks preceding Operation Iraqi Freedom, I repeatedly asserted that we would go to war only to "disarm" Saddam Hussein's regime, not to seize the country and take over its oil fields.

And yes, we ended up seizing the country and taking over its oil fields. So, in the absence of weapons of mass destruction, I certainly understand how some folks might be a tad suspicious.

I am outraged, however, that Democrats in Congress are calling for hearings to investigate whether this administration hyped the threat of a biological, chemical, or nuclear attack in order to justify military action against Iraq.

Okay, so maybe Saddam wasn't as tight with Al Qaeda as we'd made him out to be.

And maybe I did stand up in front of the whole nation and say that Saddam might produce a nuclear warhead within a year. And yes, it turned out to be total hogwash based on a lame tip from discredited informants.

But neither Defense Secretary Rumsfeld nor myself intentionally pressured the CIA, DIA, NSA, FBI, or even FOX News to exaggerate the Iraqi menace for the purpose of mobilizing public opinion behind the war.

I still firmly believe that our worst fears about Saddam Hussein will prove well founded. And I'm sure that he had a perfectly good reason for not using his secret stash of poison gas and deadly germs against invading allied troops, even though he was desperate to avoid defeat.

It's very possible that Saddam took a few weapons of mass destruction with him when he fled Baghdad. A lethal supply of smallpox, for example, could have fit easily in the glove compartment of his Range Rover. As time passes, we must seriously consider the possibility that Saddam now intends to peddle these smuggled weapons to terrorist groups or countries hostile to the United States.

According to recent intelligence chatter, both Syria and Iran "really hate our guts." Radical elements within those regimes would snap up Saddam's weapons technology faster than you can say "Hans Blix."

As you're probably aware, American forces did discover two mobile biowarfare laboratories abandoned in Iraq. We know they're biowarfare laboratories because they resemble the pinlike shapes on those grainy satellite photos that Secretary of State Powell showed to the United Nations—and Secretary Powell is a righteous stand-up guy.

Frankly, I was a little disappointed that no traces of actual bio-crud were found in the mobile labs, which evidently had been scrubbed clean with the Iraqi equivalent of extra-strength Comet. But you should have no doubt, my fellow Americans, as to the sinister purpose and intent of those facilities. Nor should you doubt our resolve to track down Saddam's hidden arsenal of mass destruction no matter where the trail leads us, even to Iran.

Which, according to our most recent intelligence, is four times larger than California. So please don't get your hopes too high.

November 30, 2003
Iraq Becomes Operation Sitting Duck

A few days ago, two American soldiers in Iraq were shot, dragged from a truck, and viciously beaten with concrete blocks. Their bodies were left on a dusty street in Mosul, a city once considered one of the safest for U.S. forces.

The murder and mutilation were carried out not by hardened operatives of Al Qaeda but by a gang of Iraqi teenagers, the very generation for whom we've been battling to "liberate" the country.

For any civilians to act so barbarously shows a depth of hatred that is chilling. As the months drag on and the flag-draped coffins of fallen Americans keep arriving at Dover Air Force Base, the mission in Iraq makes less sense than ever. What are we doing there? Who are we fighting? How do we get out? The only question that now seems hollow is why we ever invaded in the first place.

The search for the phantom weapons of mass destruction has been reduced to a nightly punch line in Jay Leno's monologue. No nukes, no anthrax, and no nerve gas have been found; nothing to justify President Bush's prewar declaration that Saddam Hussein posed an immediate threat to global security.

So far, the most dangerous weapons uncovered are decidedly low-tech — pistols, rifles, homemade bombs, land mines, and RPGs fired from donkey-drawn wagons. Unfortunately, they're doing a bang-up job of maiming and killing Americans. The atmosphere in Iraq remains so perilous that on Thanksgiving Day, Bush had to sneak into Baghdad on a darkened *Air Force One*.

Whether the war was launched on false pretenses or merely faulty intelligence will be argued endlessly. The grim fact is that we're there now, and we're stuck.

In Afghanistan, the mission was so clear. We were responding to a brazen attack against Americans on American soil. We knew who did it and where they were hiding. The international community was virtually united behind us.

Iraq is another story. Saddam Hussein was a despicable tyrant, but not even the White House claims that he played a direct role in the September 11 attacks on the World Trade Center and the Pentagon.

The hijackers themselves weren't Iraqis, nor were those who planned the crime. The man who approved it, Osama bin Laden, was known to detest Saddam. Yet here we are, mired in Iraq, our troops getting picked off by snipers, sappers, and roadside rocket jockeys. Call it Operation Sitting Duck.

The hawks in the administration gripe that the media is focusing only on the bad news out of Baghdad, but where's the good news?

Last week, U.S. Col. William Darley told reporters that attacks by Iraqi insurgents against U.S. forces had declined from a high of 40 per day in mid-November to about 30 per day now. It hardly makes you want to pop the champagne, knowing that our troops are coming under fire more often than once an hour.

This holiday weekend concludes the bloodiest month for U.S. forces since the so-called end of major combat. More than 60 U.S. soldiers have been killed by hostile fire in November. As of Thanksgiving Day, a total of 183 had died since the president triumphantly jet-landed on that aircraft carrier May 1.

Technically, though, the White House was correct. Major combat in the conventional sense ended in Iraq. These days our soldiers are dying by ambush and assassination.

Despite somewhat muted media coverage—Michael Jackson's arrest received more attention than the GI murders in Mosul—polls show that the war is increasingly a political liability for the White House. Efforts are accelerating to put a new Iraqi government in place.

Bringing the troops home, however, will be a long time

in coming. As long as Saddam Hussein remains at large, Bush will keep a sizable fighting force on the ground. His insistence that occupying Iraq is central to the war on terrorism grows more preposterous by the day. Saddam has disappeared, but the much larger evil of Al Qaeda has been lethally busy in Saudi Arabia, Turkey, and Pakistan. Meanwhile, bin Laden himself is still alive and making dire threats. He's certainly not in Iraq, and nothing that happens in Iraq will bring us closer to catching him.

The grisly scene in Mosul last week recalled that infamous horror in Mogadishu a decade ago, when a Black Hawk helicopter was shot down and the mangled remains of U.S. servicemen were dragged through the streets by a celebratory mob.

It was a demoralizing episode for this country, but at least the soldiers in Somalia went down fighting. In Iraq the enemy is often unseen, indistinguishable from friendly civilians, and the shots and grenades come out of nowhere.

Troops who were trained to wage war are now courageously trying to wage peace. In such a role, they must be visible and ubiquitous in a land where they aren't universally welcome.

The results have been deadly, though not unanticipated. The question for Bush is how long before the American people decide that the best exit plan is to elect a president with an exit plan.

February 22, 2004
Iraq War Is Boon for Halliburton

McDonald's sells Happy Meals. Halliburton Co. sells invisible ones.

The mammoth defense firm once headed by Vice Presi-

dent Dick Cheney has suspended outstanding food bills of
$174.5 million until it can resolve an embarrassing dispute
with the Pentagon. According to military officials, Halliburton invoiced the government for four million phantom meals
that were never served to U.S. troops in Kuwait.

A Halliburton subsidiary, KBR, has the contract to feed all
American service personnel in the war zone. Soldiers eat lots
of food, and Halliburton has been making lots of money. Too
much money, according to the army.

Earlier this month, Halliburton agreed to repay the U.S.
government about $27.4 million that it had overbilled for
meals at five military bases in Iraq and Kuwait. Auditors are
currently reviewing the records at 53 other dining instal-
lations operated by KBR. The company says it has done
nothing wrong and "is a good steward of taxpayers' dollars."

Back when Halliburton was given such a large and lucrative role in U.S.-occupied Iraq—it also got the contract to
repair and refit the oil fields—the Bush administration denied
that it was handing out favors to the Texas-based conglomer-
ate. Americans were assured that the selection of Halliburton
had nothing to do with the Cheney connection, a line that
nobody with an IQ over 75 believed.

Not surprisingly, the decision is now backfiring. First
came allegations that the firm was overcharging for gasoline
being shipped to Iraq, a matter now under investigation
by the Pentagon inspector general. Then, in January, the
company admitted that two of its employees had pocketed
enormous bribes from a Kuwaiti subcontractor servicing
U.S. troops. Halliburton promptly coughed up a $6.3 million
reimbursement check.

Americans aren't naive about war. They know it's a highly
expensive enterprise and a profitable one for defense contractors. Still, there will be little public tolerance for findings of

price-gouging and overbilling by an outfit with ties to the vice president, who is nearly as invisible as Halliburton's troop meals.

As the war in Iraq grows increasingly unpopular, the company's windfall looks increasingly obscene. Democrats are already urging voters to connect the dots:

* In 2000, Cheney agrees to leave Halliburton and become George W. Bush's running mate.
* Halliburton says goodbye to Cheney with a stupefying retirement package worth more than $20 million.
* When Bush decides to invade Iraq, Cheney's old company gets the biggest chunk of the business.

The White House wants us to believe it's all coincidence, and maybe it is. Maybe someday I'll win the Daytona 500, too. In a golf cart.

The war has been a spectacular boon for Halliburton, which last year raked in $3.4 billion for its work in Iraq—about 20 percent of the company's total revenue, according to *Bloomberg News*. Wall Street investors are jolly as well. The price of Halliburton stock has shot up about 61 percent since the invasion.

Those are grand statistics indeed, until you stack them up against the half-trillion-dollar deficit that the country is now stuck with, thanks in large part to this pointless war. Or the zero weapons of mass destruction that have been found. Or the 545 U.S. soldiers who have so bravely given their lives on Iraqi soil. Two more were killed Thursday, blown up by a coward's bomb on a road near Khaldiyah, 50 miles west of Baghdad.

The night before, the U.S. base at Abu Ghraib prison was

shelled for 20 solid minutes by unseen insurgents. Thirty-three mortars and five rockets were fired at our troops. Miraculously, none were killed.

Every day brings new attacks, and often a new bloodbath. The latest trend is suicide car bombers who target Iraqi police and civilians. Speaking of which, that's one statistic nobody has nailed down—exactly how many thousands of Iraqi citizens have died since the bombs began to fall almost a year ago. Perhaps nobody in command knows for sure, or wants to.

Faced with gloomy polls, the Bush administration is eager to start withdrawing forces before the November election. It wouldn't be the first time that a military exit strategy has been accelerated by political pressure. In the meantime, as U.S. diplomats and local religious leaders debate what kind of democracy the new Iraq should have, our troops will stay where they are—getting sniped at and bombed and rained with mortars.

Halliburton will get richer, even as it argues with the Pentagon over how many meals it's actually serving to American units.

This week, sadly, there are at least two fewer soldiers on the food line.

June 20, 2004
Why We Went to War Awaits Honest Answer

It's a good thing that Dick Cheney's pacemaker doesn't have a built-in polygraph.

The guy just can't stick to the truth.

Last Monday he gave a speech in which he declared for the umpteenth time that Saddam Hussein had "long-established ties with Al Qaeda." Two days later, the bipartisan commission investigating the 9/11 attacks reported precisely the opposite, shooting another hole in the Bush administration's flimsy rationale for invading Iraq.

The White House has steadfastly claimed that Hussein maintained close and sympathetic connections with Al Qaeda operatives. Staff reports released last week by the commission say that no such ties—long-standing or otherwise— can be found. This isn't good news for the White House, which has righteously touted the Iraqi invasion as a blow against a strategic Al Qaeda ally. The vice president was, and continues to be, the loudest peddler of this myth.

While President Bush has never publicly suggested that Hussein played a role in the September 11 plot, Cheney hasn't discounted the idea. As recently as January, he contended there was no proof "one way or another" regarding an Iraqi connection to the suicide hijackings.

Yet the 9/11 panel had very little trouble reaching a conclusion. It found no "collaborative relationship" between the Hussein regime and Al Qaeda and "no credible evidence" that Hussein was involved in the September 11 conspiracy. Moreover, the oft-cited April 2001 meeting between hijacker Mohamed Atta and an Iraqi intelligence officer never occurred, according to the commission staff. Telephone records and other evidence positively locate Atta here in Florida at the time he was supposedly in Prague, conspiring with the Iraqi operative.

The 9/11 panel, which includes Democrats and Republicans, portrays Osama bin Laden as the main architect of the September 11 plot. Not a single e-mail, cell-phone call, or even a fruit basket was found to have passed personally from bin Laden to Hussein, either before or after attack. According to the commission, bin Laden did meet with an Iraqi intelligence officer in 1994, but nothing came of it. The Al Qaeda leader is reported "to have requested space to establish training camps, as well as assistance in procuring weapons, but Iraq apparently never responded," according to the commission staff.

In recent months, as the 9/11 panel's investigation has unfolded, Bush himself has said little about the increasingly imaginary Hussein–Al Qaeda connection. Cheney, however, hasn't eased up. Never one to let facts clutter a good speech, the vice president is pitching the same line today that he did in advance of the war. And no one pitched the war more enthusiastically—to Congress, to foreign leaders, to Bush himself. The vice president is a persuasive fellow, and lots of folks believed what he told them. Maybe he believed it himself.

Unfortunately, the reasons given for invading Iraq, the reasons eventually embraced and promoted by the president, have been exposed one after another as bunk.

Hussein's nuclear program? Can't seem to find one.

Banned biological weapons? Can't find them, either.

Chemical stash? Ditto.

To all those never-minds, we now add one more. The theory of a sinister Hussein–bin Laden covenant has been officially discredited, leaving the Bush administration batting .000 on its prewar hype.

We weren't just misled, we were duped.

Most Iraqis feel the same way. Fifteen months after the invasion, a paltry 2 percent of Iraqi citizens consider U.S. forces to be liberators. That's according to a survey arranged by the Coalition Provisional Authority—our own guys.

Following last week's disclosures, President Bush insisted there had been a relationship between Iraq and Al Qaeda, though he offered no new details. He noted the current presence in Iraq of Abu Musab al-Zarqawi, the notorious Jordanian terrorist who has sought help from Al Qaeda.

As for Cheney, he refuses to back away from his previous claims, no matter how speculative or unproved. In a doomed effort to justify this messy and sapping war, the vice president is sticking to his original script.

So far, 832 U.S. soldiers have died in Iraq, and many more will die in the long months ahead. Most Americans are eager for us to pull out, but how we got there is a question that still awaits a full and honest answer.

Don't expect to hear one from Cheney.

May 15, 2005
Iraq's Numbers, Bodies Keep Piling Up

The number is there. Hunt hard enough through the newspaper stories and you'll find it.

Last week it surpassed 1,600. This week it will go higher.

You could write it on the blackboard in a hundred classrooms, and probably in 99 of them, nobody could tell you what it stood for.

Here's the answer: As of Thursday, 1,609 was the number of American soldiers who died in Iraq since we invaded 26 months ago.

That works out to more than two soldiers killed every day, which in actuarial terms isn't a huge toll when compared with other long wars. Unless it's your son or daughter or wife or husband coming home in the coffins, in which case the number is devastating.

Americans haven't completely lost interest in what's happening to our troops in Iraq, but an inevitable numbness has set in as the casualty figures rise steadily. The tragic has become the routine. Lots more people could tell you the score of the Heat–Wizards play-off game or where the Dow Jones closed on Friday than could tell you how many soldiers died last week in roadside bombings.

They could tell you who got the most votes on *American Idol*. They could tell you how many times that "runaway bride" from Atlanta has been busted for shoplifting. They could tell you who won the NASCAR race at Darlington and even the new Nextel Cup standings. That kind of stuff isn't hard to find. Just park yourself in front of the TV or laptop and relax. It's one big happy avalanche of entertainment.

Obviously, we in the media have gone numb, too. And let's be honest—it's much more fun to write about Paula Abdul than Ibrahim al-Jaafari. He is Iraq's new prime minister, struggling to put together a cabinet to appease the various religious factions that have detested each other as long as anyone can remember.

The last few weeks have been a bloodbath, with upward of 400 Iraqi civilians and security forces murdered in car bombings and armed attacks. Fourteen American troops were killed between May 7 and May 12, some of them in a bold Marine offensive along the Syrian border. Currently, the insurgency is being led by members of the Sunni minority who are extremely unhappy about having to surrender their long-held political power to the Shiites and the Kurds.

Also at work is an active Al Qaeda cell that, according to our own intelligence analysts, did not exist in Iraq before we invaded. Because of the U.S. military presence, the country is now attracting assassins and suicidal zealots from all over the Muslim world.

As detached about Iraq as Americans seem to be, polls show that many still doubt our reasons for being there. Originally, the stated mission was to "disarm" Saddam Hussein, but even a presidential panel of experts now says there was nothing to disarm. Saddam hoarded no weapons of mass destruction and had no connection whatsoever to the 9/11 hijackings.

Thus, it became necessary to devise a new face-saving reason for invading Iraq. Today the White House says that U.S. troops are there to establish a beachhead for democracy in the Mideast—this, as Bush strolls hand in hand with Crown Prince Abdullah of Saudi Arabia, one of the most repressive and undemocratic regimes in the world.

Still, it's significant that nine million Iraqis risked their lives to vote in January. There's bedlam and carnage in the streets, but the country at least has the framework of an elected government. It's also got a foreign army of occupation, historically not a beneficial ingredient in the making of a new democracy.

So how long do we stay, and at what final cost? Nobody has a clue. U.S. troops are busily training the Iraqi military and security forces, but the Pentagon has provided no timetable for returning control of the country to the people who live there. Meanwhile, the heavy numbers keep piling up, although some are even more difficult to find than the death toll.

In addition to the 1,609 U.S. soldiers lost, the Department of Defense lists 12,350 as wounded in action. Many have crippling injuries, and others are returning home with emotional damage that will take years to heal, if ever. As for the Iraqi casualties, we don't even count them. Nobody is sure how many civilian noncombatants—men, women, and children—have died since the night we started bombing Baghdad.

Here in the United States, we're a long way from the

car bombs and the mangled corpses, horrific images briefly glimpsed on CNN. Most of us remain comfortably buffered from the war by the reams of fluff and celebrity scandal that now pass for front-page news.

Yet the coffins quietly keep coming home from Iraq, on the average of two a day. That's two more funerals, two more families left to mourn and wonder and hope that someday it all adds up to something noble and enduring.

Something more than another stark number in a history book.

January 28, 2007
In Veep's World, We're Safer Now Than Before Iraq

The wacky, upside-down world of Dick Cheney keeps getting weirder. Last week he went on CNN and defiantly declared that the situation in Iraq is not so terrible.

This must have been surprising to the families of the 88 Iraqi civilians who were slaughtered the day before by car bombers at a busy Baghdad market.

Surprising to the loved ones and comrades of the 27 American troops who died last weekend, one of the costliest for coalition forces since the occupation.

Surprising to Lt. Gen. David Petraeus, soon to be commander of U.S. forces in Iraq, who two days earlier had informed a Senate panel that the situation there was "dire."

Surprising to Sen. John Warner and other top Republicans who have warned that Iraq is sliding into chaos, and have publicly questioned the decision to send more troops.

Surprising to Cheney's own boss, President Bush, who in a recent interview conceded that the administration's original game plan for Iraq was heading toward "slow failure."

Yet in his interview with Wolf Blitzer, Cheney brushed away as "hogwash" any suggestion that the war has been mishandled. "Bottom line is that we've had enormous successes, and we will continue to have enormous successes," he said.

There are several possible explanations for the vice president's bizarre performance:

He's crazy as a loon.

He's a compulsive liar.

He's gotten his prescriptions mixed up with Rush Limbaugh's.

Whatever the clinical reason might be, Cheney continues to float blissfully through a smug and surreal fog. "The pressure is from some quarters to get out of Iraq," he said. "If we were to do that, we simply validate the terrorists' strategy that says the Americans will not stay to complete the task, that we don't have the stomach for the fight."

Oddly, Cheney's stout appetite for battle never manifested itself when he was of draft age, during the Vietnam War. Five times he declined his country's call to serve there. Now, as the last cheerleader for the fiasco in Iraq, Cheney revels in the self-imagined role of Tough Guy. In fact, he is simply the Guy Who's Never Been Right.

Before, during, and after the invasion, it was Cheney who most strenuously promoted the fiction of Saddam Hussein's stockpile of weapons of mass destruction. It was Cheney who insisted there was a link between Hussein and Al Qaeda's 9/11 coconspirators, long after U.S. intelligence agencies had discredited the idea. It was also Cheney who predicted that American soldiers would be welcomed as "liberators" on the streets where they are now being blown up. And it was he who in 2005 confidently asserted that the insurgency was in its "last throes."

On the topic of Iraq, the vice president has been uncannily wrong about everything, yet he seldom bypasses an opportunity to play the pompous stooge. Here are some true statements that you will never hear from Cheney's lips:

The war has so far cost American taxpayers at least $500 billion, or 10 times more than the administration's initial estimate.

The combat toll on our military now exceeds 3,065 dead and more than 22,000 wounded, many permanently disabled.

No one is sure how many Iraqi civilians have perished since the invasion, but at least 34,000 are known to have died in 2006. About two million Iraqis have fled the country to escape the continuing violence.

Osama bin Laden, the man who green-lighted the 9/11 attacks, is still alive and free—and he's not hiding in Iraq. Meanwhile, the Taliban fighters who harbored Osama and his cohorts in Afghanistan are resurging with a vengeance.

And the next murderous generation of Al Qaeda fanatics has a new outpost of operations, a place where they were unwelcome for years. It's called Iraq.

This is the truth that the vice president would prefer not be reported, much less discussed openly. Naturally, he blames the media for turning the public against the war, a trick borrowed from the old Vietnam hard-liners.

Hey, what about all those markets in Baghdad that *weren't* car-bombed last week? How come you guys don't write about them?

Without cracking a smile, Cheney told Blitzer that "the world is much safer today" because Bush took military action against Iraq.

That the invasion has galvanized Islamic extremists worldwide seems not to concern the vice president even slightly.

We're all safer than we were before—that's what the man said. If Hussein were still in power, Cheney added somberly, "we'd have a terrible situation" in Iraq.

In contrast to the peaceful, safe, and stable situation that exists now . . .

Only in the daffy, disconnected mind of Dick Cheney.

March 23, 2008
Iraq: No Light at the End of the Tunnel

On the five-year anniversary of the invasion of Iraq, President Bush declared that the United States is on the way to winning the war.

He made this stupefying pronouncement in the safe confines of the Pentagon, where it's unacceptable to question the commander in chief, no matter how dense or self-deluded he might be. If Bush had dared to make the same speech in a public town hall, among civilians, the reception would have been chillier. According to almost every opinion poll, about two-thirds of all Americans now stand opposed to the war in Iraq. When reminded last week of this statistic, Vice President Dick Cheney responded: "So?"

Bush sent Cheney to Baghdad to mark the dubious anniversary of their costly, misbegotten adventure. What better way to buoy the spirits of the 160,000 U.S. soldiers who are now stuck in Iraq—a surprise visit by the Man Who's Never Been Right.

True to form, the vice president repeated his dark assertion that former Iraqi leader Saddam Hussein had close ties with Al Qaeda, a claim discredited and rejected by every U.S. intelligence agency. Cheney also described the American effort to bring stability and democracy to Iraq as "a successful endeavor." Compared to what—the landing of the *Hindenburg?*

There's still no stable, functioning democracy in Iraq. Provincial elections might finally be held in October, although the Kurds, Sunnis, and Shiites continue to fight about how power should be apportioned. It's an ancient argument that won't subside anytime soon.

After years of training, the Iraqi armed forces still aren't prepared to keep order in the country, and senior U.S. military commanders don't know when that particular miracle will come to pass.

Bush acts like there's a light at the end of the tunnel. The problem is, it's not a tunnel—it's a pit.

As of March 19, the American toll in Iraq stood at 3,982 deaths and nearly 30,000 combat injuries. An additional 145 U.S. soldiers have committed suicide there. Such heavy losses are difficult to absorb, impossible to rationalize. Nobody knows for sure how many innocent Iraqi civilians have been killed during the U.S. occupation—at least 18,600 are known to have died in 2007 alone.

The monetary cost of the war is so high that the administration cannot—or will not—give Congress an accurate figure.

Five years ago, the Bush-Cheney brain trust said the invasion and reconstruction of Iraq would cost between $50 billion and $60 billion. That number was every bit as reliable as the assertion that Saddam had stockpiled weapons of mass destruction. The Pentagon now says the war has cost about $600 billion, while congressional estimates put the sum in excess of $1 trillion—roughly 20 times more than the administration predicted. Currently, Bush and Cheney's Iraq rodeo is sapping between $8 billion and $12 billion every month from U.S. taxpayers, just what a battered and shaky economy needs.

Five years ago, we were assured that Iraqi oil revenues would finance the rebuilding of the country after we bombed it to rubble. It was one more false promise to be discarded with all the others.

The president is feeling upbeat these days because the troop surge, which he initially resisted, has succeeded in reducing sectarian bloodshed in Baghdad, as well as U.S. casualties. Other forces have been able to leave the city and hunt down insurgents who've been targeting our troops.

However, equally important factors in the lower death toll are a cease-fire declared by a key Shiite militia and an unexpected Sunni backlash against extremists. These two key ingredients for peace could evaporate soon if the Iraqi government doesn't get its act together. The fact that fewer U.S. soldiers are dying is welcome news, but it's not the same as winning the war. We're more deeply mired in Iraq today than we were in the spring of 2003. Suicide bombings against civilians and police continue, and less than two weeks ago, five American soldiers were blown up inside a house rigged with bombs.

In the bitterest of many ironies, the American occupation has given Al Qaeda a foothold in a country where the terrorist organization had never previously been tolerated. Meanwhile, the spiritual father of the 9/11 attacks, Osama bin Laden, remains alive and well, delousing his beard somewhere in the caves of Afghanistan.

Among the presidential candidates, only John McCain shares the president's view that the tide has turned in Iraq and that it is there we must ultimately fight until jihadist terrorism is vanquished. McCain has said that the United States should keep its forces in Iraq for a hundred years, if necessary.

It's a statement bound to haunt him in the coming months, no matter who his opponent turns out to be. The American people have had enough.

No matter who the next president is, the road out of Iraq will not be swift or smooth. Long after Bush is chopping brush back on the ranch in Texas, young American men and women will still be coming home from Baghdad in coffins.

No. 3,982 was Lerando J. Brown, 27, an army specialist from Gulfport, Miss.

You can put the number beside his name, but you can't put a true price. The same can be said for this war.

September 10, 2011
The Dumb Deed Before the Terror Attack

Osama bin Laden knew what he was doing when he implanted several of the key 9/11 hijackers in Florida. There was no better place for his suicide crews to be overlooked, as they not so invisibly prepared for the attacks on the World Trade Center and Pentagon.

On the day after Christmas in 2000, flight controllers at Miami International Airport were annoyed to peer out at one of the crowded taxiways and see a small Piper Cherokee. The plane wasn't moving, and the cockpit was empty. One official in the flight tower spotted two men walking away, crossing the airfield in the direction of the main general aviation hangar.

Even in Miami, this doesn't happen every day. Even rookie pilots know to radio the tower if their aircraft conks out while rolling toward the runway. Nobody just abandons a plane in a line of waiting commercial jetliners. The men who pulled this stunt were named Marwan al-Shehhi and Mohamed Atta. Nine months later, they would be infamous, but on December 26, 2000, they seemed just like two more knuckleheads in the Knucklehead Capital of America.

They had learned to fly at Huffman Aviation in Venice, near Sarasota. According to the report of the 9/11 Commission, both men earned their private pilot licenses on August 14, 2000. Atta spent only 69 minutes on the test and scored 97 out of 100. Al-Shehhi scored an 83 and took 73 minutes to finish.

The Piper Cherokee that stalled at MIA had been rented from Huffman that day by the two future hijackers. They weren't supposed to fly it all the way to Miami, so the general manager of Huffman was surprised to get a phone call from the men, asking how to restart the plane. Not long afterward, a flight official at MIA dialed Huffman to say the Piper had been abandoned, forcing other aircrafts to taxi around it. It was about 5:45 P.M., one of the busiest periods for commercial takeoffs and landings. "Any time the tower calls, they are not in the best of moods," the manager of the aviation firm told Jim Yardley of *The New York Times*.

Meanwhile, Atta and al-Shehhi were renting a car to drive back to Venice.

The Federal Aviation Administration later demanded the maintenance records of the Piper. It turned out that the engine might have flooded because of a loose spark plug. In grim hindsight, it's natural to wonder why authorities evidently made little or no effort to track down Atta and al-Shehhi after the MIA incident. The reality is that not much would have happened to the men, anyway—perhaps a small fine or a warning. Even in the unlikely event that their pilot licenses had been yanked, it wouldn't have prevented the horrific events to come. These guys would have already gained what they'd come to Florida to get: working knowledge of aircraft controls.

On the morning of September 11, Atta steered American Airlines Flight 11 into the North Tower of the World Trade Center in lower Manhattan. Seventeen minutes later, al-Shehhi crashed United Airlines Flight 175 into the South Tower.

During the months preceding the attack, Atta and several hijackers had moved their base of operations from the Sarasota area to South Florida, where they continued to blend in splendidly. The martyrs-in-waiting worked out in local gyms, hung out at sports bars and even strip joints, presumably not searching for virgins.

In April 2001, Atta got pulled over in Broward County for driving without a license. A month later, he legally got a Florida license, as did al-Shehhi and 11 other hijackers. But in the manner of thousands of scofflaw Floridians, Atta blithely ignored the driving ticket he'd received. When he didn't show up in court, a bench warrant was issued—again, no cause for alarm. His puny case was but one in a judicial system swamped by bigger ones. Atta had a better chance of dying from a bee sting than of being arrested.

Bin Laden and his organizers clearly anticipated that the young hijackers would make some mistakes in America. That's why Florida was such an obvious staging area—the bar of dumb behavior here is so high that it's almost impossible for bumbling newcomers to get noticed.

Even if you abandon a plane between runways at an international airport.

So comfy were Atta and al-Shehhi in their new locale that they didn't consider the Piper fiasco a close call. When they returned to Venice, the first thing they did was ask the manager of Huffman Aviation to reimburse them for the rental car.

He said no way. Days later they were back in Miami, practicing on a Boeing 767 simulator. The rest is awful history.

PSEUDONEWS

September 9, 2001
Frenzy by the Media, Not the Sharks

The governor and other officials have complained that the frantic media coverage of shark attacks is scaring tourists away from Florida.

To this charge, we must plead no contest.

Every summer sharks bite people, and every summer we pump the story as if it's something new and extraordinary. We're really not that lazy, we're just bored.

Traditionally, this is the slowest time of the year for serious news, so journalists are on the prowl for something juicy and hair-raising.

At the risk of overstating the obvious, let's just say we're suckers when it comes to wild critters—especially critters with teeth. Take alligators. They aren't rare, elusive, or cunning. They're big, pea-brained, and ubiquitous. Yet local TV stations will use any cheap excuse to run alligator footage. The stories tend to fall into three categories:

a) Gator in sewer drain.
b) Gator under neighbor's car.
c) Gator in pond behind the condo.

It must seem like the TV folks are trying to insult your intelligence by passing this stuff off as news, but don't take it personally. Most journalists in Florida come from places that don't have large predatory reptiles, so they get a little carried away. You'd probably see more gator stories if only they'd bite more people, but they won't. They'd rather eat garfish.

Which brings us to sharks. As inconceivable as it might seem, your average journalist knows even less about sharks than he or she does about alligators. This is evident from the way they scramble for the satellite truck every time some nitwit nails a dead hammerhead up on the board at the charter docks.

There's no reason to kill such a fish except to get your big fat face on television or in the papers, and it seems to work. Last week, an eight-foot shark that was caught in California somehow made the local news in Miami, where eight-foot sharks are about as unusual as two-legged chickens. The public's fearful fascination with sharks is matched only by the media's goggle-eyed gullibility. Hype is the inevitable result.

In Florida, the typical victim is a surfer who gets bitten once on the foot or leg while paddling in turbid water. We're delighted to call these "shark attacks," even though it's a silly exaggeration. In such cases the shark isn't stalking humans; it's hunting bait fish. Upon realizing its mistake, the shark swims away, unaware that it will be starring in tomorrow's headlines. Meanwhile, the surfer gets stitched up and heads back to the beach.

Once in a while, a large shark attacks in the true sense of the word, and we've got a legitimate news story. That's what happened on Labor Day weekend off North Carolina and Virginia, with tragic outcomes.

The deaths of two swimmers should have put our minor, everyday shark encounters into perspective, but we weren't about to let that happen. Instead the incidents were treated as the grisly culmination of a season-long siege.

NBC opened its nightly news touting "The Summer of the Shark," a phrase poached from an earlier cover of *Time* magazine. The implicit message: Watch out, America— they're not just nibbling anymore!

Statistically, you've got a much better chance of being flattened by a beer truck on your way to the beach than you do of being bitten by a shark. It's also true that the frequency of shark attacks worldwide is down from last year's rate. We in the media have dutifully reported these facts, though not so prominently as to put a damper on the hype. Heck, two more weeks of summer, and we're back on gator duty.

Sharks might be bad for tourism, but they're good for the news business. They're also good for the helicopter business. All up and down Florida's shorelines, TV and police choppers are swooping low in search of the telltale sinusoidal silhouettes.

Some of the video has been impressive, too—large schools of lemon sharks, blacktips, and other species lazing along within a few hundred yards of popular beaches.

Let's be honest. Sharks have been migrating along these routes for millions of years, and the only thing new about the phenomenon is the presence of humans in helicopters.

But hey, isn't it more exciting than the rush-hour report from I-95?

December 30, 2001
Blame This Bad Reporting on "the Fog of War"

Slowly but surely, America is learning to laugh again.

Thank you, Geraldo. And thank you, FOX News, for sending him to Afghanistan.

Let's admit it. Ever since the Taliban crumbled and the bombing slacked off, television coverage of the war on terrorism has been grindingly monotonous. Lucky for us, Geraldo Rivera is on the scene. FOX lured the mustached dandy away from CNBC with the irresistible promise of a pay cut and a chance to be shot at during a live broadcast.

Upon arriving in the war zone, Geraldo breathlessly announced that he'd be carrying a gun at all times and that he personally would plug Osama bin Laden if the opportunity presented itself. During one satellite dispatch, Geraldo frantically ducked for cover, claiming a bullet had narrowly missed his noggin. Viewers were left to wonder whether it had been fired by an Al Qaeda sniper or a disgruntled member of Geraldo's own crew. In another memorable segment, our daring correspondent lithely descended a cave to hunt for signs of bin Laden, a search that die-hard Geraldo fans hoped would end at Al Capone's vault.

So far, though, the highlight of his Afghan adventure was an emotional report from the "hallowed ground" where three U.S. soldiers accidentally had been killed by an errant American bomb. Reported Geraldo: "It was just, the whole place, just fried really, and bits of uniforms and tattered clothing everywhere. I said the Lord's Prayer and really choked up."

One tiny problem: Geraldo wasn't anywhere near the site of the fatal bombing. He transmitted his story from Tora Bora, hundreds of miles from Kandahar, where the friendly-fire tragedy occurred.

This rather humongous factual error was pointed out in a critical article by David Folkenflik, the television writer for *The Baltimore Sun*. In response, Geraldo blamed "the fog of war." He said he had "confused" two separate incidents and actually had been at the scene where two or three Afghan fighters—not the American troops—had been killed. Unfortunately, that version of the story hasn't held up well, either. The Pentagon told Folkenflik that the friendly-fire deaths at Tora Bora occurred three days after Geraldo filed his initial report. Wrote Folkenflik: "FOX News did not have any explanation for how Rivera could have been confused by an event that had not yet occurred."

It's not the first time that Geraldo's credibility has been questioned, so he is well experienced at defending himself. "The time has come to stop the Geraldo-bashing," he fumed to *The Washington Post* and offered to resign if an independent panel of journalists found he had acted unethically. Of Folkenflik, Geraldo said: "This cannot stand. He has impugned my honor. . . . He is going to regret this story for the rest of his career."

You can understand why Geraldo's knickers are in a knot. If the *Sun* hadn't blown the whistle, nobody would ever have known that his dispatch from Tora Bora was crapola.

No good excuse exists. If the friendly-fire segment was deliberately staged, then Geraldo is a liar and fraud. If it was just a mistake, as he claims, then he's an even bigger bonehead than he has demonstrated in the past. This time he got everything wrong—the location, the identity (or even existence) of the victims, and the origin of the "tattered clothing."

No wonder he choked up over the Lord's Prayer. He was hoping for divine salvation.

Most network news operations would have been so humiliated by Geraldo's screwup that he would have been canned or exiled to some remote bureau where there was no hope of getting back on the air. FOX, however, is standing by its man. Calling the episode "an honest mistake," the network said: "Based on Geraldo Rivera's 30-year track record, FOX News has full confidence in his explanation and journalistic integrity."

Meanwhile, FOX hasn't told its viewers about the big bungle. A spokesman said there is no plan to broadcast an apology or a correction. And heck, why should they? It's not journalism; it's showbiz. NBC sent Jay Leno to entertain the troops. FOX sent Geraldo to entertain the rest of us.

Give him a gun, send him down a hole, and let the comedy begin.

We'll watch. We'll laugh. And when it's time to get serious, we'll change the channel.

February 8, 2004
A Parent's Guide to J. Jackson's Halftime Crisis

A Parent's Guide to the Janet Jackson Crisis: Questions that your children might ask and how you should answer them:

Besides her incredibly lame lip-synching, what exactly did Janet Jackson do that was so wrong?

She exposed a private part of her body on national television, with millions of kids watching.

Big deal. It was just a breast. Everybody's got 'em, everybody's seen 'em.

True, but Janet was still out of line. Some people find nudity offensive, even during halftime of a game in which grown men are cussing, spitting, and pounding each other senseless over a pigskin.

But remember that time you took us to some big museum to see all those old paintings and statues? Remember I counted 27 breasts on one floor?

Let me explain: That was art. This is flashing.

But don't they show worse stuff than that on those raunchy cable stations you and Dad watch late at night?

Whoa, that's different. Grown-ups are allowed to watch people peeling off their clothes on TV— Hey, how do *you* know what we're doing late at night!

Getting back to this Janet Jackson thing, why'd she do it? Didn't she know that impressionable kids like me could be traumatized for life?

It's called a publicity stunt. Sometimes when show-business people are trying to be noticed, they go for something really tasteless and pathetic.

Even when they know it's going to make people mad? I don't get it.

It's called desperation. Janet has a new CD coming out next month, and she's trying to sell zillions of copies and make tons of money. It isn't easy competing for headlines with a freakazoid brother who's up on felony charges.

So, what's going to happen to Janet now?

Oh, she'll probably sell zillions of CDs and make tons of money.

You mean her cheap publicity stunt could really work?

Sure. Janet might be tacky, but she's not stupid. She knew that flashing a Super Bowl audience would gain her more attention than anything else that happened on the planet last Sunday.

Something else actually happened that day besides the football game?

For starters, 109 innocent people were blown up by suicide bombers in Iraq. Of course, a massacre like that isn't nearly as much fun to show on TV as the digitally obscured breast of a fading pop singer.

This is confusing. If what Janet did was so bad, why do they keep replaying the videotape over and over again?

Hmmm, good question. Maybe they just want to give everyone a chance to see her performance and make up their own minds.

Oh, I'm so sure.

Okay, okay. The real reason they keep replaying the Janet clip is that the media has the judgment and maturity of a slobbering, hormone-crazed adolescent—no offense.

They go wild over a bare boob, a bare butt, a bare anything, especially if it belongs to a famous person.

Aren't they worried about upsetting the viewers?
Just the opposite. The TV industry learned long ago that many people who claim to be morally offended by something will tune in to watch it over and over again, if given the opportunity.

Wow, that's bizarre.
It's called hypocrisy, and actually, it's not so uncommon among grown-ups.

With all the terrible stuff going on in the world, I still don't understand why people are making such a fuss about Janet.
To you and your friends, hers might seem like just another celebrity breast, but for some adults, it represents a mountainous threat to decency, good manners, and core family values.

But what about that Nelly dude grabbing his crotch onstage? Nobody's complaining about that.
That's because compulsive crotch-grabbing has become a respected form of artistic expression, while baring a breast is still considered taboo. Hey, we've got to draw the line somewhere.

So, how can I tell if I've been corrupted by Janet or not?
Don't worry, we'll let you know. Any more questions?

Just one. It's about that weird, star-shaped thingie she had fastened on her you-know-what.
They're calling it a "nipple shield."

Cool. Can I get one?
That's it. You're officially corrupted.

February 6, 2005
Memo from Grandpa: Please Don't Eat Worms

I'm standing at the window of the hospital nursery gazing at you, nine pounds and four ounces of snoozing pink innocence and boundless possibility.

Naturally it's my hope that you grow up to be happy, caring, generous, productive, principled, and unselfish. Your parents will have much to say about that, and there's no doubt they'll steer you wisely through childhood, as they are doing with your brother and sister. Like most mothers and fathers, they're reluctant to risk dampening their children's aspirations by heaping too much grim reality upon them too soon. This is a worthy and loving instinct.

However, being a grandfather invests me with a cranky candor that you may have to indulge from time to time as you grow older. We might as well begin now.

The world into which you have so hungrily arrived is a complicated, troubled, and sometimes heartbreaking place. You were fortunate to have been born in the richest and most tolerant country, though it's far from perfect. You'll get a chance to make it better, and I hope you do.

Waiting down the road are opportunities so plentiful and varied as to throttle the imaginations of those of us born in the '50s. The choices you make ought to be yours alone, but it would be baloney for me to say that I'll be bursting with pride no matter what you do.

Example: While flipping TV channels the other night, I came upon a program called *Fear Factor*. Believe it or not, the show features young men and women swallowing live worms and repulsive parts of dead animals—the ultimate goal being to get famous and win a wad of cash.

You will learn that this sort of witless self-degradation

is what passes for entertainment in some parts of modern American culture.

Surely the parents (and grandparents) of *Fear Factor* contestants never dreamed those kids would someday show up on national television with cow entrails dangling from their expensively straightened teeth, but there you have it.

That's what I mean about choices. When I was growing up, it wasn't nearly so easy to make an ass out of oneself in front of millions of people. Today almost anybody can do it. It's practically an industry.

For what it's worth, it would be just fine with me if your ambitions led you in other directions. I could coast happily into old age knowing that you never groveled in Donald Trump's boardroom or chose your fiancée from a gaggle of strangers on the lawn of a French castle.

A few weeks ago, something called a tidal wave smashed into the coasts of Asia and Africa, killing more than 160,000 persons. It was a horror that you have no reason to contemplate at your tender age. But here's what happened afterward: Millions and millions of people around the world reached into their own pockets and sent whatever money they could afford to help the survivors of that tragedy. And thousands more — nurses, doctors, rescue workers, volunteers — hopped on planes and flew to lend a hand. I couldn't tell you the names of these people because they didn't do it in order to become celebrities or win a prize. They did it because they were needed and because it was decent and humane and right.

Now, I'm not suggesting that you can't gobble live worms on TV and still be a good person. I'm just asking you not to be fooled into believing that sort of thing is remotely important, no matter how much attention it gets.

I've spent most of my adult life writing about screwups, the usual flaws being greed, arrogance, and stupidity. I've

reported on crooked lawyers, doctors, cops, pro athletes, cler-
gymen, journalists, and, of course, politicians.

Any one of those callings would be fine, if that's where
your passion and talents lie. No matter what you eventually
decide, the best way to stay out of the headlines is to be hardworking and honest. Sounds simple, but you'll be surprised at
how many people never quite grasp the concept.

Counting you and the other babies in this nursery, there
are now about 6.3 billion human beings on the planet. I'd
be lying if I said we've taken good care of the joint, because
we've trashed it. I hope that your generation will do better. I
would've liked to take you hiking or fishing in some of the
cool places I knew as a kid, but they are mostly gone now,
replaced by shopping malls and subdivisions. You might want
to spend some time fighting to prevent such mistakes from
happening again, for the day when you have kids of your own.

It seems silly to be laying all this on you now, when your only
worldly concern is scoring a dry diaper and some warm milk.

I trust that your father will spare you from this column
until you're much older and well on your way.

I'm not too worried. After all, your dad turned out just fine.

And if he ate any worms, he was smart enough not to
broadcast it.

June 19, 2005
With Michael Acquitted, We'll Have to Settle for Real News

I read the news today, oh boy.

No more Michael Jackson trial.

What do we do now? The King of Muscle Relaxants has
floated back to Neverland, and the rest of us are stuck here in
the real world. You know what that means: real news.

It's scary. There were 2,200 journalists credentialed to

cover Michael's trial, and now they've all got to find something else to do. Some of them will stumble into real stories that actually affect the lives of their viewers and readers. It's inevitable.

All those acres of newsprint and eons of TV time devoted to the Jackson trial now must be filled with something else. Sure, there's always Brad and Angelina or Tom and Katie. But they make a red-carpet splash, and then they're gone. Before you can say Kim Jong Il, the grown-up headlines start scrolling back through our lives.

Michael, you've no idea how much you'll be missed. You kept us so blessedly distracted from the serious events of the world. Every evening we could safely switch off our brains, sit back, and enjoy the freak show from Santa Maria.

Oh, how the fans would shriek when you emerged from that black Suburban—you in that wine steward's vest and the armband and the dragonfly shades. Having a bodyguard carry your umbrella was delicious camp, Mary Poppins with a concealed-weapons permit. And that morning you showed up in pajamas! Priceless.

But now the circus is winding down. The talking heads on the networks have run out of jurors and lawyers and lawyers pretending to be experts. It's gotten so pathetic that Geraldo is interviewing himself.

And the news, Michael—talk about a bummer.

Five more U.S. Marines got blown up in Ramadi, which is a city in western Iraq. Another roadside bomb, the Pentagon says. That's 1,705 U.S. troops who have died since the war began. They printed the total in the newspaper. It made me sick to think about.

What else? Oh yeah, those wacky Iranians have admitted they've been messing around with plutonium. Apparently, they're working on a nuclear device, which is just what the world needs.

Then there's some awful story about the Taliban—remember them? Well, it turns out that we didn't come close to wiping out all of those creeps when we bombed Afghanistan. A Taliban gang broke into a medical clinic in Kandahar and murdered a doctor and six assistants. Later, the leader of the party went on TV to assure all aspiring suicide bombers that Osama bin Laden is alive and well.

So, if you're a jihadist, the news isn't all bad.

Likewise if you're a tobacco tycoon. The Bush administration just ordered the Justice Department to whack $120 billion off the government's settlement demand in its case against cigarette makers. An early Christmas present for Joe Camel, I guess.

See, Michael, you can't bail on us now. Don't disappear behind those gilded gates and leave us out here twisting in the unsurreal world.

Remember what happened after the O. J. Simpson trial ended, when the country spiraled into a mass depression? Reporters stared emptily at their notebooks; joke writers for Leno and Letterman were put under a suicide watch. For nearly three dismal years, there was nothing to talk about except important stuff, like soaring health-care costs and welfare reform and the genocide in Africa.

But then came Monica Lewinsky, and it was showtime—sex in the White House! Once again we were a nation intellectually at peace, blissfully obsessed by scandal. That's why we're begging, Michael. As arduous as the trial was for you, it was an opiate for the rest of the country.

Think of what you spared us. Every day for three months, 2,200 reporters who could have been digging up serious stories elsewhere were instead camped out with the tabloids at the courthouse. No case could have been more insignificant to our everyday lives, our well-being, or the future of the planet—which is why we couldn't get enough of it. We're hopelessly, hungrily hooked on squalid spectacle. We crave the inane and irrelevant. It's our national dope; a legal way to stay stoned.

So, what depressing headlines are we left with today?

Body counts from Baghdad. The murder trial of a senescent ex-Klansman. Terri Schiavo's autopsy report.

O, where art thou, Macaulay Culkin? Whither goeth Tito and La Toya?

You might be a free man, Michael Jackson, but the rest of us are prisoners of reality.

Come back soon. Before the civil trial.

March 4, 2007
We Have Seen the Future, and It's Not Pretty

Now that Anna Nicole Smith is at long last departed from Florida, it's time to confront a simmering disgust over the media's salivating treatment of this dreary event.

Was the press coverage excessive? You bet.

Mindless? Inevitably.

Tasteless? Rapturously so.

But this is the *new* New Journalism, which is steered by a core belief that people would rather be smothered by seedy gossip about dead ex-Playmate junkies than be bothered with the details of North Korea's nuclear program. Like the Don Henley song says, crap is king. We are merely here to serve.

If you Googled Anna Nicole's name last week, you got 28.8 *million* hits—10 times more than that of Condoleezza Rice, who is only the U.S. secretary of state.

Debate all you wish about whether the public's interest is fueling the Anna Nicole overkill or the overkill is inflating the public's interest. The fact is, lots of people are hungry for the story—and not because they care one bit about this poor woman or her child. It's necro-tainment, that's all. The five-car pileup on the interstate. The stunt plane crashing at the air show. The train derailment caught on tape.

As soon as Smith's death became known, a small army of print and broadcast reporters swarmed to Fort Lauderdale, grabbed spots in the shade outside the courthouse, and began tracking the day's legal proceedings, which they dutifully regurgitated to their readers and audiences. Not since the O. J. Simpson murder trial have so much manpower and so many resources been thrown at a story of so little ultimate consequence to society.

Scoff, if you will, at the hyperventilating TV coverage of the Smith case. You think it's easy trying to make Anna Nicole sound important enough to justify three minutes and twenty seconds of airtime? That's a tough job, folks. Here you've got this deceased person who had no discernible talent whatsoever, a pitiable and often incoherent soul who perished in a shabby and unoriginal way. Yet day after day, you must with all seriousness face the cameras and present Smith's demise (and its messy, freak-filled aftermath) as a matter of pressing significance.

How does such a forlorn cliché become elevated to major breaking news? Many journalism students are probably pondering the same riddle. The answer isn't pretty. In a nutshell: Former *Playboy* centerfold turned rich widow turned reality-TV star suddenly dies, leaving an infant of uncertain paternity and a potential fortune up for grabs.

Story-wise, the angles are beauty, sex, money, and greed—classic tabloid ingredients and now a premium formula for mainstream media. For a competitive industry that's fighting to maintain profit levels and market shares, covering Anna Nicole is relatively cheap and easy, a quick hit; modest investment, maximum return.

Another factor heightened the frenzy: She expired in South Florida, which in February is a dream destination for any journeyman reporter. Had Smith passed away at a Holiday Inn in Buffalo, the throng of invading media would have been much smaller—and far more eager to leave.

Now the circus shifts to Nassau, where visiting journalists face a dicey new challenge: how to conceal their windsurfing lessons and casino losses on their expense accounts. It's money that could be spent in pursuit of serious news in Darfur or Pakistan, or even back home, where there is likely some crime and corruption waiting to be exposed. But this is a new dawn for modern journalism. The smelly stuff that was once left to the capable vultures at the *Star* and the *Enquirer* is now front-page fodder in your hometown paper and the lead story on the six o'clock news.

Dead or alive, celebrities rule. And it's never been easier to become a celebrity.

Although the Anna Nicole blitz hasn't much illuminated or informed, neither has it been a total waste of time. For example, attentive readers and viewers picked up some helpful information about how quickly the human body decomposes, both before and after embalming.

CSI Miami, eat your heart out.

Don't make the mistake of dismissing the Smith story as an anomaly; it's a media watershed. If the death of a hapless, doped-up ex-model can knock two wars out of the headlines, there's no end to the squalid possibilities.

We have seen the future, and it's in the gutter.

November 29, 2009
Johnston's Fifteen Minutes Are Up

Times are hard, but the pathway to fame in America has never been easier.

No talent is required—you can go on a shooting spree, give birth to octuplets, or launch a homemade balloon from your backyard and tell the cops that your little boy is trapped inside. Gripped by a stubborn recession and war anxiety, Americans remain the world's most ravenous consumers of a celebrity journalism that features nitwits and naïfs over Nobel laureates.

Exhibit A is a person named Levi Johnston, who ascended to junior stardom by knocking up Sarah Palin's oldest daughter. He's not the first teenager who forgot to use a condom, but few others have milked their dumb mistake with such gusto.

There's Levi on CBS's *The Early Show*, ominously suggesting he knows dark secrets about Palin.

There he is being interviewed in *Vanity Fair* as if he were a matinee idol, and there he is again in the pages of *GQ*, diapering the new baby.

There he is on *Tyra* and *Larry King Live*. And there he is at the Teen Choice Awards, a hope-affirming presence for all young unwed fathers.

There he is again in a national TV commercial, breaking pistachio nuts while the announcer wryly says, "Now Levi Johnston does it with protection."

And finally, there he is in *Playgirl* magazine, displaying every part of his anatomy except the one that propelled him into the headlines.

The spectacle isn't entirely Levi's fault. He didn't set out to be famous, but last fall he suddenly found himself in the spotlight—presented to the world as the future son-in-law of the future vice president of the United States.

He was a popular kid, but he quit high school and had family problems, including a mother battling a drug habit. The McCain-Palin campaign dressed him up and gave him a prominent place next to pregnant Bristol at the Republican National Convention. The couple would soon be married, Palin announced brightly, although Levi's facial expression didn't exactly radiate serenity.

He and Palin's daughter both deserve some sympathy. The out-of-wedlock pregnancy was a potential embarrassment to the campaign, which had been working to portray Palin as a conservative Christian crusading for traditional family values. Levi and Bristol were given upright roles to play, and they hung in there until Election Day. Afterward, the wedding plans were scuttled, baby Tripp was born, and Levi says the Palins began to treat him coldly. Instead of going back to Alaska and politely fading away, he hired a manager-slash-bodyguard. This, of course, is the American way. Nobody settles for just 15 minutes of fame.

Obviously, it was explained to Levi that his marketability would be enhanced—and fame prolonged—if he could dish some dirt about Palin. It was a brand-new role, but he warmed to it. Levi now asserts that Palin isn't the all-American mom that she makes herself out to be—for example, she doesn't really cook much at home!

At first she wanted to hide Bristol's pregnancy, he claims, and adopt the child herself. Worse, he says, she sometimes referred to her own infant with Down's syndrome as "the retarded baby."

That Levi was saying such things wasn't nearly so disturbing as some of the media's reaction, which was to treat the kid like he was Ben Bernanke expounding on long-term interest rates. Even if Levi's stories are true, he isn't sharing them to save the country from a Palin presidency. He's hustling, period.

The irony is pungent. He owes his own overnight fame to the overnight fame of the woman he's bad-mouthing. They are forever joined as family by his fathering of a Palin, and are destined to orbit the tabloid universe in tandem.

Once Palin quit the governorship to give speeches and sell books, she refueled Levi's dubious celebrity. It's no accident that his *Playgirl* photo spread coincided with the rollout of her memoir. The snippy war of words benefits both of them. She sells more books, he gets more face time on television. What other kid from Wasilla ever heard himself called out on *Oprah*?

Certainly the media can be blamed for overhyping Levi, but he'd evaporate like a moose burp if the public quit paying attention. We are easily and shamelessly intrigued.

So, for all you Levi Johnston fans, here's the latest: While hanging out at Hollywood's trendy Chateau Marmont, he said he might soon be *Dancing with the Stars*, and he's also considering—hang on to your hockey sticks—a gig on *Survival*.

The networks say it's not true, but who are you going to believe?

A book deal can't be far off and, after that, maybe a reality show with Octomom and Balloon Boy.

Rock on, Levi. Give the people what they want.

December 14, 2009
What Was Tiger Thinking?

Rejected first draft of a statement by Tiger Woods prepared for his website.

Two weeks ago on this page, I apologized for my personal transgressions and pleaded for the media to give me and my family some privacy.

Who was I kidding?

Now I've got helicopters buzzing my house, paparazzi staking out the gym, and even that dog Letterman is making fun of me. Each day some new babe is holding a press conference or selling her story to a tabloid.

Clearly, I need a new public relations strategy. Maybe the time has come to be totally honest and set the record straight.

To all the women who claim to have had wild sex with me: Enough already! I give up. There are so many that my lawyers can't sort out the real girlfriends from the phony girlfriends. I suppose it's possible that I slept with all of them, but I honestly don't remember. That Ambien—it seriously kicks butt.

But hey, I'm not blaming drugs. Whatever happened in all those hot tubs and elevators was my fault and mine alone. I'm basically just a hound, okay? Another sex-crazed jock who can't say no when the opportunity presents itself.

Anybody who grows up hitting a thousand golf balls a day never dreams of becoming a sex magnet for hotties. Let's face it, the PGA ain't exactly the NBA.

But now I've hurt my family and messed up my life, and somehow I've got to make things right. Instead of hiding out like a billionaire coward, I'm going to man up.

Concerned fans have been flooding my website with

e-mails, and I'd like to candidly answer a few of the most frequently asked questions.

John F., in Akron, writes: "Dear Tiger, what exactly is a
VIP club hostess?"

Well, John, VIP club hostesses are gorgeous single women
who work at fancy nightclubs where ordinary mokes like you
can't get past the front door.

But that's a good thing, because these slinky vixens would
only seduce you and promise not to tell a soul and then call
your BlackBerry in the middle of the damn night and wake
up your wife and . . .

Anyway, stay away from those hostesses!

Rick K., in Phoenix, writes: "Dear T.W., what really happened the night you crashed your Escalade?"

Dude, I don't remember anything except the sound
of breaking glass and then somebody hollering at me in
Swedish.

Louise W., in Orlando, follows up: "But why wouldn't you
agree to be interviewed by the Highway Patrol?"

Good question, Louise. For days after the accident, I
wasn't even able to speak. When my SUV struck that tree, a
three-iron must have fallen out of the branches and crashed
through the windshield and smashed me right in the mouth.

It's possible, right?

Mary M., in Atlanta, writes: "Dear Tiger, is it true that
you're losing sponsors because of the scandal?"

That's absolutely false! All my corporate sponsors are
loyally supporting me, including that big sports equipment
company, the razor company, and the high-energy beverage
company. I'd mention them all by name, but they've asked
me not to do that (or be photographed using their products)
for at least the next six months. Their lawyers have been very
nice about it, though.

Jerry L., in New York, writes: "Dear Mr. Woods, I was shocked by the explicit text messages that you exchanged with some of your girlfriends. What do you have to say to all your disappointed fans?"

Look, Jer, I'm not perfect, and I'm obviously not as smart as everyone thought.

None of my cool buds like Jeter or Jordan ever explained to me that text messages just sort of float around cyberspace forever. Is that the scariest thing you ever heard?

No wonder I've got insomnia.

Tanya L., in Las Vegas, writes: "Hey, Tiggy, remember me from that time in the penthouse at Caesar's when—"

Nice try, Tanya. Or whatever your real name is.

Mike G., in Miami Beach, writes: "Dear Wood Man, you are my hero! I mean, like, porn stars? Seriously?"

Whoa, Mike. They didn't tell me they were porn stars. They said they worked for Cirque du Soleil. I guess all those dragon tattoos should have tipped me off.

Tony R., in Pebble Beach, writes: "Dear Tiger, I can't hit a downhill bunker shot to save my life. Should I switch to a 60-degree wedge?"

Stick with your 56-degree, Tony, but play the ball in the center of your stance with the clubface slightly open.

And by the way, God bless you for asking.

April 30, 2011
The Donald Makes (Almost) Humble Speech

Rejected first draft of Donald Trump's final announcement about his political intentions in 2012.

First let me say how proud I am of myself for heckling Barack Obama until he produced the "long form" of his birth certificate, something no white president managing two wars and a budget crisis has ever been asked to do. At long last, the national debate can move on to other idiotic conspiracy theories, which I may or may not exploit to boost my TV ratings.

Tonight, though, belongs to the 50 billion Donald J. Trump fans who've tuned in to see the season's last episode of *Celebrity Apprentice*. To all my fellow Americans watching at home, and to all of you gathered here in the boardroom, the waiting is over.

[Pause for spontaneous applause from studio audience.]

Before I reveal my decision about whether or not to seek the presidency of the United States, I want to say a few words to all those pundits and bloggers who've been viciously attacking my integrity during these last few weeks.

To start with, I'm not a racist.

What I am is an egotistical gasbag who will say or do anything for attention. There's a big difference!

Just because I needlessly insulted a black president and fired La Toya Jackson (and, okay, Dionne Warwick), that doesn't make me a racist. I fired Gary Busey, too, didn't I? And he's as white as they come.

Other critics have questioned my truthfulness regarding my enormous, mind-boggling wealth. It's true that on occasion I have exaggerated my net worth by a few billion dollars, and also perhaps overstated my stake in certain high-profile real-estate projects.

Does that make me a liar and a poseur? No. It makes me a guy who talks big, and that's just what this nation needs: more bigheaded white guys talking big.

Now for the announcement that all of you are awaiting: After consulting with my family, my political advisers, and of course my close personal friend Martha Stewart, I've reluctantly decided not to seek the Republican nomination for president.

[Dramatic pause for a collective groan of disappointment from the audience.]

Let me give you my reasons for this very difficult decision.

Ever since I braced President Obama about his birth certificate, I've been hounded by the media to produce my own birth records (which is fine), my tax returns going back five years (which I'm looking for), my contract with NBC (which I've misplaced, though I'm pretty sure it's in my golf locker down at Mar-a-Lago), a list of all current corporate holdings and mortgage positions (like I keep track), and a sworn affidavit from my hairstylist stating that no orangutans were harmed during the weaving of my toupee.

Make no mistake: These petty demands are meant only to distract voters from the more serious issues I've raised, such as whether or not I'm richer than Mitt Romney (I am!).

Tragically, the frivolous and mean-spirited nature of the debate has taken a toll on my family, which is the second most important thing in my life. In good conscience, I can't put my kids through a grueling presidential campaign in which they'll hear their father maligned as a publicity-grubbing charlatan who couldn't find Yemen on Google Earth.

The truth is, I did find Yemen on Google Earth. It was Bahrain that gave me fits.

Don't get me wrong. I know I'd be a fantastic president, just like I'm a fantastic billionaire reality-show host.

Before the bloggers start in, let me set the record straight. My choice not to run for the highest office in the land has absolutely nothing to do with the fact that the job pays only $400,000 a year, which is, frankly, a joke.

When Donald Jr. told me what the president's salary was,

I gotta admit, I thought he'd been spending a little too much time on Willie Nelson's bus.

[Pause for audience laughter.]

Just kidding. Willie's a close personal friend.

But seriously, can you believe that the most powerful guy in the free world gets paid a lousy 400 grand a year? The bat-boy for the freaking Yankees makes more than that!

I understand that by bowing out of the presidential race, I'm disappointing billions and billions of Americans who'd been counting on me to save the country. Two of them are sitting in this boardroom tonight. Meat Loaf, what can I say? I know I promised that you could be Secretary of Defense in the first Trump administration. And Lil Jon, you were my first choice to replace Bernanke at the Federal Reserve.

Gentlemen, you're both fantastic patriots and close personal friends of mine.

Be patient. Your time will come.

Meanwhile, to all the fans who've cheered for me on this brief but overhyped journey, all that's left to say is: I'm almost humbled.

God bless me, and God bless America. Good night.

[Remain seated for thunderous applause.]

June 4, 2011

Here's the Lowdown on "Weinergate"

Now comes before us in indignation one Rep. Anthony D. Weiner, Democrat from New York, who, through Twitter, launched an unseemly photograph to a female college student in Seattle.

Weiner, a feisty liberal who hopes to become mayor of New York, is an avid user of social networks on which he dispenses quips and commentary. He says he's the victim of a hacker who sent out a "gag photo" of a man sporting a suggestive bulge in his underwear. In the lofty vernacular of our times, this is called a crotch shot, also known as a Favre.

Weiner vigorously denies tweeting the waist-down picture and says he has never met or spoken with the young woman who received it. The woman says the same thing. Yet "Weinergate," as the bloggers have tagged the scandal, refuses to go away. Here's why: When asked about it last week, the congressman stated that he couldn't say "with certainty" whether or not it was his crotch in the picture.

This raises, so to speak, a couple of possible scenarios. Perhaps Weiner is photographed so often from the waist down that he can't recall all the different pictures. Or perhaps the snapshot in question was taken from an angle that makes it difficult for him to identify himself in bedroom lighting.

For whatever reason, the congressman isn't sure if it's him in the wayward tweet. Most folks caught in the same predicament would know at a glance. Unless you're a Calvin Klein model, a porn actor, or a rock star, you can probably count on one hand the number of times somebody aimed a camera point-blank at your groin.

Back in 1971, the Rolling Stones released a classic album called *Sticky Fingers*. The jacket art, conceived by Andy Warhol, was a pair of jeans with a zipper that really unzipped, revealing a photograph of a male torso in tight white briefs.

The rumor was that the man posing for that photo was Mick Jagger, the band's lead singer. That wasn't true, but nonetheless, many album covers were ripped open on the shelves of record stores by young female fans who lusted for a peek.

It's safe to say that a different sort of frenzy has been stirred by the alleged crotch shot of Congressman Weiner. In an interview with CBS News, the most he would say is "The photograph does not look familiar to me."

Not exactly a blistering denial.

In a stab at humor, he also alluded to his friend Jon Stewart's joke that the tweeted picture featured such a robust weiner that it couldn't belong to Weiner.

As this is being written, the congressman still hasn't settled the debate over whether or not it's him in his skivvies. Obviously, there's no law against photographing yourself in underwear or having a friend do it. For a public figure, however, the dumb thing is to send out such an image electronically, or to leave it in a computer file that could be hacked. Yet brainless indiscretion does seem to be trending.

In February, another New York congressman, Rep. Chris Lee, resigned after it was revealed that he had e-mailed a suggestive photo of himself to a woman he'd contacted on Craigslist. In his creepy self-portrait, the married Republican lawmaker was posing shirtless and flexing his muscles.

Most infamously, NFL superstar Brett Favre got in trouble for sending inappropriate texts and voice mails to a woman who worked for the New York Jets while Favre was the team's quarterback. Included in his Neanderthal seduction efforts was a graphic picture he'd taken of his locker-room pride and joy, a gesture that failed to impress the young lady and also was likely not a big hit with Mrs. Favre.

It's common for men to behave like knuckle-dragging morons, but cyber-technology is presenting new opportunities for self-humiliation and disgrace. Tiger Woods, who had no qualms about sending raunchy texts to the women he was boinking, was unaccountably flabbergasted, stunned to learn that some had archived these messages and shared them with others.

Rep. Weiner was known as a popular bachelor until last year, when he married a longtime aide to Hillary Clinton. It's possible that the disputed close-up was taken by Weiner himself, or a past girlfriend, or even his wife. Or maybe it's not even his personal junk in the photo, which would leave the mystery of how it got posted on his account with yfrog, an image service affiliated with Twitter.

If the congressman is being truthful when he says he didn't send the picture, the story is worthwhile only as a lesson to all prominent persons who occasionally get stupid with their smartphones.

Spare us, please, from your homemade crotch shots.

The delete button is your friend.

July 9, 2011
Casey-Mania and the Talking Heads

A true headline among the flurry of stories posted on Yahoo! following the Casey Anthony verdict: "Kim Kardashian Weighs In."

It's fairly horrifying that anyone gives a rat's ass about Kim Kardashian's take on the Anthony case. On the other hand, she couldn't be more clueless than some of the motormouths who landed TV gigs as "legal experts" during the trial coverage. Never have the airwaves and bandwidths of this country been so clogged with gasbags posing as seasoned courtroom veterans, or lightweight has-beens seeking to jump-start their careers.

High on Casey-mania, cable networks such as HLN were frantic to fill airtime with talking heads, and by the end of the trial, you wondered if they were just yanking random lawyers out of the hallways and shoving them in front of the camera.

The prevailing tenor of the coverage, embodied by Nancy Grace and others, was that Anthony was guilty as sin of killing her daughter, Caylee. This wasn't an unreasonable view, considering Anthony's many lies, her busy social life after Caylee's disappearance, and the circumstantial evidence compiled by prosecutors. Despite the acquittal, there remains no plausible set of circumstances to explain Caylee's death that would not directly and criminally involve her mother.

So what went wrong with the jury? Nothing.

The public's expectations were jacked up by all the TV yakking about this dreadful crime and the train wreck of a mom accused of committing it. With some sharp exceptions, like Jeffrey Toobin of CNN, most of the "legal experts" continued shooting from the lip, feeding the hype.

But here's what smart trial lawyers knew from the beginning: Proving Anthony guilty of first-degree murder would be very difficult.

In the shell-shocked outcry last week after the verdict was announced, many were comparing the surprise outcome to that of the O. J. Simpson murder trial. The truth is, the Simpson prosecutors had much more evidence to work with, a veritable gold mine. They had a cause of death. They had a time of death. They had blood evidence, DNA, gloves, and footprints. They had two intact bodies and an actual crime scene. And still they lost the case.

Because it took so long to find Caylee's remains, Anthony's prosecutors couldn't tell the jury where, when, or how she had died. Duct tape on the skull, chloroform residue in a car trunk—that's enough for a theory, but it's not a smoking gun. Then there was the question of motive. For any experienced homicide detective, the Simpson crime scene had jealous ex-husband written all over it. But in the Anthony trial, jurors were asked to believe that this woman murdered her daughter simply so she could go out partying with her peeps. Sicker things have happened, but it's a tough sell without credible witnesses who heard Casey say she wanted her daughter dead.

Given what they had to work with, prosecutors did a solid job. Obviously, so did Jose Baez, the much maligned lead defense lawyer for Anthony. It's funny to see the so-called experts backpedaling in their estimation of both sides now that the case is over.

Shortly before the verdict came down, one row of TV legal eagles sat there predicting that the prosecution would be helped by the fact that most of the jurors were women, and women would be tougher on Anthony because of the nature of the crime.

So much for that bit of wisdom.

Watching a trial on television isn't the same as watching it from the jury box, where there's no background commentary or dramatic theme music during the breaks. However, smart lawyers and judges will tell you that a different jury could have just as easily convicted Anthony, just as a different jury could have convicted Simpson. That's how it goes.

What happens next is more predictable: Casey Anthony enters the low realm of celebrity. She'll get a ghostwriter and do a bestselling book and possibly have her own reality show. On the advice of her attorneys, she will either find Jesus or volunteer to work with abused kids. She will be strongly counseled not to start dating Alex Rodriguez or Charlie Sheen.

And at some point, she'll sit down with Diane Sawyer

or Oprah, and we'll get to hear a brand-new version of poor Caylee's death.

Millions and millions of people will watch the interview, after which a group of big-haired experts will tell us what it all means. Don't be shocked to see a Kardashian on the panel.

PARTY WITH THE
FRINGE ON TOP

Fringe Embraces "Martyr"

The man who did more damage to the anti-abortion cause than anybody in history is at peace with himself. Paul Hill, sitting on Florida's Death Row, says he's glad that he murdered an abortion doctor and would do it again.

Fortunately, he'll never get the chance. He's scheduled to die on September 3.

Opponents of capital punishment are asking Gov. Jeb Bush to halt the execution because it could make Hill a martyr to pro-life extremists.

Crackpot websites are hailing him as a patriot and a hero and warn that his death will bring bloodshed to other abortion providers, judges, and politicians. Last week, single rifle bullets were anonymously sent to prison officials, Attorney General Charlie Crist, and the judge who sentenced Hill.

Here's what brave Mr. Hill did to earn his martyrdom: On July 29, 1994, he carried a loaded shotgun to the Pensacola Ladies Center and blasted Dr. John Britton; his driver, retired Air Force Lt. Col. James Barrett; and Barrett's wife, June. Barrett, 74, and Britton, 69, died.

If mowing down senior citizens with a 12-gauge doesn't seem especially courageous or noble, remember that Hill was only following God's orders. That's what he said, anyway.

At trial, the former Presbyterian minister sought to portray his actions as justifiable homicide committed on behalf of the helpless unborn. The judge nixed that defense, noting that the operations performed by Dr. Britton were legal.

A Panhandle jury wasted no time convicting Hill, and mainstream anti-abortion groups wasted no time renouncing his crimes. Still, the assassination was a nightmare for a political movement that has claimed as its moral cornerstone a reverence for human life. The overwhelming majority of Americans who oppose abortion take a similar view of murder, and a homicidal fanatic like Hill is the worst possible poster boy for their cause.

Not surprisingly, the freak fringe has embraced him. "God's prophet," enthused one Maryland preacher, while an anti-abortion newsletter called Hill "an authentic Christian martyr, whose death proves the government of the United States has been enslaved by the forces of Satan."

If these drool-flecked screeds sound familiar, it's because the news these days is full of instant martyrs. You hear the same righteous pseudo-religious tripe about the suicide bombers in Israel and Baghdad; about the dead Hussein brothers; about the 19 creeps who hijacked those jetliners on September 11, 2001.

You'll hear more if and when Osama bin Laden ever gets whacked—remember, he's only trying to save the Islamic world from us wicked Western devils. Like Hill, all wannabe martyrs claim to be true believers. And they all try to justify their cowardly deeds with selected quotes from holy books—the first refuge of hypocrites and the oldest alibi for slaughter.

In a letter to the *Herald*, Hill wrote, "Yes, the Lord is giving me a generous measure of peace and joy as I anticipate my departure. My confidence is not in anything that I have done, but in the righteous life and the substitutionary death of Christ on the cross."

Even as he plays the Jesus card, Hill concedes that "only a relatively small number of people" have voiced support for the Britton murder. Gee, what a surprise. Predictably, Hill's sparse following has found a nest on the Internet, where the dumb notion of mailing bullets to public officials first caught on. Evidently, some rare editions of the Bible now include The Book of Remington.

In one online diatribe, an anti-abortion activist even compared Jeb Bush to Pontius Pilate. At least one death message has been sent to the governor, who told the *Herald*: "I get threatened all of the time. The execution goes on as planned."

Ironically, Bush is a longtime opponent of abortion. He's also a supporter of capital punishment. Being simultaneously pro-life and pro-death isn't easy to explain, but plenty of conservatives—including the governor's older brother—take that position.

In Hill's case, the law is unambiguous about punishment. Bush would set a reckless precedent by sparing a cold-blooded killer out of sympathy for a cause, or out of fear that his execution might instigate more shootings. If, as Hill's supporters predict, his death touches off a new "torrent" of violence against abortion providers, the pro-life movement might never recover from the backlash. On both sides of both issues (abortion and capital punishment) there are lots of decent, thoughtful people who don't feel the need to shoot somebody to advance a viewpoint.

Paul Hill is no better than any common terrorist, pious, unrepentant, and blind to his own hypocrisy. The guilt-free inner serenity that he claims to enjoy is precisely what you'd expect from a malfunctioning moral compass.

Note: Paul Hill was executed by lethal injection on Sept. 3, 2003.

October 8, 2006
Foley Contrite, but Only After He Got Caught

New rule for all members of Congress: Keep your hands where we can see 'em.

In a dubious feat of multitasking, then-Rep. Mark Foley

engaged in online sex with a former congressional page in April 2003 while Foley was on the floor of the House of Representatives, preparing to vote on an appropriations bill for Iraq.

Afterward, Foley asked for a "good kiss good night," and suggested that the boy visit him over the Veteran's Day weekend. "We may need to drink at my house so we don't get busted," Foley chirped.

Now unmasked and disgraced, Foley has rabbited off to rehab, where he is said to be remorseful, shattered, etc. Meanwhile, his lawyer spins a woeful tale of an unnamed clergyman who supposedly abused Foley in his youth. Whatever. It's not as if the West Palm Beach Republican voluntarily marched forward and confessed to making lewd passes at high school boys. He got contrite only after he got caught.

Even if Foley really has an alcohol problem, which would be news to many of his friends, it doesn't alter the unforgivable fact that he used his position as a congressman to troll for teenage sex partners. A congressman who bragged about his high marks from the Christian Coalition and American Conservative Union, a congressman who co-chaired the caucus on missing and exploited children, railing against Internet pedophiles . . . Perfect cover for the secret Foley, who was sending out electronic messages asking, among other things, for a young male page to provide the measurements of his penis.

That's not a drunk talking. That's a predator.

Foley has disappeared into Detox Mansion, but no such refuge is available to the Republican House leadership. With each day's tawdry headlines, Speaker Dennis Hastert struggles to appear suitably shocked and disgusted, while clinging to his job like a bear up a tree. His credibility is zero, his memory worse than Condoleezza Rice's. Kirk Fordham, Foley's ex–chief of staff, says he warned the speaker's office three years ago that Foley was getting too chummy with the pages.

Hastert denies it. Three other top Republican lawmakers say they told him last spring about a troubling Foley e-mail. Hastert says his colleagues spoke not with him but with his staff and that nobody passed the information along to him. Either the speaker's lying or his staff is full of chowderheads.

The incident involved a 16-year-old page from Louisiana who was disturbed by chatty online messages from Foley that included a request for the boy's photo. "Sick . . . sick . . . sick . . . sick," the teen had typed in response. "Overly friendly" was how the congressman later described it.

You know—like when your neighbor's poodle gets overly friendly with your leg.

The page's parents complained to Rep. Rodney Alexander of Louisiana, who told Majority Leader Rep. John Boehner and New York Rep. Thomas Reynolds. All have said they informed Hastert, whose recollections might be less hazy if Foley were not a member of his own party.

Foley was eventually questioned by House officials, and he agreed to stop communicating with the page. Hastert said the matter was handled quietly because neither the page nor his family wished to publicize it.

In defending himself, the speaker noted that editors at two Florida newspapers—*The St. Petersburg Times* and *The Miami Herald*—knew the content of the 2005 e-mail and decided not to write anything. It wasn't a stellar moment for the *Times* or this paper, although nailing down the story would have been difficult—but not impossible—without the teen's cooperation.

Hastert or any of the GOP big shots who knew of the e-mail were in a better position to investigate; with a single call, they could have put the FBI on Foley's computer trail to find out if there was a pattern to his creepy correspondence. As it turned out, there was a pattern. The congressman (aka "MAF54") resigned abruptly after Brian Ross of ABC News confronted him with graphically sexual electronic messages that he'd sent to an ex-page in 2003 and 2004.

More such revelations are bound to seep out in the days ahead, which is grim news for GOP incumbents as the midterm election approaches. This, after all, is the party that has declared itself morally superior; the party that lectures all of us about conservative family values; the party embraced by the Christian right as God's political arm in America. The party that spent $47 million of taxpayer money investigating the Clintons, ultimately impeaching the president for lying about consensual sex with an adult woman who wasn't his wife.

How much will these pious stiffs spend to ferret out the truth about one of their own who sought out underage boys? Will they bring back Ken Starr to track down those on Capitol Hill who knew what Foley was doing?

The young page who received that request for a photo last year thought it was sick, sick, sick, sick.

But not sick enough to concern the Republican leaders who shrugged it off. They were waiting for something sicker, and now they've got it.

September 2, 2007
Sen. Craig Tells What Really Happened . . .

Rejected first draft of Sen. Larry Craig's press statement about his arrest in a restroom at the Minneapolis airport.

Ladies and gentlemen, thank you for coming out today.

I'm not.

Joined by my devoted wife, I'm here to assure the citizens

of the great state of Idaho that I am not gay and never have
been gay.

How do I know?

Because every week I answer a simple are-you-gay survey
that I clipped out of a reputable underground men's magazine and carry around in my very masculine rawhide wallet.

The survey questions are pretty easy: Can I whistle more
than three Broadway show tunes? Do I tint my eyebrows?
Can I make a quiche? Stuff like that.

The most points I've ever scored is 73, and you aren't officially gay unless you score 75 or higher. So there!

As an outspoken crusader for conservative family values,
I have extensively researched the gay lifestyle and trained
myself to identify its sinister operatives. I usually remain on
guard, but my concentration lapsed that fateful day in the
Minneapolis airport. Let me explain.

Yes, as the police report says, I peeked into an adjoining
stall in the men's room. That's because I thought I recognized the gentleman—he looked like a strapping young trout
guide who once floated the Snake River with me—and I
wanted to say howdy. That's the extra-friendly Idahoan coming out in me, but apparently, the rules are different in the
big city. The fellow rudely ignored me, so I sat down to take
care of business.

As the police report states, I did start tapping my right foot.
I have since come to learn that that is a common signal for
persons wishing to make sexual contact in public restrooms.
In my case, the explanation is totally innocent. There was
this song playing on my iPod—"Vogue," by Madonna (the
live version!)—and my feet just went crazy to the beat. Now,
I defy anyone, Democrat or Republican, to listen to that cut
(the drum work is absolutely fierce!) and not start to boogie.

And yes, as the police report alleges, my right foot veered

slightly under the divider and touched the foot of the gentleman who was in the next stall. Later, I found out that this is
another sign often employed between men trying to "hook
up." Who knew?

Back in Crested Butte, you might get your teeth knocked
out for playing footsies with another guy, but you wouldn't
get arrested and have your name splashed all over the headlines and end up as a joke in Letterman's monologue. Geez
Louise!

The police complaint goes on to say that I put my left
hand under the stall divider three times, making an overt gesture to the other fellow (who, unfortunately, turned out to be
an undercover officer).

Again, I have a simple explanation. There's a little-known
cowboy custom—even some cowboys haven't heard of it—that
says you always wave three times when saying goodbye to
strangers. Once more, my western friendliness got me into
trouble.

So why did I plead guilty to disorderly conduct if I did
nothing wrong?

I was tricked by those crafty big-city prosecutors in Minnesota. Not being a legal sharpie, I had no idea that pleading
guilty was actually the same as admitting guilt.

I apologize to my family, the voters of Idaho, and the
Republican Party, which needs another sex scandal like Lindsay Lohan needs another vodka.

Mark Foley was dumb enough to e-mail those congressional pages, and David Vittner, my Senate colleague from
Louisiana, was dumb enough to give his phone number to
that escort service. Me? I didn't tell anybody my real name
until after I was busted!

Back in 1999, when I still wasn't gay, I voted to impeach

Bill Clinton for lying about having sex with that intern (I forget her name, but she had killer hair).

At the time, I told Tim Russert of NBC that Clinton was "a nasty, bad, naughty boy" who deserved a spanking. I stand by those words, as weird as they might sound today. Clinton *was* a very naughty boy.

I'm not. I'm a hardworking senator who believes in traditional values—faith, family, and a strict justice system, except as it is applied to certain sitting members of Congress.

Standing humbly before you this morning, I can honestly say that I'm as not-gay right now as I have ever been in my whole life. In fact, I'm so not-gay that the gay community wants nothing to do with me. This silly Minneapolis restroom incident has been blown out of proportion so badly, and it's time to set the record straight.

Here's a promise to the good folks of Idaho: I am so not-gay that I will quiz myself every morning with that magazine survey and publish the results in the Congressional Record for all to see.

The day I turn gay, you will be the first to know.

Then you can spank me all you like. Please.

January 18, 2009
America Catches Up with Its History

In the spring of 2007, at a gathering of fewer than 100 people in Indian River County, the junior U.S. senator from Illinois stood up and talked about leading this country in a new direction.

The man was sharp and impressive, and I left that event feeling absolutely certain that he had no chance of winning the Democratic nomination, much less the presidency. No way, I said, will America elect a black man with a strange name like that. Not in my lifetime.

Being wrong isn't always bad. On Tuesday, Barack Obama will be sworn in as the nation's 44th president.

The fact is difficult to absorb for a white kid who grew up in the South—and don't let anyone tell you that Florida in the '60s wasn't the Deep South.

But the astonishment over what's happening in Washington this week goes beyond the breaking of racial barriers. On another level, Obama's ascent to the White House challenges the core skepticism of my generation, which we sometimes bear like a scar.

How did we become like this? It didn't happen overnight.

One day, when you're 10 years old, the teachers start crying and somebody whispers that the president got shot in Dallas.

A few years later it's Martin Luther King, Jr., and then Bobby Kennedy, and even though you're just a teenager, it dawns on you that your country can be a mighty dangerous place for leaders who dare to speak out for change.

That same year, voters choose Richard Nixon to be president because he says he has a secret plan to end the Vietnam War, the first in an avalanche of lies.

One day, a month before your high school graduation, you turn on the TV and see that four college students have been killed by the Ohio National Guard during a campus demonstration. These are American kids being shot by American troops, and now it dawns on you that your country can be a dangerous place for *anybody* who dares to speak out for change.

Later come the Watergate tapes, which confirm your darkest suspicions about Nixon and his goon squad. By the summer of 1974, when he was finally routed from the White

House, the country was desperately gasping for fresh air. Just as it is today.

America is exhausted, tapped out. The last eight years have felt like a hundred.

George W. Bush and Dick Cheney are leaving office with some of the lowest public approval ratings in the history of ratings. Somewhere, Nixon must be chuckling.

Now the nation turns, with hope, to Obama. In a recent CNN poll, a stunning 82 percent of Americans surveyed had a favorable opinion of the president-elect. That says as much about the country's punch-drunk psyche as it does about Obama's charisma. We know he's smart. We know he's a good communicator. Now we'd like to see some supernatural powers, please.

He should begin by rebuilding the U.S. economy, a flaming pile from top to bottom. Fix the banking system, which, under Bush, was allowed to gorge itself on flimsy debt. Then unfreeze the credit markets, clean up Wall Street, and revive the housing industry. As soon as possible, thanks. Then he should reform public education so that every teacher gets a decent salary and every student learns to read. Add these to the national wish list: energy independence, affordable health care for everyone, and an end to global warming.

Don't forget Iraq. Obama should withdraw U.S. forces swiftly and responsibly, while making sure that decades of sectarian atrocities are forgotten and all ancient hatreds set aside, so that the whole place doesn't erupt in civil war as soon as we're gone.

Then it's on to Afghanistan, where the new president should shut down the opium trade, neutralize the Taliban, and track down Osama bin Laden before he dies of old age.

The situation in Gaza is a bloody nightmare, but with

the right kind of persuasion, Obama should be able to bring Hamas and Israel together. Never mind that each side is a sworn mortal enemy of the other.

Then there's Iran, Russia, the narco-war in Mexico . . .

Whew.

When Bush took office, the economy was purring, the national budget showed a surplus, and we weren't at war with anybody. Those aren't conditions in which voters tend to act boldly, and a candidate like Obama probably couldn't have won the White House in 2000.

It took a total meltdown of confidence, a shattering of trust in our leadership, to bring such a long shot to the highest job in the land. Obama is inheriting problems so dire and tangled that they practically defy comprehension.

Despite the odds, lots of Americans are optimistic and even excited about the prospects of this new presidency. Among those are many in my generation, who once thought we knew better than to tie our hopes for this country to the voice and vision of one man. But it's not a bad feeling.

October 31, 2009
Dear Sarah: Keep Up the Great Writing!

Confidential response of Sarah Palin's book editor to the first draft of her upcoming memoir, Going Rogue.

Dear Sarah,

Thank you for turning in the manuscript so quickly. I thought only Stephen King could crank out 400 pages in four months! Seriously, there's some terrific material here, and all of us at HarperCollins are thrilled to be publishing your life story.

Before we move ahead, the fact-checking department has

asked me to pass along a few notes and comments that may require some revisions on your part.

1. Eric Clapton spells his last name with a C.

    More significantly, his publicists tell us that you were not the inspiration for "Layla" and that he doesn't recall ever having an affair with you. Is it possible you've got him confused with another rock star?

2. The mainland of Russia is indeed visible from parts of western Alaska during favorable weather conditions in the Bering Strait. Considering the ridicule you endured over this issue during the campaign, your desire to set the record straight is understandable.

    Still, 78 pages is a big chunk of the book. Perhaps it's possible to deal with the "I can see Russia" controversy a bit more succinctly.

3. Our researchers can find no evidence that Tina Fey belongs to the Taliban. Could you send us the sourcing for that reference?

4. John McCain's campaign staff is vehemently denying the incident you describe in Chapter 13. Perhaps you could provide our legal department with the names of persons who actually witnessed the senator placing the duct tape over your mouth.

5. Even though you quit with 18 months remaining in your term, your achievements as Alaska's governor will be of great interest to your readers and political supporters.

    How about expanding that section of the book to a full chapter?

6. On page 107 of the manuscript, you describe a frisky

interlude with Todd as taking place on a John Deere Cyclone 340 snowmobile.

However, that particular model has been out of production for several years. Is it possible that you two were cavorting on a Sprintfire?

7. Our researchers can find no evidence that Katie Couric is secretly financing the Sunni insurgency in Iraq. Could you send us the sourcing for that reference?

8. Although the passage about moose shooting from helicopters is certainly provocative, perhaps it could be re-polished to focus more on your cooking recipes—which look very yummy, by the way—than on the preferred field techniques for skinning and gutting.

9. Our copy editors are still struggling to sort out the many colorful characters in your manuscript. In one chapter, the children are called Bristol, Piper, Track, Willow, and Trig, yet only 44 pages later, they appear as Caribou, Cessna, Herring, Juniper, and Scrod.

    Maybe you could check with Todd and get back to us on that.

10. "Mexican" is not a language (see manuscript page 188).

11. Our researchers cannot verify that David Letterman is "heavily involved" in the opium trade in eastern Afghanistan. Could you provide the sourcing for that reference?

12. The details of your high school basketball career are inspirational, but would it be possible to condense that section from three chapters to one? Just a thought.

13. John McCain's office says that it was the senator, not you, who came up with the "two mavericks" campaign theme. He claims you originally proposed a slogan saying, "One Creaky Elder Statesman, One Hot Young Maverick — but Don't Worry, Folks, She Knows CPR!"

14. Tony Blair was the prime minister of Great Britain. Tony Orlando is an American pop singer (see manuscript page 341).

15. Levi Johnston emphatically denies that Mitt Romney paid him to seduce and impregnate your oldest daughter. Furthermore, he claims that you personally offered him $50 to moon Joe Biden during the vice presidential debate.

    Our legal department has suggested removing any mention of this young man (including those beer-pong photos) from the manuscript. What do you say?

Finally, on a personal note, I'm sorry you're having so much difficulty reaching the ghostwriter we assigned to this project. After your first meeting, she left me a rather frazzled message saying she "needed to take a break and do some soul searching."

We've tracked her to a sweat lodge down in Taos, New Mexico, and I'm pretty confident she'll be back on the "Going Rogue" Express in no time.

Meanwhile, keep up the great writing, Sarah. We can't wait to read the finished book!

January 17, 2010
Robertson Again Blaming the Victims

It's no secret that the Rev. Pat Robertson is a yammering fool, but last week he hit a new low.

During a chatty sit-down segment of his television program, *The 700 Club*, the prominent Christian preacher offered his viewers a unique explanation of the terrible earthquake in Haiti: "Something happened a long time ago in Haiti, and people might not want to talk about it. They were under the heel of the French. Napoleon the Third and whatever. And they got together and swore a pact to the devil. They said, 'We will serve you if you get us free from the prince.' True story.

"And so the devil said, 'Okay, it's a deal.' They kicked the French out, the Haitians revolted and got themselves free. But ever since, they have been cursed by one thing after the other, desperately poor. . . . They need to have, and we need to pray for them, a great turning to God."

Robertson was referring to Haitian voodoo rites that were supposedly conducted before a slave uprising against French colonists in 1791. Why God waited more than 200 years to unload a natural disaster of such magnitude on an innocent generation of Haitians remains a question that perhaps God will answer for Robertson during their next private conversation.

It should be noted that Robertson's idiotic comment was followed by a promise that one of his organizations, an aid group called Operation Blessing, would send medicine and workers to Port-au-Prince to help in the relief efforts.

A spokesman for Robertson has since scuttled forward to insist that the famous televangelist—a stalwart of the Christian Coalition and founder of the Christian Broadcast Network— wasn't really saying that the earthquake in Haiti was caused by God's wrath. But that's exactly what Robertson was saying. It's what he always says when something bad happens.

If you buy the gospel according to Pat, the 9/11 terrorist attacks against the United States were divine retribution brought on by homosexuals, abortion activists, feminists, and the ACLU. The same sinners were to blame for Hurricane Katrina, or so proclaimeth the Rev. Robertson. When Israeli Prime Minister Ariel Sharon was felled by a stroke, it was God's way of punishing him for withdrawing from the Gaza Strip. Again, Robertson connected the Biblical dots.

In most advanced countries, a guy like this would have been laughed off the stage long ago as a bombastic fraud, and nothing he said would be taken seriously.

Until he made it big on television, he was just another sweaty faith healer, "curing" hernias, ulcers, and hemorrhoids in exchange for cash donations. Lord, does he hate to be reminded of those days!

Another touchy subject is his dismal record as a prognosticator. Robertson announced that the world would end in the fall of 1982, one of scores of loony predictions that have fizzled. Six years later, with doomsday apparently rescheduled, he ran for president and got stomped in the Republican primaries. But he didn't fade away. He just went back on TV and kept blurting the same outrageous, offensive crap.

Amazingly, he's never been disowned by the GOP leadership. Just the opposite.

In 2008, when presidential hopefuls were trolling for the votes of fundamentalist Christians, Robertson was courted avidly by Republican candidates. Mitt Romney thought he'd won the preacher's endorsement only to see Rudy Giuliani get the nod. The former New York mayor was so excited that he joined Rev. Pat for a big announcement at the National Press Club. The impact upon Giuliani's campaign was a feeble thud. If anything, Robertson's support probably lost votes for Giuliani in Florida, a state he'd counted on winning.

But you just wait. If Robertson still has a TV show in 2012, the candidates who are trying to sell themselves as "social conservatives" will come swooning again. And as before, they'll pretend they are in the presence of a true man of God, not a toxic flake.

Among Robertson's devout followers are some pathetic souls who actually believe his pronouncement that the Haitian people invited this disaster by swearing "a pact to the devil." Perhaps blaming the victims for some imaginary sin makes it easier for Robertson's audience to absorb the overwhelming images of suffering and desperation that now fill the airwaves and the Internet. Who knows.

Even as he sends help, Robertson somberly advises the Haitian people to make a "great turning to God." The country's population happens to be 80 percent Catholic, but not all Christians are equally precious in the eyes of Rev. Pat.

The man richly deserves to be ignored, but that can't happen until those who want to be president quit groveling for his worthless blessing.

May 23, 2010
Get Guv'ment Off Our Backs . . . but Not Yet

It's fashionable to be mad at the government these days, but many folks are unclear about how to join the movement.

The first step is to master the idiom of outrage. It's not just government, it's Big Government. Or even better: Big Guv'ment. Huge, clunky, intrusive, exorbitant—that's Uncle Sam. Get off our backs, get out of our lives, and let go of our wallets!

The sentiment has been around for 234 years, but never before did we have the Internet to make it feel so fresh and original. Every red-blooded patriot should aspire to a life that's more or less free of government, which apparently can't do anything right.

Let's begin with health care. President Obama should immediately abandon health-care reform and turn the whole confusing mess back over to the insurance companies, with no federal rules or supervision. Wouldn't that be swell? The problem with such a bold plan is Medicare, which funds critical coverage for many millions of older Americans. Technically, it's a humongous government program, one of the worst drags on the deficit. But if you got rid of it, lots of people who can't afford to pay for private insurance would grow sick and die, and a public uprising would took place. Even some crotchety Tea Partiers depend on Medicare. So, okay, leave that one alone. But otherwise, government doesn't know squat about health care!

Now let's talk about this so-called financial reform that the president keeps pushing. Big Guv'ment has no business meddling with our venerable Wall Street banks and brokerage houses, even though they brought the country to the brink of a catastrophic depression. Heck, everybody makes mistakes.

And why should the Federal Reserve set monetary policy when we've got all these sharp dudes at Goldman Sachs and AIG who have at heart only the best interests of ordinary citizens.

The only snag with banishing government completely from the financial sector is something called the Federal Deposit Insurance Corporation, or FDIC. At least 240 banks have gone belly-up since the financial crash, yet most depositors didn't lose a dime. That's because the mission of the FDIC is to guarantee that your savings are safe. True, it's another layer of federal bureaucracy, but many Americans would have been ruined without it. So, fine, don't touch the FDIC. Other than that, Mr. Obama, you let the bankers run the banks!

The same hands-off philosophy should guide our national

energy strategy—where does Big Guv'ment get off telling the oil and gas companies where it's safe to drill? Washington should get out of the way and let the energy industry police itself, because it has the very best expertise and technology . . .

Okay, bad example.

Then how about that pesky Food and Drug Administration, huh? Say your child comes down with the flu. Is it really necessary for government to hassle the pharmaceutical companies over which cough syrups are safe and which are dangerous?

Never mind—that's another not-so-great example.

Along those same lines, it's also probably not a terrible idea for U.S. Department of Agriculture inspectors to take a peek at the chicken and beef that are sold in our grocery stores, just to make sure they aren't crawling with salmonella or E. coli.

Because this is getting a bit confusing, let's recap: Government is totally inept, wasteful, and useless, with the possible exceptions of Medicare, the FDIC, FDA, and USDA. We might as well add the Coast Guard, which rescued hundreds of people during Katrina and is now scrambling to contain the BP oil spill.

Come to think of it, now would also be a foolish time to chop up the TSA, CIA, NSA, FBI, or any of our national security agencies. There are too many terrorists hell-bent on killing Americans, and—no offense—most local police departments aren't geared up to screen airline manifests or track Al Qaeda's cell-phone signals.

Oh heck, I just thought of another federal bureaucracy that seems to work pretty well: the National Oceanic and Atmospheric Administration. Without NOAA, we wouldn't know how large a hurricane was or where it was heading, which is fairly useful information here in Florida. With the storm season starting next month and the Gulf of Mexico turning black with crude, let's add NOAA to the not-so-worthless list, along with Medicare, the FDIC, FDA, USDA, Coast Guard, FBI, and so on.

As for the rest of Big Guv'ment, get your shiftless boot off our hardworking necks and let us be—at least until we're old enough for Social Security.

Then we'll tell you where to send the checks.

December 5, 2010
In a Giving Mood, but Only Toward Rich

Just in time for the holidays, Congress has terminated unemployment benefits for millions of out-of-work Americans. We're told this was done as an act of fiscal responsibility, to help prune the gargantuan national deficit.

It's somewhat revealing, then, to follow another big battle on Capitol Hill. This one centers on the so-called Bush tax cuts, which are due to expire at the end of the month.

Democrats want to keep the lower rates for all Americans except individuals making more than $200,000 a year and couples earning more than $250,000. Republicans want to extend the lower tax rates for everybody, including the wealthy—their most prized constituency.

The problem with the GOP tax plan is that it would add about $700 billion to the deficit over the next decade. A few years ago this would have been business as usual, because the Bush administration was printing money as fast as the Republican leadership could spend it. Now, prodded by the renegade Tea Party, guys like Mitch McConnell and John Boehner are born-again penny-pinchers. They've rediscovered the deficit and declared war.

Well, sort of.

A few hundred billion here, a few hundred billion there—no biggie, right?

Listen to this, from a recent column in *The New York Times*: "If there were such a thing as Chapter 11 for politicians, the Republican push to extend the unaffordable Bush tax cuts would amount to a bankruptcy filing." The writer is David Stockman, a former GOP congressman and Ronald Reagan's budget chief from 1981 to 1985.

Stockman says Republicans have abandoned their fiscal principles to embrace a policy that "has amounted to little more than money printing and deficit spending." He also chides McConnell for asserting that the richest taxpayers shouldn't be burdened with a relatively modest 3 percent rate hike to reduce the nation's public debt, which is approaching $18 trillion.

To some people who are suffering in the current economy—with the worst continuing unemployment in three decades—axing jobless benefits while prolonging a fat tax cut for the rich seems not only wrong but cruel. Even some who aren't suffering feel the same way.

More than 40 wealthy Americans—including some Google executives and Ben Cohen of Ben & Jerry's ice cream—have formed the Patriotic Millionaires for Fiscal Strength. On its website, the group has urged President Obama to end the Bush tax breaks for rich folks such as themselves: "For the fiscal health of our nation and the well-being of our fellow citizens, we ask that you allow tax cuts on incomes over $1,000,000 to expire at the end of this year as scheduled." Not all millionaires share such a bighearted view, but it's refreshing to hear from some who do.

Throughout the midterm campaigns, many Republican candidates were eager to spread the fiction that taxes had gone up under Obama and the Democrats, when the opposite was true. A sizable chunk of the Big Bad Stimulus program was a tax refund in middle-class paychecks, which many people haven't noticed because it has been spread out over time.

Another boilerplate lie was that Obama was scheming to do away with all the Bush tax cuts. In truth, under the Democratic proposal, 98 percent of taxpayers would continue paying at the lower rates. Only the wealthiest 2 percent would see their tax scale revert to pre-Bush levels, but that particular 2 percent is near and dear to the GOP.

The result, playing out now in Washington, is that Republicans are threatening to smother all legislation—from the nuclear arms control to food-safety precautions—until the Obama administration caves in on the tax cuts for the rich. Although the president is willing to compromise—raising the minimum annual income threshold from $250,000 to $1 million is one option—the opposition hasn't budged. McConnell insists that preserving the tax cuts for top earners will help invigorate the economy, a notion disputed by the nonpartisan Congressional Budget Office and discredited by events of the last three years.

In the interest of disclosure, I'm one of the fortunate taxpayers who will benefit nicely if the Bush rates are kept in place for those in the higher brackets. I don't donate to political parties or candidates, though it doesn't seem to matter. McConnell and his troops are fighting tirelessly to get me more money.

I suppose I should be grateful, but something doesn't smell right.

This month alone, two million Americans will see their unemployment paychecks stop, all in the name of cost-cutting for the good of the federal budget. Meanwhile, the so-called deficit hawks want to give away a total of $700 billion to folks like me, who can get along just fine without it. "Obscene" is the first word that comes to mind. "Sad" is the second.

Bad Photos Make for Bad Politics

Rejected first draft of a memo from House Speaker John Boehner to fellow Republicans following the embarrassing resignation of Rep. Christopher Lee of New York after he sent an inappropriate photo to a woman he met on Craigslist.

Dear Colleagues,

In light of recent unsavory events, I would like to review conduct guidelines for social conservatives, laboring as we do in the unforgiving glare of public scrutiny.

Needless to say, it is unseemly for any Republican member of Congress, particularly one who's married, to attempt to "hook up" with strangers on the Internet. That's what dark hotel bars are for, and I'm told there are many such establishments in the Capitol Hill area.

Remember, we are the party of family values, the party that spent a humongous pile of taxpayer money impeaching Bill Clinton because of his fling with a White House intern. We must not allow ourselves to wander down that same sleazy path—or at the very least, we must not allow ourselves to get caught.

Rep. Lee did the honorable thing by resigning, yet the damage to our cause has been done. So what lessons can we take from this incident?

First and most important: Never get anything on Craigslist except patio furniture, golf clubs, Super Bowl tickets, riding mowers, or snow globes.

If you belong to a social network such as Facebook, don't post any information or comments that might be misconstrued by your constituents or twisted into something sinister by your political enemies. As a further precaution, I advise you to unfriend anyone whose last names you don't know, especially if they are employed by an unlicensed massage parlor.

In the wake of this recent controversy, several House members have inquired about our policy regarding photographs. I would ask you all to go back and reread the Brett Favre memorandum that I sent out last fall. Obviously, Rep. Lee misplaced his copy.

Let me reiterate that it's perfectly acceptable to send out pictures of yourself to voters and campaign donors. However, you must always be careful to pose in a dignified manner— sitting at your desk, for example, or standing on the Capitol steps. Your facial expression should be one of pensive sobriety, as if you're contemplating how to repeal Obamacare and save this great nation from ruin.

For female members, a conservative dress or suit is fine for photographs; taupe is always safe. For men, the preferred attire is a navy blue coat jacket, a club necktie, and, of course, your American-flag lapel pin (with the stripes positioned horizontally, Rep. Quayle!).

Obviously, all body piercings and tattoos should remain out of sight.

One final point, and I can't stress this strongly enough: Republican House members should never, ever use their cell phones to photograph themselves shirtless, no matter how "hot" they think they look. In the event that such a revealing picture does exist, you are absolutely forbidden from e-mailing it to somebody you just met online. No exceptions!

That might sound harsh, particularly to those of you who've been putting in a lot of time at the gym. I understand that you're proud of your new buffed self. So, evidently, was Rep. Lee. But the sad fact is, in this time of brutal partisanship, nobody can be trusted to keep a secret. Whenever you put anything on the Internet, assume the content is being leaked to unscrupulous liberal bloggers who are eager to make us look like phonies and hypocrites.

For my part, I no longer go online to order my tanning goggles or even bootleg cartons of Marlboros, even though the savings were substantial and shipping was usually free. Such caution should govern all congressional e-mails, online conversations, tweets, and text messages.

In Rep. Lee's case, he represented himself to the woman on Craigslist as an unmarried person—"a very fit fun classy guy." He also lied about his age and claimed to be, of all things, a lobbyist (no wonder she lost interest!). Unfortunately, the one fact that Rep. Lee failed to conceal was his name, which is why our party now finds itself in this squeamish posture. Every sordid scandal like this makes it more difficult to achieve our mission of branding the Democrats as reckless, undisciplined, and unfit to lead.

But to all my fellow Republicans, I say this: Have faith. After all, we survived Larry Craig, Mark Foley, John Ensign, Mark Sanford, Mark Souder, David Vitter, and the rest. We'll survive Christopher Lee, too.

Be smart, be strong, and never, ever use your real name when trolling the Internet for hot monkey love.

In time, we will retake the moral high ground. We will rise up again.

Wait, make that "prevail."

August 21, 2011
GOP Attacks on EPA Ignore the Problem

Dutifully following their Tea Party scripts, most of the Republican presidential candidates have declared war on the Environmental Protection Agency. They claim that the economy is being smothered by regulations designed to keep our air and water safe. No iota of evidence is being offered, and in fact the record profits of big energy companies indicate a spectacular lack of suffering.

But listen to Rep. Michele Bachmann's promise to an Iowa crowd about one of her first presidential priorities: "I guarantee you the EPA will have doors locked and lights turned off, and they will only be about conservation. It will be a new day and a new sheriff in Washington, D.C."

Granted, Bachmann is a witless parrot who has no chance—absolutely zero—of being elected to the White House. But her hatred of the EPA is shared by Gov. Rick Perry of Texas, who is considered a GOP front-runner. Like Bachmann, Perry refuses to accept that global warming is real. He launched a lawsuit to stop the EPA from enacting rules to limit greenhouse gases from oil refineries, power plants, and other industrial sources.

Perry likes to whine that "EPA regulations are killing jobs all across America," a statement that draws more cheers in his native state than in the rest of the country. In fact, polls show that a large majority of Americans are worried about air and water pollution and hold a positive view of the EPA.

Nothing kills jobs like an environmental catastrophe, as the Gulf Coast gravely experienced during (and after) the BP oil spill last year. The true cost of that accident to the economies of Louisiana, Alabama, Mississippi, and Florida is probably incalculable, although surely many billions of dollars were lost. The cleanup wasn't perfect, but it's absurd to think that BP would have worked faster or more efficiently if the Obama administration and the EPA hadn't been leaning on the company, both publicly and behind closed doors.

Forty-one years ago the agency was formed, and for good reason: Toxins by the ton were being flagrantly pumped into this country's rivers, bays, and oceans, and blown through smokestacks into the air. People were getting sick and dying only because some companies were too greedy to spend money cleaning up their own mess.

The corporate mentality toward pollution has changed because the alternatives are heavy fines, criminal penalties, and savage publicity. A reminder of why we still need the EPA was last month's oil spill on the Yellowstone River, which affected ranchers, farmers, fishing guides, and rafting companies. It also occurred seven months after ExxonMobil insisted that its pipeline would never rupture because it was buried too deep.

Of all the reasons government exists, none is more crucial than trying to keep its citizens safe, whether from a terrorist attack, Wall Street's recklessness, or industrial poisoning.

Not surprisingly, surveys show that most Americans want their children to grow up drinking clean water and breathing clean air. How, then, to explain the radical hostility of Bachmann, Perry, Newt Gingrich, and some of the other Republican candidates?

First, it's about raising money. The petroleum and coal conglomerates are huge GOP donors, and they'd love to have a president who would gut the EPA.

Second, it's about politics. To win Republican primaries—the theory goes—a candidate must fire up the Wing-nut Right. The easiest way to do that is to brainlessly bash whatever government does. Perry specializes in this, even though almost half of Texas's vaunted employment growth has been in the public sector—government jobs, in other words. You won't hear the governor complain about the $200 billion that U.S. taxpayers pump into his state's economy annually for military bases and related industries.

One thing to emerge from the Republicans' attacks on the EPA is the early campaign path of Mitt Romney. Clearly, his strategy is to appear less loony and misinformed than his rivals. Romney says the EPA has an important role; furthermore, he has actually conceded that global warming is a fact. As governor of Massachusetts, Romney expressed interest in a carbon cap-and-trade program and proposed a plan to cut back on greenhouse gas emissions.

Predictably, with the primaries looming, Romney now says he opposes regulating carbon dioxide and other gases linked to climate change. As he and the other GOP candidates begin piling into Florida for the long campaign, pay attention to their rhetoric about the dreaded EPA.

The economy here would crumble if the environment were left unprotected. Florida can't survive without tourism, and tourism dies when tar balls and rotting fish turn up on the beach. What remains of the long-polluted Everglades would also be doomed without a federal regulatory presence, however cumbersome. Doomed, too, would be South Florida's chief source of fresh water, upon which business growth depends—not to mention the future of about eight million people.

Yet don't be surprised if Perry and Bachmann arrive here clinging to the Tea Party narrative that government oversight is inherently evil. They'd like us to kindly forget about that little mishap in the Gulf of Mexico last year, as well as other manmade though preventable disasters.

It's easier to ignore the past and stick to the script, especially if someone else is writing it.

October 2, 2011
All Aboard Herman Cain Bandwagon

An absolutely true news item: Herman Cain, former CEO of Godfather's Pizza, has won the Republican presidential straw poll in Florida.

My fellow Americans,

Welcome to the Herman Cain bandwagon!

All you devoted Tea Party folks know who I am, and know where I stand. Same goes for all the fans of my syndicated column and my commentaries on the FOX Business Network, as well as all the good God-fearing people at the Baptist church where I'm an associate minister.

But the rest of America is probably wondering: Who the heck is this Herman Cain, and how does running a pizza company qualify him to be president of the United States? What makes him so much smarter than Papa John or that super-rich dude who owns Domino's?

First thing you should know: Herman Cain isn't just about pizza.

I also worked for Coca-Cola and Pillsbury and supervised a whole bunch of Burger Kings. I've served on the board of Nabisco, Whirlpool, and even *Reader's Digest,* a solid conservative publication.

Not that I'm trying to downplay all those great years at Godfather's. Make no mistake: Pizza has been very good to Herman Cain. I can't think of a better background to prepare a candidate for the formidable and complex challenges of the modern presidency.

Imagine the Mideast, for example, as a large mozzarella pie with an extra-crispy crust. Each slice is loaded with different exotic ingredients, and occasionally, one slice clashes with the others to which it is geographically linked.

Let's say the pizza slice we call Israel is diced mushrooms and bell peppers. Perhaps Syria is bacon with pineapple chunks. Will there be harsh words and strife? It's inevitable.

Now, throw in Jordan (ham with kalamata olives) and Egypt (pulled chicken on spinach leaves) and of course Saudi Arabia (artichoke hearts, tomatoes, and ground lamb).

What you have, my fellow Americans, is a recipe for trouble.

Which is why we need a president who has firsthand experience in the delicate balancing and mixing of life's condiments. Let me say this loud and clear: Herman Cain is a man who can make pineapple chunks work with anything!

Now let's talk about our struggling economy. Again, you might be wondering how an executive career in food services translates to instant expertise on the global debt crisis, domestic tax policies, or Social Security reform. Don't forget that I was once chairman of the Federal Reserve Bank in Kansas City. I also single-handedly rescued Godfather's Pizza from bankruptcy, although I had to shut down more than 120 restaurants and fire a whole bunch of folks.

I don't deny saying that I'll turn America around the same way I turned Godfather's around, but naturally, the left-wing media has twisted this into something snarky. Of course you can't run the biggest economy in the world exactly the same way you run a pizza company. The secret to Godfather's resurgence was basic: More topping. The secret to saving America is equally simple: Less topping.

Imagine the federal budget in slices, and what do you see?

Cheese, my fellow Americans, a veritable mudslide of cheese.

Then, on top of all that goo, you've got a virtual mountain of pepperoni, jalapeños, prosciutto, capers, eggplant, onions, salami, and anchovies. And where is President Obama? He's in the kitchen cooking up more marinara sauce, probably with garlic and rosemary!

As you know, the biggest, sloppiest pieces of our budgetary pizza are Social Security, Medicare, and the Pentagon. Herman Cain is the only candidate who isn't afraid to reach into that hot oven and scrape off all the wasteful toppings until there's nothing left but the dough.

To those who think I'm a long shot, let me remind you that the same was said about a certain B-list Hollywood actor who became one of our best presidents (and who also liked a slice of deep-dish from time to time).

It's true that I've never held public office. It's also true that I've fumbled my facts a bit when it came to sensitive topics like Palestine or, more recently, the Fourteenth Amendment of the Constitution.

That's okay. Herman Cain can take a fair hit.

But I've detected even among fellow party members a humoring attitude toward my candidacy. I can't help but wonder if they'd be treating me the same way if my background wasn't pizza but, say, calzones.

In any case, thanks to those 986 Republicans who voted for me in Florida's straw poll, Herman Cain is now a crusty force to be reckoned with.

Bring on the heat.

August 25, 2012
GOP Delegates: Don't Go Near the Strippers

It's been widely noted that Tampa is the strip-club capital of America, and this week vigilant media will be scrutinizing arrest reports in search of Republicans who strayed too far from the convention center (not to mention the party's puritanical agenda).

Hillsborough County actually has a law that strippers must keep a six-foot distance from patrons, but wanton groping is bound to occur as delegates celebrate the wild and crazy nomination of Mitt Romney.

Hopes that Missouri Congressman Todd Akin would be caught with a naked dancer writhing on his lap have been put on hold. As of this writing, Akin says he won't come to the convention, a monumental relief to Romney but a disappointment to those who are curious to hear Akin clarify his odd theories of female biology.

Party leaders would rather deal with a Hurricane Isaac than a loose cannon who, with one ill-timed monologue, illuminated the chilling gap between the Republicans' radical social agenda and mainstream voters. Akin is one of those self-righteous meddlers who oppose abortion even in cases of rape and incest, a view supported by only 17 percent of Americans (according to the latest *Washington Post* poll) but championed by right-wing Christians. In fact, it's part of the GOP platform that will be presented to delegates.

What got Akin in trouble with his own party wasn't his punitive stance against rape victims; it was saying on TV that women's bodies have a natural way of "shutting down" to prevent pregnancy after a "legitimate rape." Issue number one is Akin's boggling stupidity, which Republican leaders never worried about until he opened his mouth and embarrassed them. Issue number two is his destructive insensitivity. Driving away female voters is the last thing the GOP needs before a tight election, and even the bad hairpieces on FOX News are twitching in dismay.

Akin, who is running for the U.S. Senate, has so far refused to drop out of the race, and he continues to stoke the abortion debate. This is what happens when you pander to extremists while trying to sell your party as compassionate and levelheaded—the extremists don't always shut up when you want them to.

As the Republican delegates this week struggle to stay six feet from the strippers, Romney is trying to put about 600,000 light-years between himself and Todd Akin. However, the presidential nominee has a big problem, and that problem is his running mate, Paul Ryan.

The Wisconsin congressman, another "social conservative," joined with Akin to cosponsor anti-choice legislation in the House. The bill would ban all abortions "unless the pregnancy is the result of an act of forcible rape or incest." Last week, during the Akin fiasco, Ryan clammed up when he was asked to explain the term "forcible rape" in relation to other rapes. "Rape is rape," he said over and over in the tone of a constipated macaw.

Like Akin, Ryan doesn't really believe rape is rape. He and many anti-abortionists favor a narrow definition of the crime. For example, they think statutory rape involving teens is different and that pregnancies resulting from those acts should not be terminated. The philosophy is pure Akin and Ryan. They want to be in your bedroom, in your doctor's office, in your church. Forget privacy. Forget personal decisions.

A 14-year-old girl who gets pressured into having sex with her boyfriend must have the baby. Same goes for a wife forced by threat to have sex with a violent husband. Same goes for any woman with a medical condition that makes pregnancy dangerous.

Meet your new Republican Party, hijacked by reactionaries.

Poor Mitt Romney. To placate the Bug-eyed Right, he has flip-flopped on so many issues that he's got ideological whiplash. He even put Ryan on the ticket to fire up the Tea Party and religious conservatives who are wary of his moderate past and also of his Mormonism.

And what did Mitt get for all his trouble? Ten weeks before the election, the national debate has been diverted away from the sputtering economy to the emotional subject of women's rights and free choice.

Romney's mission at the convention is daunting. He must make a speech that shows he's different from the Akins and Ryans while at the same time sucking up to the rabid factions whose votes he will need in November.

And this pivotal appearance will occur after four days in Tampa, of all places, where the rains of Isaac could chase the party faithful and morally upright into lurid dens of cheap champagne and pole dancers.

Sin and Facebook fame are only six feet away.

October 27, 2012
Not an Easy Makeover for Allen West

After less than two years in Congress, Rep. Allen West has raised $15 million to get himself reelected.

That's a mountain of money, but you'd need every dime if your job was to make West look like a calm, responsible person. His wack-job ranting hasn't hurt him among the Tea Party faithful, but it threatens the prospects of the 51-year-old Republican since he switched to a new district that includes Martin and St. Lucie counties and part of Palm Beach.

The task for West's campaign managers is daunting because he has said so many phenomenally offensive and factually indefensible things. Every time the man opens his mouth there's a moment of high drama: Please, Al, just stick to the script. We're begging you.

Back in July, appearing as he does with hungry regularity on FOX News, West likened Social Security disability benefits to "a form of modern, 21st-century slavery." In one coldhearted breath, the retired army colonel managed to insult 828,000 fellow veterans under the age of 66 who report receiving disability funds from Social Security. These include both active-duty and retired military.

West's lame effort to mop up his mess occurred the following night (again on FOX) and featured his now standard attack on the liberal media for twisting his words. The recurring migraine for West's handlers is that his words don't require any twisting. They just spill out of his head that way, usually in front of a television camera, allowing them to be painfully replayed over and over.

It's been a gold mine for West's young Democratic opponent, Patrick Murphy, whose most effective campaign ads are a running montage of West's indelible sound bites. A favorite is his 2011 speech to a conservative women's group in which he declared that those who support Planned Parenthood "have been neutering American men and bringing us to the point of this incredible weakness." What in the world was West babbling about? Are there mandatory spay clinics for guys?

Who knows what he meant, but it was weirdly fascinating to watch.

He actually went on—and some of this you don't see in the commercial—to urge his audience "to let them know that we are not going to have our men become subservient . . . because if you don't, then the debt will continue to grow . . . deficits will continue to grow."

Oh, now it all makes perfect sense.

Is West insane? That's a natural question, but the answer is no. He's just a fringe gasbag who spices his macho act with a little right-wing paranoia.

Still, it's possible he really believes that American men are being psychologically emasculated by evil birth-control advocates and that this is somehow responsible for the nation's budget deficit. Likewise, it's possible West was dead serious when he told a Jensen Beach town hall meeting last April: "I believe there's about 78 to 81 members of the Democratic Party who are members of the Communist Party. It's called the Congressional Progressive Caucus."

This was a stupendously dumb remark in a community where many are old enough to remember Sen. Joe McCarthy. (Among the current House members whose patriotism West attacked is a Lutheran farmer from Maine, that well-known hotbed of sedition.)

You can see the problem facing West's campaign team, and you can see why it needs at least $15 million. This is not an easy makeover. What do you do with a guy who blogs that voters with Obama bumper stickers are "a threat to the gene pool"? There are many Obama stickers to be seen in the 18th District along Florida's Treasure Coast, a fact lost on the arrogant West, though not on his pollsters.

Unsurprisingly, most of his money is coming from outside the state. He's raised about five times more than Murphy, thanks partly to big checks from the PACs of ExxonMobil, Northrup Grumman, Citizens United, and OSI Restaurant Partners, which owns Outback and Carrabba's. Floridians who buy their groceries at Publix might be interested to learn that the company's executives apparently have no problem with West's wild slurs. So far Publix has sent him $12,500, through individuals and PACs.

The question is, will all that be enough?

Can $15 million create in the minds of voters a new, unembarrassing Allen West?

If not, he'll know who to blame: Planned Parenthood, the secret Communists in Congress, and all those slaves getting disability checks.

September 29, 2012
Billionaire Koch Brothers Try to Buy State's Court

The new stealth campaign against three Florida Supreme Court justices is being backed by those meddling right-wing billionaires from Wichita, Charles and David Koch.

They couldn't care less about Florida, but they love to throw their money around.

Last week they uncorked the first of a series of commercials from their political action committee, Americans for Prosperity. The targets are Justices R. Fred Lewis, Barbara Pariente, and Peggy Quince. They were three of the five-vote majority that, in 2010, knocked down a half-baked amendment slapped together by state lawmakers seeking to nullify the federal Affordable Health Care Act.

The Florida Supreme Court upheld lower-court decisions in finding that the proposed amendment contained "misleading and ambiguous language," the hallmark of practically everything produced by this Legislature. Stoned chimpanzees have a keener grasp of constitutional law.

Conservative groups have gone after local justices before. In Iowa, a place that has nothing but vowels in common with

Florida, three state justices were fired by voters after being vilified for ruling against a ban on gay marriage.

On the November ballot, Lewis, Pariente, and Quince are up for merit retention, meaning voters can choose to retain them or not. This simple system was put in place to keep the state's high court above the sleaze of political races. The mission of the Kochs, hiding as always behind their super PAC, is to get the three justices dumped at the polls so that Gov. Rick Scott can appoint replacements.

This is worth repeating: If the Kochs have their way, Rick Scott—yes, that Rick Scott—gets to pack the Supreme Court with his own handpicked crew.

"Yikes" is right.

The head of the Florida chapter of Americans for Prosperity is a person named Slade O'Brien, whose job is to keep a straight face while saying things like: "We're not advocating for the election or defeat of any of the justices. What we're attempting to do is call more attention to them advocating from the bench." Meanwhile, the state GOP's executive board is less coy. It voted to oppose the retention of Quince, Lewis, and Pariente, branding them "too extreme."

Well, let's have a peek at these dangerous radicals.

Justice Pariente, 63, has been on the court for 15 years. She graduated from George Washington University Law School and clerked in Fort Lauderdale under U.S. District Judge Norm Roettger, Jr., who was no softie.

Justice Lewis, 64, who graduated cum laude from the University of Miami Law School, has been on the court almost 14 years. Both he and Pariente were appointed by Gov. Lawton Chiles, not exactly a wild-eyed liberal.

Justice Quince, also 64, is the first African-American woman on the Supreme Court. A graduate of the Columbus

School of Law at Catholic University, she worked for years prosecuting death-penalty cases in the state attorney general's office. In 1999, she was jointly selected for the high court by Chiles and that wacky left-winger Jeb Bush.

Twice before, Floridians have voted to keep these justices, but now the Kochs from Wichita say they know better. You won't see David or Charlie in any of the campaign commercials, because they don't like people to know they're prying.

Their multinational fortune comes from oil refineries, fertilizers, cattle, commodities, chemicals, and paper mills. Next time you reach for Angel Soft toilet paper, think of the Koch brothers.

Both are MIT grads, philanthropists, unabashedly ultra-conservative, and anti-Obama. They're spending hundreds of millions of dollars trying to defeat the president and lesser officeholders all over the country who won't bend to their will. Some Florida Republicans—respected judges and lawyers—are disturbed by the sneak attack on the Supreme Court, which they view as a bald attempt to politicize the judiciary.

The two other justices who voted against the inept Obamacare amendment were similarly singled out two years ago, when they were up for merit retention. Tea Party groups bought TV time blasting justices Jorge Labarga and James Perry, and urging voters to remove them from the court. It didn't work.

Labarga was retained with about 59 percent of the vote, Perry with 61 percent. Those aren't bad margins, considering that the justices can't campaign in their own defense.

This time is different, because Americans for Prosperity has a bottomless war chest to use against Lewis, Pariente, and Quince. Be assured that Gov. Scott is rooting for the Kochs. He'd love to have three openings to fill on the court. The last thing these guys want is fair judges who know the law; they want partisan judges who'll obediently support their political agenda.

It's worse than just trying to buy an election. It's trying to hijack Florida's justice system at the highest levels.

And all the Angel Soft in the world won't wipe away the stink.

Note: By lopsided majorities, Florida voters returned Justices Pariente, Lewis, and Quince to the state Supreme Court.

February 16, 2013
Rubio and the GOP's Thirst for Leadership

Secret Valentine's Day memo to Sen. Marco Rubio from the Strategy Office of the Republican National Committee.

Dear Marco,

One simple word sums up your unorthodox rebuttal to the president's State of the Union address: Genius.

Pausing in the midst of a speech that nobody would otherwise remember, lunging off-camera for a bottle of water, and then slurping it like a demented hummingbird . . . *Time* magazine was right. You are the savior of the Republican Party.

Was the whole country laughing at you? Possibly. Okay, yeah. But was it the most unpresidential thing you could have done? No! You could have walked out with your fly unzipped (whoa, don't get any ideas!).

Truth be told, all of us here at the RNC started freaking out when we saw you stop and take that sip. What's that goofball doing? we wondered. Does he think it's a rehearsal? Doesn't he know he's on live TV in front of, like, 50 million voters?

But once we stopped throwing our coffee cups and kicking our garbage cans, we calmed down and thought about what you'd done. And we finally got it, Marco—the sheer brilliance. The water grab wasn't really a spontaneous and awkward moment, was it? You'd planned the whole darn thing, right down to your deer-in-the-headlights stare at the camera.

Of course you did, because that's what saviors do. They see the big picture.

The script we gave you to read the other night was incredibly lame. In fact, it was basically Mitt Romney's stump speech for the last three years. Didn't work for him, and let's face it, it wasn't going to work for you, either.

Truth is, we don't have any new ideas in the Republican Party. Our plan was to retread all our stale old ideas through a sharp, young Hispanic dude—you!—and hope people would think they're hearing something fresh.

Obviously, you read through the script ahead of time and realized it was a turkey. So you improvised a visual distraction, something so ditzy that all of America would instantly stop paying attention to what you were saying.

In retrospect, it was the best thing that could have happened to our party. Thanks to you, Marco, nobody's talking about that moldy little speech. They're talking about you jonesing for that water bottle. The video clip has gone totally viral. On YouTube, you're getting more hits than that adorable piano-playing hamster!

Here at RNC headquarters, we're receiving thousands of e-mails and tweets, including some from GOP donors who haven't yet grasped the subtle cleverness of your "message." Which is: Yes, Sen. Rubio is really thirsty. The whole country is really thirsty!

Thirsty for a new direction, a new vision for the future.

We're still ironing out some wrinkles, but you get the idea. You've struck gold, Marco, and we're on it.

THE JOKE STATE

The Greatest Show in Miami

The Miami mayoral race is like that famous circus act in which a midget car speeds into the tent and clowns start piling out. This year, 10 candidates have emerged from the city's metaphorical midget car to amuse us before next week's election.

The most colorful of the pack is incumbent Joe Carollo, fondly known as Crazy Joe. He's ruthless, paranoid, demagogic, divisive, and unabashedly bankrupt of conscience. We love him. If journalists alone were allowed to vote, Carollo would win in a landslide because he makes our jobs so easy.

Still, it's only fair to mention the other leading candidates, who are themselves not without entertainment value.

Among the front-runners is Maurice Ferré, an ex-mayor who promotes himself as a visionary and a healer, reaching out to all factions of the community.

While Ferré might be more polished and presentable than Carollo, he's probably not the steadiest hand to be guiding Miami toward long-term fiscal solvency. After his family's concrete business tanked in the 1970s, Ferré transferred all his assets to his wife. In 1983, when the State Attorney's Office tried to collect an unpaid campaign fine of $65,000, no funds could be found in Ferré's own name.

Ten years later, he still hadn't paid the fine. He claimed to have no personal assets but admitted enjoying "a very nice lifestyle" supported by his wife's holdings. Today, Ferré happily reports that his finances are under control and lists a private net worth of $3 million. Inspiring as this dramatic change of fortune might be, voters should still be wary of entrusting the city's fragile budget to someone with Ferré's checkered-checkbook past.

Another familiar figure trying to unseat Carollo is Xavier Suarez, fondly known as the former Mayor Loco. The last election "won" by Suarez was nullified after it was revealed that absentee ballots had been phonied to his benefit. A court removed Suarez from office after 111 bizarre days, during which he appeared to be auditioning for a dinner-theater production of *One Flew Over the Cuckoo's Nest*.

These days, Suarez campaigns on the assertion that Miami's fiscal crisis was a hoax and that the city is actually rolling in dough, despite the contrary findings of professional auditors. As evidence of the nefarious plot, Suarez excitedly points to $148 million in unused bond and special project funds recently unearthed by city officials.

Unfortunately, most of that money was long ago marked for specific capital commitments and cannot legally be diverted to cover Miami's operating expenses or balance its budget. Suarez, however, seldom lets hard facts stand in the way of a juicy conspiracy theory. In such twitchy ramblings, he is nearly Carollo's equal.

One surprise among the mayoral front-runners is lawyer Manny Díaz, a first-time candidate who is not yet known by any derogatory nickname.

At first glance, Díaz would seem an unlikely pick for Miami's top job in Miami. He doesn't appear to be insane, dysfunctional, or arithmetically challenged.

Díaz's civic résumé is distressingly impressive, especially his work on behalf of Haitian refugees in the 1980s. Though he has the requisite anti-Castro credentials—he was part of the legal team representing the Miami relatives of Elián González—he's also shown an apparently sincere concern for Miami's neglected minorities. A recent poll suggests that Díaz will be one of the top vote-getters on November 6 and would beat Carollo in a runoff. That's unsettling indeed for those of us who've been counting on another four years of slapstick at City Hall.

One hopeful note: Díaz has raised more money than all the other candidates, thus increasing the potential for trouble later on, when fat-cat donors come whining for favors.

A longtime pal and fund-raiser of Sen. Bill Nelson, Díaz prospered while Nelson was Florida's insurance commissioner. During those years, Díaz's law firm received more than $1 million worth of business from the state Insurance Department—merely a happy coincidence, we're told.

Let's hope not. We need a reed of hope for future scandal, should Díaz get elected. The prospect of having a mayor who is both uncompromised and unimpaired is too dreary for a writer to contemplate.

This is Miami, for heaven's sake. You can't have a circus without the clowns.

June 9, 2002
First Draft Needs Tweaks on Content, Facts, Title

An absolutely true news item: Florida Secretary of State Katherine Harris, now a candidate for Congress, is writing a book about her controversial role in the 2000 presidential election.

Dear Katherine,

The first draft is terrific! All of us here at Delusional Press are thrilled to be working with such an exciting new talent.

We do have a few minor editing suggestions, however, that might better serve to underscore your diligence and objectivity during this turbulent episode in American politics.

To begin with, we're not entirely comfortable with any of your proposed titles, which I will discuss in order of stated preference.

Tell Al Gore to Kiss My Smokin' Hot Chad is too wordy to fit on the book's cover. Also, the tone is a bit brash for our conservative readership.

While your second choice, *Recount, Shmecount!* has a nice wry ring to it, the title struck some of us as flippant, considering the heavy historic event about which you're writing.

Of all the titles you suggested, by far the catchiest is *How I Saved America.* Unfortunately, the folks in marketing feel that it could scare off potential readers who might mistake the book for a gloating and self-aggrandizing political tract, which of course it isn't!

So, we all put our noggins together and came up with what we believe is a positive, inspiring title: *Center of the Storm: Practicing Principled Leadership in Times of Crisis.*

What do you say, Katherine, does that reach out and grab you by the tonsils or what? Think Churchill during the blitzkrieg. Or maybe Reagan during Grenada.

Now, let's move on to your manuscript, which needs only a little tweaking: Our copy editors have noted that you refer to former Vice President Gore as "a drip" (pp. 13, 27, 88, 92, 107, 185, 310–76), "a dweeb" (pp. 14, 44, 98–107, 224, 288, 410), and "a whiny Ivy League wimp" (pp. 1, 5, 9, 55, 67, 71, 123, 144, 233, and throughout the epilogue).

For consistency, we should settle on a single pejorative name for Gore. Personally, I'd say that "drip" covers a lot of territory and still gets your point across. No more than half a dozen references are probably sufficient.

Similarly, some of us remain uneasy with your frequent characterizations of the Bush brothers as "godlike" (pp. 46, 75, 221, 388), "heroic" (pp. 1, 32, 113, 150, 244), and "saintly" (pp. 28, 67, 183, 209–14). Let's consider toning down those sections. Same goes for the dream sequence in which Jeb appears as a golden unicorn, "his rippled flanks glistening in the moonlight." There's some interesting writing there, to be sure, but it's best saved for a different book.

Look, we're not trying to be sticks in the mud. Nor would we ever seek to dilute your deeply felt convictions about what happened during the presidential election.

Still, we are in the business of selling books. Thus, you can understand our disquiet to see the term "left-leaning Metamucil heads" (p. 169) applied to the Palm Beach County retirees who mistakenly cast ballots for Pat Buchanan instead of Gore. That group, according to our calculations, represents 6,000 to 10,000 voters who won't likely be lining up to purchase your opus, no matter what the title.

So, exactly who is your potential audience? Good question, Katherine, and one we've been asking ourselves daily here at the publishing house.

Market surveys tell us that most people would rather undergo amateur liposuction than read another word about the 2000 presidential election. This aversion seems to cut broadly across party lines.

Our target customer base seems further limited because Gore actually outpolled your candidate by more than 500,000 votes nationwide—a fact only recently unearthed by our crack research department.

But don't fret for even a moment. Our sales force loves a challenge!

You recently inquired about advance orders, and I do have some figures to report. So far, 537 customers have prepurchased your book online—coincidentally, the exact number that was George W.'s disputed margin of victory in your home state.

While that doesn't seem like many sales, we suspect that

thousands of readers got you confused with another famous Harris (Thomas, in this case) and accidentally ordered *Hannibal* instead.

We are confident that we'll get this sorted out soon. Amazon, unlike the bureaucracy of Florida, is quite amenable to recounts.

Meanwhile, take a look at the manuscript changes we've suggested, and try not to worry about the bestseller lists. As you know better than anyone, Katherine, numbers never tell the whole story.

January 11, 2004
Rush's "Fans" Say Loyalty Has Limits

Dear Mr. Limbaugh,

As president-elect of our local Rush Limbaugh Fan Club, I've been deputized to write this letter regarding your recent legal problems.

Here in Gopher County, some of your loyal followers are upset about what they've been reading and hearing in the media, which (as we all know) is run by a bunch of liberal pansies (except for your radio show, of course!).

Anyhow, we were all real sorry to learn about you being a dope addict. Naturally, we didn't believe a word of the story until it came from your own lips.

Seeing how you've been so hard-core against drug users on your radio show—saying that they ought to be locked up with murderers and rapists—it must've been hard on you to sneak around all those years, pretending like you were some straight-up, sober citizen.

According to Palm Beach prosecutors, in only six months you got about 2,000 painkiller pills from pharmacies in your neighborhood (and that's not including what you scored on the sly from your maid). When you do the arithmetic, that works out to at least 11 hits of opiate-based analgesics a day—enough to put any lily-livered liberal in the emergency room—yet it didn't even slow you down! Speaking on behalf of your devoted radio listeners, most of us never suspected that you were ripped to the gills. You always made perfect sense to us.

Still, we were sympathetic when you explained that you'd been popping pills because your back was hurting and then your eardrums were hurting, and I forget what else was hurting. Hey, it's a hard job, sitting in front of that microphone. You don't get much exercise, except for the jaw muscles.

Admittedly, we got worried when you went into rehab, since the concept was pretty much invented by mushy-hearted liberals who wanted to help drug users instead of punish them. Thank goodness you were still a die-hard conservative when you came out!

But that, Mr. Limbaugh, is when the trouble began.

The authorities in Palm Beach have been investigating a drug ring that allegedly supplied some of your pain pills. However, instead of cooperating with law-enforcement officials, you've recently instructed your attorney to stonewall.

To those who have followed you faithfully, it's mighty confusing. You've always said that you were pro-law-and-order, ranting about criminal suspects who complained that their constitutional rights were being violated. Yet that's exactly what you're doing now, and you haven't even been charged with anything.

Prosecutors want your medical records in order to make sure you didn't scam overlapping prescriptions from different doctors, which is illegal. You say the state attorney's request is an invasion of privacy, and you want the medical files sealed permanently. It sure is strange to hear you talk about privacy as something so important. Remember all the laughs you got out of Monica Lewinsky's situation? Imagine what would've happened if the special prosecutors had listened to her pleas for privacy. There would have been no impeachment of Bill Clinton, and America would have been deprived of hours of your laser wit and acid commentary.

Speaking of Ken Starr, why didn't you hire him to be your defense lawyer? A solidly upright, uptight ultraconservative. This Roy Black fellow might be one of the country's best trial attorneys, but are you aware that he has represented murderers, thieves, drug kingpins, and—worst of all—one of the Kennedys! You can't get more liberal than that. Now you and Mr. Black claim that the authorities in Palm Beach are persecuting you because of your political beliefs.

"The Democrats still cannot defeat me in the arena of political ideas," you said on your radio show. "And so now they are trying to do so in the court of public opinion and the legal system."

Whoa.

Even for the most dedicated Limbaugh listeners (and here in Gopher County, we've been steadfast), this is too much to swallow.

All of a sudden you're the innocent victim of a vast, nefarious political conspiracy—for God's sake, you sound just like Hillary!

Next thing we know, you'll be telling us that Dick Gephardt spiked your Lipitors with Xanax. Or that Howard Dean got you hooked on those OxyContins (he is a doctor, right?).

Please, Rush, don't go down this slippery slope. With every passing day, you act more like the "whiny wimps" you've been ridiculing all these years. Here in the land of the right-wing and the righteous, we're loyal, but we have our limits.

We can forgive you for being a pillhead—but never for being a liberal.

April 18, 2004
Might as Well Call It the Manuel Yip Bill

Long live Manuel Yip!

The legacy of Miami's most famous dead voter is being revived—and just in time for the presidential election.

Determined to keep Florida in the national spotlight, legislators are poised to pass a law that will make it infinitely easier to corrupt the voting process again. The proposed measure would do away with the meager requirement that absentee voters have their ballots signed by a witness.

Finding a witness doesn't seem like such a hardship—a relative can do it, and the signature doesn't even have to be notarized. Yet apparently, many Floridians are so lonely and cloistered that they can't dredge up a single soul to watch them seal their ballots.

Or so election officials and legislators would have us believe. They say the witness requirement is burdensome and unnecessary.

To which Manuel Yip might say: Hear, hear!

The former Miami restaurateur passed away in 1993. Four years later, he voted for Xavier Suarez in a city mayoral election that turned out to be an orgy of forgery and ballot stuffing. Being deceased, it was only logical that Yip should vote as an absentee. You can't get much more absent than he was.

No one would have noticed his posthumous participation except for the fact that his ballot request came not from the cemetery but from a small house on Southwest 26th Road. In fact, 11 other absentee ballots were sent to the same place. The man who owned the house, Alberto Russi, was listed as a "witness" on Yip's ballot and at least 75 others. "I do not understand how my signature ended up on the vote of a dead man," Russi insisted at the time. He later pleaded no contest to vote fraud.

Investigators for Joe Carollo, Suarez's mayoral opponent, unearthed other oddities. Officials eventually examined nearly 5,000 absentee ballots—11 percent of the total vote. The results were so disturbing that the original vote tally was scrapped and Carollo was installed as mayor.

It wasn't the first time an election had been stolen using absentee ballots. After a 1993 vote-rigging episode in Hialeah, Miami-Dade forbade a person from signing out more than one absentee ballot for others, except immediate family. The regulation was easily evaded by so-called ballot brokers. Employed by the candidates, the brokers typically are paid $25 to $30 for every absentee ballot they collect and turn in.

In the 1997 election, they simply ordered the ballots by phone, then showed up at voters' homes on the day the ballots arrived. Many of the absentees were elderly and, it later turned out, coached on how to fill out the ballot forms.

A spate of new rules adopted after the Miami scandal were stalled or weakened because Justice Department officials worried about their constitutionality. Among the discarded reforms: more reliable ways to verify a voter's identity.

As weak as it is, the lone-witness requirement has proven useful. Those who fixed the Miami mayoral race would never have been caught—or successfully prosecuted—if their names hadn't turned up over and over again as witnesses on the disputed absentee ballots. No such trail of evidence will exist in future elections if the Legislature has its way. Ballot shenanigans would be almost impossible to detect.

Astoundingly, election supervisors throughout Florida support abolishing the witness requirement for absentee forms. They say it's pointless, because clerks only check whether the voter's signature on the ballot matches the one on the voter rolls. Furthermore, they say, nobody ever bothers to verify the address given by a witness.

That's thinking like a true bureaucrat. Our staff is too swamped, preoccupied, or befuddled to do a thorough job, so what the heck. Let's just make every election a free-for-all!

Secretary of State Glenda Hood (a worthy successor to Katherine Harris) says that absentee voters shouldn't be penalized because they don't have their ballots witnessed. About 2,300 were disqualified in the March 9 primary because of problems with witness signatures or lack thereof. So, thanks to a relatively small number of voters who are too lazy, stoned, or stupid to find a witness, the state is ready to throw out the one rule that addresses the rather crucial issue of authenticity. Without it, we are left only with the voter's signature and the hope that election clerks will be skilled enough to spot every forgery. Dream on.

The hurried timing of the absentee-vote legislation is suspicious, in advance of a presidential vote that promises to be close. Not surprisingly, the measure also neglects to toughen criminal penalties for election fraud.

During the 2000 Gore-Bush debacle, the handling and legitimacy of absentee ballots was a sticking point in the recount debate. Clearly, lawmakers in both parties are hoping to capitalize on similar confusion this November. It's no accident that so many election scandals involve absentee ballots. Tampering with them is easy, though apparently not as easy as some Florida politicians would like it to be.

If they get their way, the votes of deceased persons—and others of dubious veracity—will count the same as yours, in the absence of telltale witnesses.

While the late Manuel Yip has been purged from voter rolls, the thieving spirit of those who faked his signature is alive and well in Tallahassee.

June 27, 2004
In This Election, Nothing Will Go Wrongg

Late-night comedians are already making snarky jokes insinuating that Florida will botch the upcoming presidential election.

Enough already. One little fiasco that changed the course of history and dumped democracy on its ear, and they just can't let it be.

Well, forget what happened back in 2000. This is a new day, a new year, and a new era of modernized voting technology. No more butterfly ballots, no more hanging chads, no more frenetic recounts. As Gov. Jeb Bush declared last week, "Floridians can be confident our state is fully prepared for the upcoming election season and the ones to come."

All Americans should share that hearty confidence.

After the 2000 mess, Florida was one of the first states to rush out and purchase touch-screen voting machines. These babies weren't cheap, either, even though we didn't spring for the top-end model that gives each voter a paper receipt.

You might have read recently about a minor problem with the new machines being used in 11 counties. Not to worry—the bugs are being worked out.

Here's what happened. During two municipal elections in Miami-Dade, the touch-screen devices failed to provide a full electronic log of ballot activity. Simply put, the machines were unable to re-create a complete record of who voted and how they voted. Admittedly, without such a log, it would be difficult to do an accurate recount in the event of a close election. Nor do we dispute that tests conducted on the new machines found that, on other occasions, votes simply vanished when the totals were transferred for tabulation.

The manufacturer of the machines, Electronic Systems & Software, says that it has invented a software "patch" that will fix the glitch, although the state has yet to install it. In the meantime, ES&S suggests that election workers download vote totals from each touch-screen unit onto laptop computers. This will take at least five minutes per machine, and there are 7,200 machines in Miami-Dade alone.

That means a full statewide recount might not be finished until, oh, the winter of 2007. But don't worry—should you die of old age while waiting for the recount, your vote will stand. Unless, perhaps, you're one of the convicted felons whose name may be summarily erased from the voter rolls.

Last month, the state ordered local election officials to begin purging 47,000 voters as possible felons who had served their sentences but hadn't yet gotten their civil rights reinstated. Because many of the applicants were African-Americans, who tend to be Democrats, critics accused Gov. Bush of trying to disenfranchise those who might vote against his brother in the November presidential election.

Bush responded by speeding up clemency requests, and recently, he announced that voting rights have been restored for 20,861 Floridians with past felony convictions. Approximately 50,000 others with more serious criminal records must appear personally before the governor and the cabinet. However, there's absolutely no truth to the rumor that those wearing Bush-Cheney sweatshirts will be moved to the top of the list.

Here in Florida, our new motto is: No voter left behind.

To that end, the governor has signed a law abolishing the requirement that all absentee ballots must be witnessed by a third party.

You might recall that contested absentee ballots played a

large role in George W. Bush's puny 537-vote margin of victory four years ago here in the Sunshine State. Among our 67 counties seemed to exist oddly differing standards for ballots sent in by absentee voters. What was accepted and counted in one jurisdiction was sometimes rejected and discarded in another.

Who says our political leaders didn't learn from the 2000 debacle?

But by eliminating the witness requirement, our Legislature has generously made it possible for practically anyone—living or dead, real or imaginary—to cast an absentee vote in Florida. No more costly investigations of ballot brokers who prey on senior citizens and immigrants. No more embarrassing revelations of deceased citizens rising up to vote. From now on, the legitimacy of each absentee vote can be determined only by visually comparing the signature on the ballot with that on the registration roll.

More than 416,000 Floridians voted absentee in 2000, and the number will be higher this fall. Obviously, there aren't enough election workers to check the authenticity of every signature, which is the whole point.

The second-best thing to a free election is a scandal-free election, and ballots that can't be investigated can't very well blow up into a scandal. So let the comics make their snide little jokes.

Touch-free voting machines that leave no paper trail, absentee ballots that need no witnesses—who says Florida's political leaders didn't learn anything from the debacle of 2000?

Just wait and see.

September 19, 2004
Debate? What Debate? You Mean Me?

An absolutely true news item: The first presidential debate is set for September 30 at the University of Miami, but as of late last week, President Bush still had not confirmed his attendance.

"Aw, do I have to go?"

"Sir, it'll look bad if you don't."

"But Florida's a disaster area. The humane thing to do is postpone the debate until the hurricane season is over."

"Mr. President, hurricane season doesn't end until four weeks after the election."

"Perfect!"

"Sir, we need to RSVP as soon as possible. Sen. Kerry will be at the debate, rain or shine."

"He's taller than me, isn't he? Can't we do something about that?"

"Yes, Mr. President, that's one of our key negotiating points. Either you get to stand on a Miami phone book, or the senator has to speak from a kneeling position behind his podium."

"What about two phone books? Just to be sure."

"All right, sir, I'll run that by the Kerry people."

"Say I agree to do this thing. Isn't there a way to arrange it so I can make up my own questions?"

"Not likely, sir. It would be somewhat unorthodox for a debate format."

"Then we've gotta get some friendly faces on board. Hey, how about Laura? She's real smart. You know, she used to be a librarian . . ."

"Mr. President, I'm not sure it's a great idea to have your own wife on the panel."

"Then what about Jeb? Heck, he lives only five minutes down the road from the University of Miami. He could stop by and toss me some softball questions about the Everglades. Like: 'Mr. President, the people of Florida want to thank you for saving our precious wilderness!'"

"Sir, that's not technically a question."

"Oh, really? Maybe you'd like to go work for an English professor instead of a commander in chief. Maybe you didn't enjoy those box seats at the Orioles games or those backstage passes to Toby Keith."

"With all due respect, Mr. President, try to chill out. Remember how well you did four years ago in your debates with Vice President Gore. Remember that even the Democrats were impressed."

"Yeah, but Gore was shorter than Kerry."

"That's true, sir. But Kerry seems to be more boring."

"No way!"

"That's what our focus groups are telling us, Mr. President."

"Heck, Al nearly put me into a coma. How'm I supposed to stay awake for this guy?"

"Coffee, sir. By the gallon."

"Okay, let's say I show up for this shindig. I don't want to hear one single smart-ass question about where are Saddam Hussein's weapons of mass destruction. Or why the prescription-drug bill is gonna cost so much more than we first said. Or how I spent my summers in the National Guard. Understand?"

"Those are all on our do-not-ask list, Mr. President. We're playing hardball, trust me."

"Am I leaving anything out?"

"Well, there's Osama, Enron, Halliburton, the environment, the jobless rate, the trade imbalance, the budget deficit . . ."

"Geez, the budget deficit! I almost forgot. What's it up

to now, like, a gazillion dollars? My head hurts, just thinkin' about it."

"Don't worry, sir, there won't be any math questions. We've already told them it would be a deal-breaker."

"Know what would go over like gangbusters? Since we'll be in Miami? A slam on Fidel Castro!"

"It's already in the pipeline, Mr. President. A guy from FOX News has promised to ask about Cuba if we can get him on the panel."

"That's fantastic. I can do five killer minutes on Fidel, no sweat. Maybe this won't be such a tough gig after all."

"It'll be fine, Mr. President. But, before we start preparing for Miami, there is something you should be aware of—Sen. Kerry was the star of the debate team at Yale."

"Get outta here. There was a debate team? Go find my yearbook."

"I'm afraid there was a debate team, sir. A fairly good one, too."

"Uh-oh. I think I smell another hurricane coming. Can't Cheney jerk a few chains over at NOAA? Who's in charge of all those weather satellites, anyway?"

"I'll make some calls, Mr. President."

December 17, 2006
Comic Echo of 2000 Election—It's Not Funny

The first time I tried a touch-screen voting machine was November 7. It was not an experience that inspired confidence.

When I pressed a finger down to select my choice for governor, a mark appeared beside the name of a different candidate at the bottom of the list. A poll worker insisted that the device was working properly and suggested that I'd accidentally touched it in the wrong place with my "wrist."

I'd done no such thing. The machine screwed up.

I hit another command to nullify the wrong vote, corrected it, and moved on through the remainder of the ballot. After I finished, the machine allowed me to recheck all my selections to make sure they were right. Whether or not the votes actually were recorded that way, I'll never know. No paper receipt was provided.

For almost 18,400 people in the Sarasota area, it didn't matter whether they touched the screen with their fingers, wrists, noses, or toes. No votes were recorded for them in the hottest political race in the region, the battle for the District 13 congressional seat.

The "undervote" in the expensive and widely publicized contest between Republican Vern Buchanan and Democrat Christine Jennings was a staggering 14 percent in Sarasota County.

In nearby counties where the District 13 race was on the ballot, the undervote was only 1 to 5 percent. The discrepancy is statistically jarring and more than a little suspicious.

Buchanan was declared the winner by 369 votes. As expected, Republican leaders say the touch-screen machines were functioning perfectly, and it's not their problem if 18,000 people happened to skip over that section of the ballot.

Also as expected, Jennings is challenging the outcome in court, citing numerous complaints about the machines from voters and some poll workers. She has said she'll ask the House of Representatives to investigate.

It's one of the last unsettled political races in the country, and naturally, it would be in Florida, the same state that spectacularly botched the 2000 presidential election and spawned the national stampede to electronic voting.

At the time, many people warned against switching to touch-screen devices—and costly ones—that offered no paper trail. But the numbskulls prevailed, the machine manufacturers got rich, and now here we are.

Gas pumps give receipts. ATMs give receipts. Yet the most crucial instrument in the cog of modern democracy isn't equipped to spit out a simple slip of paper that verifies a vote.

Fittingly, the disputed congressional district in Sarasota is the one represented by Katherine Harris, who, as secretary of state, ratified George W. Bush's hairbreadth victory here and then threw herself in front of recount efforts. A manual recount last month upheld Buchanan's slender margin, but critics say it's pointless to recount electronic data that might be inherently flawed. When a paperless machine fails to record a vote, it's impossible to know if that was a mistake or if the voter intended to pass over that race.

In another comic echo of 2000, the Sarasota County ballot was apparently designed by kindergartners on cough syrup. The Jennings-Buchanan race was positioned without a headline at the top of the second page, above the brightly highlighted governor's contest. So many voters complained that the election supervisor notified poll workers to remind people to look for the District 13 race.

Another theory about the exceptionally high undervote is that many voters got disgusted by the nonstop media fusillade between Jennings and Buchanan and skipped the race in protest. Yet there was an abundance of vicious, degrading political campaigns throughout the state, and no one can explain why Sarasotans would be offended in disproportionately higher numbers than other Floridians.

According to *The St. Petersburg Times*, 13 percent of those who voted in Sarasota County in 2004 took a pass on a state Senate race, but only 6 percent skipped the District

13 congressional battle between Harris and her Democratic opponent. It's hard to believe that 14 percent of those who took the trouble of going to the polls this year snubbed the highest-profile local race on the ballot. Maybe they all tried to vote with their wrists instead of their fingers.

A test of 10 touch-screen machines, five of which were used in the Sarasota election, showed no serious malfunctions. Jennings has argued that the testing should focus exclusively on machines used on Election Day.

If nothing else, the fiasco in Sarasota has accelerated the national momentum to dump paperless voting machines. A panel advising the U.S. Election Assistance Commission recently came out in favor of phasing out devices that don't provide paper verification of votes. The transition would take years and be costly for taxpayers, but the integrity of the entire election process is at stake. Several studies have stated that paperless voting machines are subject to errors, fraud, and hacking.

Governor-elect Charlie Crist supports a statewide upgrade to touch-screen machines that give paper receipts, which is smart. Because the next time there's a mysterious razor-thin vote, it could just as easily be the Republicans, not the Democrats, who get shafted.

And it'll probably happen right here in Florida.

November 2, 2008
Deliver Us from Scandal, Lord

An Election Day prayer for the Sunshine State.

Dear Lord, have mercy on Florida. Please don't let it happen again here.

Not that we're blaming You for the voting debacle back in 2000. You're not the one who designed the ridiculous butterfly ballots that started the whole mess. It wasn't You who put Katherine Harris in charge, and it certainly wasn't You who caused all those silly chads to hang.

And don't worry—we know You're not the one who stopped the recount and handed the presidency to You-know-who. That was the Supreme Court.

The rest, as they say, is history. Not that You need reminding, but the last eight years in this country have been basically a train wreck. Iraq, Katrina, the economic crash—we're not whining, Lord, but our nerves are shot.

Everybody knows somebody who's lost their job or their pension or their home. Meanwhile, the government is spending $10 billion a month on a war that should never have been started, and hundreds of billions more to bail out banks for bad loans that shouldn't have been made.

Oh, did we mention that Osama bin Laden is still alive and well and cranking out home videos? Next time You have a spare lightning bolt . . . Well, it's just a thought.

Anyway, back to the election. During that long tense November eight years ago, lots of folks prayed for You to make an appearance in Tallahassee, or at least give us a sign. Apparently, You were preoccupied with more pressing disasters, and that's okay.

The world is profoundly screwed up, and Your to-do list must be as big as a phone book. There probably was a horrible famine or plague breaking out somewhere at the same time as the Bush-Gore fiasco, and You were too busy to intervene here, divinely or otherwise.

All we're asking now—and we surely don't mean to impose—is that You keep a wise and watchful eye on us Tuesday. In case You haven't been following the presidential race, many of the pundits are predicting Florida will again play a decisive role in the outcome.

God, we sincerely apologize in advance. After what happened in 2000, we never EVER wanted to face another November when the fate of the entire republic depended on the integrity of the voting system.

The possibilities are terrifying. We've got 67 counties, which means 67 chances for shenanigans, careless tabulating, or simple machine failure. Heck, they still can't run an election in Palm Beach County without losing boxes and boxes of ballots!

People are so nervous that more than two million showed up for early voting, many waiting in the sun for hours. In theory, filing a ballot this way would allow more days for the counting and take pressure off polling officials who might be unduly ponderous, myopic, or technologically challenged.

The public turnout has been an amazing phenomenon that underscores how seriously Floridians are taking this election and how determined they are to make their votes count.

But there's one other reason for the long lines: atonement. For eight grinding years, we've had to live with the knowledge that it was our fair state that put George Bush and Dick Cheney in the White House and set the nation on this rocky course. Nationally, they'd lost the popular vote by 544,000, but it was Florida's electoral votes that tipped the scale.

So, every political season we suffer stoically through a fresh round of "Flori-duh" jokes, and the predictable snarky wisecracks from late-night television hosts.

In truth, the 2000 travesty wasn't the fault of our voters. They tried, Lord, they really did. The thousands who accidentally voted for nutty Pat Buchanan wouldn't have made that mistake if the ballots had been designed by a third-grade art class instead of some clever bureaucrat.

Yet the guilt lingers, and there's no sense denying it. The throngs who lined up to vote early went there to prove something. We can never erase the dismal consequences of Bush-Gore, but we've got a chance to help make history without mucking it up.

Despite what the crazy TV preachers say, we don't really know whether You're a red God or blue God, Republican or Democrat or independent. All we want is an even break.

So please remember Florida in Your blessings on Tuesday.

Deliver us from scandal, Lord. Let our optical scanners perform flawlessly. Let the trucks that carry our precious ballot boxes not be hijacked and later abandoned behind a strip joint, and let those who count those ballots be pure of character and pretty good with math.

Most of all, Lord, let there be no need for lawyers.

But if, in Your infinite wisdom, You see a need to test the faith of this great country with another electoral crisis, please consider doing it in Virginia or Ohio or maybe North Carolina.

God, anywhere but here. Amen.

July 18, 2010
Medicare Corruption Gusher Worsens

Among South Florida's fearless Medicare rip-offs—and there are thousands—is the story of Guillermo Denis Gonzalez.

After serving 14 years in prison for murdering a man with a silencer-equipped handgun, Gonzalez decided in 2006 to try the medical supply business.

For $18,000, the Hialeah resident bought a Medicare-licensed company called DG Medical Equipment, and within a year he'd submitted $586,953 in false claims for supplies that were never provided to patients.

Medicare, using federal tax dollars, reimbursed Gonzalez $31,442 before he was tracked down and arrested.

Last summer, after pleading guilty to defrauding the government, Gonzalez was marched over to state court to face another murder charge—this one for allegedly stabbing and dismembering an acquaintance during a monetary dispute. He is scheduled to go on trial next month.

No one familiar with Florida was surprised to learn that a murderer had been welcomed into the health-care trades. Indeed, the most shocking thing about the Gonzalez case was that Medicare hadn't forked over the full half a million bucks in bogus claims that he'd sought.

South Florida remains the Deepwater Horizon of Medicare corruption in the United States, and the gusher is getting worse. No other place even comes close to matching the number of crooked health-care businesses or the immense dollar amounts that wind up in the pockets of criminals. While overworked prosecutors crack down on operators like Gonzalez, the latest wave of Medicare cheats is specializing in fictional billing for mental health services, rehab sessions, and physical therapy.

As Jay Weaver reported in the *Herald* last week, mental health clinics in Florida billed Medicare for $421 million in 2009. That's four times more than was billed in the same period by mental health clinics in Texas, and 635 times more than was billed by clinics in Michigan. As crazy and depressed as Floridians can be, there's no way that we're four times crazier than Texans or 635 times more depressed than Michiganders. The only plausible explanation for such a staggering discrepancy in mental health claims is stealing—thieves in Florida are simply more adept at fleecing Medicare.

Our dubious distinction as the sleazebag capital of America brought Attorney General Eric Holder and Health and Human Services Secretary Kathleen Sebelius to Miami last week for the first ever national summit on health-care fraud. It wasn't quite as flashy or upbeat as the LeBron James–Chris Bosh–Dwyane Wade summit at the American Airlines Arena, but the mission is nonetheless worthy of attention.

Medicare is the biggest drain on the federal budget, and epidemic fraud is the biggest drain on Medicare. Most older Americans depend on the program to cover many health-care expenses, but the system is sagging and bloated.

Experts say Medicare fraud in South Florida costs U.S. taxpayers between $3 and $4 billion annually. It's predictable that Miami-Dade, Broward, and Palm Beach counties would be the hotbed, and also the venue for one of every three federal health-care fraud prosecutions.

Part of the problem is that Medicare pays claims first, then asks questions later. That leaves criminals with a time gap that often allows them to bank the money, shut down their storefronts, and scurry on before they get caught.

In 2008, Medicare paid $520 million to home-health-care agencies in Miami-Dade, just for treating diabetic patients. That was more money than the agency spent on that particular illness throughout the rest of the country combined. The feds then changed the rules and put a cap on claims for homebound patients receiving insulin injections. The scammers simply turned their energies toward other exploitable areas—in particular, mental health and physical therapy treatments.

Records show that Florida rehabilitation facilities billed

$171 million to Medicare last year for physical and occupational services, which was 23 times more than California and 26 times more than New York—two other states with no shortage of fraud artists.

For years, the Justice Department has been locking up Medicare fraudsters in Florida, yet business is booming. More FBI agents and prosecutors would help, but you'd need an army of them to dismantle all the bogus Medicare operations in South Florida.

Despite all the individuals indicted, including 94 nationwide on Friday, the risk of getting nabbed for Medicare fraud remains relatively small, and the potential profits from the crime remain large.

That's why health care is such an appealing career move for local felons, even the occasional murderer. Why use a gun when you can make lots more money with a pencil?

May 28, 2011
GOP Won't Let Democracy Get Out of Hand

According to a new Quinnipiac University poll of Florida voters, Rick Scott is now one of the country's most unpopular governors, a dubious feat after only four months in office.

It's bad news for Republican Party bosses, but all is not lost. Scott recently signed a new election bill that is callously designed to suppress voter turnout, making it harder for many disgruntled Floridians to cast a valid ballot in 2012.

Democrats outnumber Republicans in the state, so GOP leaders are desperate to find ways to keep certain people away from the polls. One of the Legislature's top priorities was to change the voting rules to avoid a repeat of 2008, when Barack Obama won the state's 27 electoral votes on his way to the presidency.

Obama benefited from early-voting days, which proved popular among minorities, college students, and retirees. Republican officials became incensed during the election when then-Governor Charlie Crist—one of their own—decided to extend polling hours to accommodate the long lines.

The nerve of that guy, making it easier for common citizens to vote!

Determined not to let this whole democracy thing get out of hand, the GOP-held Legislature crafted a bill that reduces the number of early voting days from 15 to eight and requires some voters who have moved to cast provisional ballots, a deliberate inconvenience aimed at students.

Historically, provisional ballots are counted at a much lower rate than regular ones, meaning many young voters won't get heard—exactly what Scott and the Republican leadership want. The new bill also throws out a rule that had been in effect for 40 years, allowing Floridians to update their legal addresses when they arrive to vote. Now you can only do that if you moved within the same county.

To hinder community groups that register first-time voters, the law requires volunteers for organizations such as the League of Women Voters to register with the state as if they were sex offenders.

Upon signing the anti-voting bill into law, Gov. Spaceman said the following: "I want people to vote, but I also want to make sure there's no fraud involved in elections. All of us as individuals that vote want to make sure that our elections are fair and honest."

Those who recall what happened here in the 2000 presidential election can't help but chuckle at the comic aspect of a Republican governor pretending to fret about voter fraud.

Interestingly, the officials who are most familiar with the

fraud issue—the county supervisors of elections—are mostly opposed to the new voting law and say current voter databases are fairly accurate. They actually asked the Legislature for more early-voting sites and were, of course, rebuffed.

The statewide association of election supervisors also warned Scott that imposing the restrictive provisions could cause a fiasco at the polls in 2012, just what we need to reinforce our national reputation for electoral dysfunction.

When the governor promised to bring all those new jobs to Florida, who knew he was talking about lawyers?

Nobody except a handful of GOP honchos thought the punitive new voting law was a good idea. The League of Women Voters, labor unions, and other citizen groups lobbied against it, to no avail. Scott's office reported receiving more than 15,300 calls and e-mails, with opposition running 10 to one. It's significant that the governor's own overseer of elections, Secretary of State Kurt Browning, never once spoke in favor of the legislation. Only after Scott signed the bill did Browning offer a lukewarm endorsement.

The effort to manipulate elections by making it difficult for some people to vote has been around since the nation was founded. It's a strategy that was infamously codified in the Deep South by "literacy tests" intended to disenfranchise black citizens, which prompted the Voting Rights Act of 1965.

Congressional Democrats have asked the Justice Department to block Florida's new law, which already took effect in all but five counties—Monroe, Hendry, Hardee, Collier, and Hillsborough. There the federal government must approve changes to voter-eligibility rules.

In addition to impeding potential Democratic voters, Republican lawmakers have tacked several items on the November 2012 ballot in hopes of galvanizing their own base.

You'll see an anti-abortion amendment, an anti-Obamacare amendment, and still another measure that would allow tax dollars to be funneled to religious institutions.

The GOP's dream scenario is a low turnout dominated by a grumpy, aging core of conservative white people who can't stand Obama. With their party outnumbered on Florida's voter rolls, top Republicans hope that rigging the voting rules will improve their chances to recapture the White House.

You could call it democracy with selective exclusion.

Or you could call it what it is.

November 5, 2011
GOP Laff-fest Coming Soon to Our State

When Florida's Republican 2012 presidential primary was moved up to January 31, the reaction was mixed.

Some voters were glad to be getting past it sooner than later. Others were dismayed that the holiday season would be polluted by vicious campaign commercials and distracting barnstorm visits from candidates.

Now it's clear that many of us underestimated the redemptive entertainment value of the GOP race. Floridians are in need of a good laugh, and this particular ensemble will deliver plenty of those.

Rick Perry, the Texas governor, spent last week denying that he was drunk or high when he gave a speech punctuated by odd giggles and twitches in New Hampshire. The video has become a YouTube sensation, and it's hilarious stuff—at least until you consider that this goober might someday have his finger on the button that controls America's nuclear arsenal.

In the governor's defense, his campaign staff said that Perry was simply being "passionate" in front of the New Hampshire crowd. Jerry Garcia liked to perform in a passionate state, too. Before he went onstage with the Grateful Dead, he'd go straight to his dressing room and drop some heavy passion.

After that weird speech, Perry's strategic mistake was claiming to be straight when it happened. He should have just said, "Yeah, okay, I had a few beers." Or even "Shoot, I must've accidentally popped a Xanax instead of my Lipitor."

Then people would have thought: Oh, that explains it.

But the possibility that he was totally sober isn't quite as funny. In fact, it's semi-terrifying.

This isn't the sergeant at arms of your local Kiwanis Club who's nervous about speaking in public. This is a career politician who wants to be the freaking commander in chief of the United States.

With Perry polling only slightly ahead of Dr. Conrad Murray, the New Hampshire debacle should have sunk his hopes for the White House. No way. The Texan will be rolling full steam into Florida, and for that we have Herman Cain to thank.

Last week it was revealed that the pizza king turned front-runner had been twice formally named in sexual-harassment complaints when he was head of the National Restaurant Association. (There was a time in this great nation's history when a background in franchise-food services wasn't considered a springboard to the U.S. presidency, but this is a new day.)

Cain denied the damaging charges and accused his rival Perry of leaking the information to the press. Things can only get uglier between now and January, which means Floridians can look forward to a blaring, venomous, low-class campaign.

The trick is not to get depressed but, rather, to enjoy the show for what it is.

Michele Bachmann will be here, and God only knows

what will come out of her mouth. Don't be surprised if she confuses the Seminole tribe with the Apaches.

And then there's undersedated Rick Santorum, moldy Newt Gingrich, invisible Jon Huntsman, and dependably amusing Ron Paul, who hovers like a benign but addled Yoda on the fringe of every debate. The race is Mitt Romney's to win. All he has to do is appear halfway sane, which should be easy, considering the competition.

Romney's biggest hurdle will be trying to explain his pandemic flip-flopping, and that might prove impossible. His best shot at victory is to stick with two basic talking points:

1. Obama's a terrible president.
2. I'll be a terrific president.

As Cain and Perry stumble, a Romney win is looking like a done deal. However, Florida is a land of unpleasant surprises where front-runners can crash and burn.

Ask Gary Hart, whose bid for the Democratic nomination began unraveling with his antics aboard a Miami yacht called *Monkey Business* in 1987. Less titillating but equally final was the collapse of Rudy Giuliani during the last presidential campaign. The former New York mayor staked everything on winning Florida, and he virtually camped out here for weeks. But the more stump speeches he gave and the more hands he shook, the lower he dropped in the polls. To know Rudy was to lose interest. As a result, John McCain captured the state and, ultimately, the Republican nomination.

Romney is less prickly than Giuliani, and he definitely has better hair, no small advantage in national politics. His advisers will coach him to stand tall, stay cool, and avoid getting dragged into the mud pit with Cain, Perry, and the others. However, the mud pit is where all the fun happens. That's why so many TV viewers are watching the GOP debates, waiting for somebody to melt down or fly into orbit.

People say they want civility in politics, but that's a pipe dream. The presidential campaign is way too long and silly.

Being connoisseurs of the absurd, Floridians should welcome the candidates as fountains of comic relief. For voters here, the road to the primary will be difficult to endure without a sense of humor or 50 milligrams of "passion."

November 10, 2012
Once Again, Florida's the National Punch Line

The bad news is that Florida screwed up another big election.

The good news is that it doesn't matter this time.

By now, we Floridians have stoically accepted our laughingstock role in the Electoral College. To comedy writers, we're the gift that keeps on giving. What would Jon Stewart and David Letterman do without us?

We are the Joke State.

And by a stroke of good fortune, it's much easier to smile today than it was 12 years ago.

Gov. Rick Scott should send a bushel of oranges to every voter in Ohio as thanks for getting Florida off the hook and sparing the nation from another *Bush v. Gore* debacle.

The 2012 presidential race was basically over last Tuesday night when precincts in Cleveland and other key areas began reporting. President Obama's victory was announced shortly after 11 P.M., while many Miami voters were still waiting in long lines. To their honor, lots of them stayed and voted anyway.

On Wednesday, Floridians awoke to learn that thousands of ballots remained uncounted in Miami-Dade and several other counties. As the sorting process dragged into Thursday, we all began hearing from friends and relatives living in normal places where elections are conducted without scandal or farce. Whether it was by text, e-mail, or phone call, the gist of the inquiry was the same: What is wrong with your state?

CBS asked me the same question, and all I could say was: "It's a freak show."

Yes, Florida's ballot was ridiculously long, stacked with dense constitutional amendments.

Yes, exceptionally long poll lines were made worse by the Legislature's decision to cut the early-voting period from 14 days to eight days. It was one of several Republican strategies to stifle turnout in the cities, and it backfired.

And yes, Gov. Scott could have made the election go smoother if he hadn't refused to extend polling hours for early voting. However, there was scant chance of the governor lifting a finger to help urban Hispanics or African-Americans cast ballots, because they often vote Democrat.

Adding to those factors last week were the same demons that helped send the 2000 presidential contest to the Supreme Court—random bungling, lack of preparation, and free-floating confusion.

Chads or no chads, Florida simply isn't equipped to run a major election. We're in way over our heads, and we should admit it.

Mixed among all the smart, hardworking people in county election offices are a few witless boobs, some of them in supervisory positions. All it takes is one to gum up the works.

While Miami-Dade is no stranger to treachery in its elections, last week's fiasco is more likely the result of unpreparedness. Poll workers were swamped with last-minute absentee ballots from voters who got weary of standing in line. Once more, Florida found itself in the humiliating position of being the only state in the union that couldn't get its act together and add up the votes of its citizens on time.

By midnight Tuesday, every other state on the electoral map was blue or red. We were the only blank one on the board and stayed that way late into the week. This time all of America wasn't anxiously waiting. It was chuckling and shaking its head.

We can't count on Ohio or any of the swing states to bail us out again in 2016, so what are our options?

In case you were wondering, the U.S. Constitution makes no allowance for a state to exempt itself from presidential elections in order to avoid national ridicule. Nor is there any legal mechanism by which Florida's 11 million registered voters might have their ballots shipped somewhere safe to be counted—say, Kansas.

Maybe we just hold our heads up high and try again, bracing for the inevitable screwup and the snarky one-liners to follow.

If the next presidential campaign proves as exhausting and dispiriting as this one, the country will sorely need a laugh or two when it's over. Perhaps that is Florida's true electoral destiny—to be the comic relief, the perpetual punch line.

It's way less painful than being the decider.

ACKNOWLEDGMENTS

As always, I'm deeply indebted to Bob Radziewicz, formerly of *The Miami Herald* and now at the University of Miami School of Communication. His sharp editing eye has improved my columns for more years than either of us care to count.

I'm also boundlessly grateful to the newsroom staff of the *Herald*, which even in these lean times puts out a damn good paper. In particular I want to thank Juan Vasquez, Dora Bain, and Myriam Marquez in the Op-Ed department, and also the publisher, David Landsberg, who honors the sacred but fragile wall between editorial and business operations. David leaves me alone to write what I feel, no matter what kind of grief the columns might bring his way.

Lastly, I must once again thank the inexhaustible Diane Stevenson for sifting through a small mountain of tirades and riffs to choose some favorites from the last dozen years. This is the third time Diane has put together a collection of my newspaper work, yet her energy and enthusiasm remain unflagging. It's baffling to a dark Nordic soul like mine, but I count myself lucky to have her as a reader and a friend.

If nothing else, these columns should strip away any remaining mystery about where I find the inspiration—and source material—for my warped comic novels. I can't imagine living anywhere as corrupt, overrun, mismanaged, and freak-infested as Florida. I also can't imagine living anywhere as beautiful or so worth fighting for.

Carl Hiaasen
Vero Beach
June 7, 2013

BASKET CASE

Jack Tagger's years in exile at the obituaries desk of a South Florida daily haven't dulled his investigative reporter's nose for a good story. When Jimmy Stoma, the infamous front man of Jimmy and the Slut Puppies, dies in a fishy scuba accident, Jack sees his ticket back to page one—if only he can figure out what really happened. Standing in his way are, just for starters, his ambitious young editor, who hasn't yet fired anyone but plans to "break her cherry" with Jack, and the rock star's pop-singer widow, who's using the occasion of her husband's death to relaunch her own career. The soulless, profit-hungry Jack becomes so obsessed with unraveling the lies surrounding Jimmy Stoma's strange fate that he's willing to risk his career, even his life.

Fiction

THE DOWNHILL LIE
A Hacker's Return to a Ruinous Sport

Bestselling author Carl Hiaasen wisely quit golfing in 1973. But some ambitions refuse to die, and as the years passed and the memories of slices and hooks faded, it dawned on Carl that there might be one thing in life he could do better in middle age than he could as a youth. So gradually he ventured back to the rolling, frustrating green hills of the golf course, where he ultimately—and foolishly—agreed to compete in a country-club tournament against players who can actually hit the ball. Filled with harrowing divots, deadly doglegs, and excruciating sandtraps, *The Downhill Lie* is a hilarious chronicle of misadventure that will have you rolling with laughter.

Memoir/Sports

A DEATH IN CHINA

From Carl Hiaasen and the distinguished foreign correspondent Bill Montalbano comes a relentless novel of treachery and murder set in the clenched society of China, where even tomorrow's weather is a state secret. David Wang, a Chinese-American art historian, dies shortly after a visit to an ancient tomb housing priceless artifacts. Officials diagnose death by duck, a fatal confluence of culture shock and rich cuisine. But Wang's friend Tom Stratton suspects something more sinister, especially after the dead man's brother, a highly placed Party official, tries to have him kidnapped. From a nightmarish interrogation to assassination by cobra, *A Death in China* takes readers on a trip with no rest stops through a world of claustrophobic mistrust and terrifying danger.

Crime Fiction

TRAP LINE

With its dozens of outlying islands and the native Conchs' historically low regard for the law, Key West is a smuggler's paradise. All that's needed are the captains to run the contraband. Breeze Albury is one of the best fishing captains on the Rock, and he's in no mood to become the Machine's delivery boy. So the Machine sets out to persuade him. It starts out by taking away Albury's livelihood. Then it robs him of his freedom. But when the Machine threatens Albury's son, the washed-out wharf rat turns into a raging, sea-going vigilante. In *Trap Line*, Hiaasen and Montalbano pit a handful of scruffy Conchs against an armada of drug lords, crooked cops, and homicidal marine lowlife. The result is a crime novel of dizzying velocity, filled with wrenching plot twists, grimily authentic characters, and enough local color for a hundred tropical shirts.

Crime Fiction

VINTAGE BOOKS
Available wherever books are sold.
www.vintagebooks.com